CLIFFS

SAT I ☜ W9-DHL-200

Reasoning Test

PREPARATION GUIDE

by

Jerry Bobrow, Ph.D.

Contributing Authors

Bernard V. Zandy, M.S.

William A. Covino, Ph.D.

INCORPORATED

LINCOLN, NEBRASKA   68501

ACKNOWLEDGMENTS

I would like to thank Michele Spence of Cliffs Notes for her many hours of final editing and her careful attention to the production process. I would also like to thank my office staff for their typing assistance: Joy Mondragon, Dana Lind, Brenda Clodfelter, and Cindy Fisher. Finally, I would like to thank my wife, Susan, daughter, Jennifer (15 and almost driving), and sons, Adam (12) and Jonathan (8), for their patience, moral support, and comic relief.

ISBN 0-8220-2074-2

FIRST EDITION

CONTENTS

Ability Tested • Basic Skills Necessary
Directions • Analysis of Directions
Suggested Approach with Samples
Summaries of Strategies

Ability Tested • Basic Skills Necessary
Directions • Analysis of Directions
Suggested Approach with Samples
Summaries of Strategies

PART III: PRACTICE-REVIEW-ANALYZE-PRACTICE
Three Full-Length Practice Tests

PREFACE

Your SAT I: Reasoning Test score can make the difference!

And because of this, you can't afford to take a chance. Prepare with the best! Since better scores result from thorough preparation, your study time must be used most effectively. *Cliffs SAT I Preparation Guide* has been designed by leading experts in the field of test preparation to be the most comprehensive guide that you can realistically complete in a reasonable time. In keeping with the fine tradition of Cliffs Notes, this guide is written **for the student.** It is direct, precise, compact, easy to use, and thorough. The testing strategies, techniques, and materials have been researched, tested, and evaluated and are presently used in SAT I test preparation programs at many leading colleges and universities. This book emphasizes the *Bobrow Test Preparation Services* approach, developed over the past twenty years with thousands of students in preparation programs. The *Bobrow* approach focuses on the six major areas that should be considered when preparing for the SAT I:

1. Ability Tested
2. Basic Skills Necessary
3. Understanding Directions
4. Analysis of Directions
5. Suggested Approaches with Samples
6. Practice-Review-Analyze-Practice

This guide combines introductory analysis sections for each exam area with lots of practice—three full-length practice tests. These practice tests have complete answers, in-depth explanations, analysis charts, and score range approximators to give you a thorough understanding of the SAT I.

Cliffs SAT I Preparation Guide was written to give you the edge in doing your best by giving you maximum benefit in a reasonable amount of time and is meant to augment, not substitute for, formal or informal learning throughout junior high and high school.

Don't take a chance. Be prepared! Follow the Study Guide Checklist in this book and study regularly. You'll get the best test preparation possible.

STUDY GUIDE CHECKLIST

_____ 1. Read the SAT I: Reasoning Test information bulletin.

_____ 2. Become familiar with the New Test Format, page 3.

_____ 3. Familiarize yourself with the answers to Questions Commonly Asked about the new SAT I, page 6.

_____ 4. Learn the techniques of the Successful Overall Approaches, page 9.

_____ 5. Carefully read Part II: Analysis of Exam Areas, beginning on page 15.

_____ 6. Strictly observing time allotments, take Practice Test 1, section by section (take Section 1, check your answers; take Section 2, check your answers, and so on), beginning on page 123.

_____ 7. Review the answers and explanations for each question on Practice Test 1, beginning on page 187.

_____ 8. Analyze your Practice Test 1 answers by filling out the analysis charts, page 182.

_____ 9. Review your math skills as necessary.

_____ 10. Review or reread Part II: Analysis of Exam Areas, beginning on page 15, to see if you applied some of the strategies.

_____ 11. Strictly observing time allotments, take Practice Test 2, beginning on page 229. Take a very short break after each hour of testing.

_____ 12. Check your answers and use the Score Range Approximator (page 439) to get a very general score range.

_____ 13. Analyze your Practice Test 2 answers by filling out the analysis charts on page 290.

_____ 14. While referring to each item of Practice Test 2, study all of the answers and explanations that begin on page 295.

_____ 15. Selectively review some basic skills as necessary.

____ 16. Strictly observing time allotments, take Practice Test 3, beginning on page 337. Take a very short break after each hour of testing.

____ 17. Check your answers and use the Score Range Approximator (page 439) to get a very general score range.

____ 18. Analyze your Practice Test 3 answers by filling out the analysis charts on page 400.

____ 19. While referring to each item of Practice Test 3, study all of the answers and explanations that begin on page 405.

____ 20. Again, selectively review Part II: Analysis of Exam Areas, beginning on page 15, and any other basic skills or exam areas you feel are necessary.

____ 21. **Carefully read** "Final Preparation" on page 443.

Part I: Introduction

GENERAL FORMAT OF THE SAT I: REASONING TEST

Section 1	Verbal Reasoning	30 Questions
30 Minutes	Sentence Completions Analogies Critical Reading (2 passages)	9 Questions 6 Questions 15 Questions
Section 2	**Mathematical Reasoning**	**25 Questions**
30 Minutes	Multiple Choice	25 Questions
Section 3	**Verbal Reasoning**	**35 Questions**
30 Minutes	Sentence Completions Analogies Critical Reading (1 passage)	10 Questions 13 Questions 12 Questions
Section 4	**Mathematical Reasoning**	**25 Questions**
30 Minutes	Quantitative Comparisons Grid-ins	15 Questions 10 Questions
Section 5	**Verbal Reasoning**	**13 Questions**
15 Minutes	Critical Reading (paired passages)	13 Questions
Section 6	**Mathematical Reasoning**	**10 Questions**
15 Minutes	Multiple Choice	10 Questions
Section 7	**Verbal or Math**	**25–35 Questions**
30 Minutes		25–35 Questions
Total Testing Time 180 Minutes = 3 Hours		Approximately 163–173 Questions

Note: the **order** in which the sections appear and the **number of questions** may vary, as this is a **new** test and there may be many forms. Only three of the verbal sections—two 30-minute sections and one 15-minute section (about 78 questions)—and three of the math sections—two 30-minute sections and one 15-minute section (about 60 questions)—actually count toward your SAT I score.

One 30-minute section is a "pretest," or "experimental," section that does not count toward your score. The "pretest," or "experimental," section can be a verbal or math section and can appear **anywhere** on your exam. It does **not** have to be section 7. **You should work all of the sections as though they count toward your score.**

GENERAL DESCRIPTION

The SAT I is used along with your high school record and other information to assess your competence for college work. The test lasts 3 hours and consists of mostly multiple-choice type questions, with some grid-in questions. The verbal sections test your ability to read critically, to understand word relationships, and to understand words in context. The math sections test your ability to solve problems in arithmetic, algebra, and geometry.

Comparing the New SAT I and the Old SAT

	SAT I	Old SAT
	Approximate Number of Questions	*Number of Questions*
Verbal		
Sentence Completions	19	15
Analogies	19	20
Reading	40	25
Antonyms	none	25
Total Verbal Questions	78	85
Math		
Multiple Choice	35	40
Quantitative Comparisons	15	20
Grid-ins	10	none
Total Math Questions	60	60

Special Notes for the SAT I

- Calculators may be used.
- On grid-in questions, there is no penalty for guessing.
- There is no TSWE (Test of Standard Written English) on SAT I.
- Verbal sections are now more reading and reasoning oriented.
- Math sections are now more reasoning oriented.

5

QUESTIONS COMMONLY ASKED ABOUT THE SAT I

Q: WHO ADMINISTERS THE SAT I?

A: The SAT I is part of the entire Admissions Testing Program (ATP), which is administered by the College Entrance Examination Board in conjunction with Educational Testing Service of Princeton, New Jersey.

Q: HOW IS THE NEW SAT I DIFFERENT FROM THE OLD SAT?

A: See the comparison chart on page 5.

Q: IS THERE A DIFFERENCE BETWEEN THE SAT I AND THE SAT II?

A: Yes. The SAT I assesses general verbal and mathematical reading and reasoning abilities that you have developed over your lifetime. The SAT II measures your proficiency in specific subject areas. The SAT II tests how well you have mastered a variety of high school subjects.

Q: CAN I TAKE THE SAT I MORE THAN ONCE?

A: Yes. But be aware that ATP score reporting is cumulative. That is, your score report will include scores from up to five previous test dates. It is not uncommon for students to take the test more than once.

Q: WHAT MATERIALS MAY I BRING TO THE SAT I?

A: Bring your registration form, positive identification, a watch, three or four sharpened Number 2 pencils, a good eraser, and your calculator. You may *not* bring scratch paper or books. You may do your figuring in the margins of the test booklet or in the space provided.

Q: IF NECESSARY, MAY I CANCEL MY SCORE?

A: Yes. You may cancel your score on the day of the test by telling the test center supervisor, or you may write or telegraph a cancellation to College Board ATP. Your score report will record your cancellation, along with any completed test scores.

Q: SHOULD I GUESS ON THE SAT I?

A: If you can eliminate one or more of the multiple-choice answers to a question, it is to your advantage to guess. Eliminating one or more answers increases your chance of choosing the right answer. To discourage wild guessing, a fraction of a point is subtracted for every wrong answer, but no points are subtracted if you leave the answer blank. On the grid-in questions, there is no penalty for filling in a wrong answer.

Q: HOW SHOULD I PREPARE FOR THE SAT I?

A: Understanding and practicing test-taking strategies will help a great deal, especially on the verbal sections. Subject-matter review is particularly useful for the math section. Both subject matter and strategies are fully covered in this book.

Q: WHEN IS THE SAT I ADMINISTERED?

A: The SAT I is administered nationwide six times during the school year, in November, December, January, March, May, and June. Some special administrations are given in limited locations.

Q: WHERE IS THE SAT I ADMINISTERED?

A: Your local college testing or placement office will have information about local administrations; ask for the *Student Bulletin.* The SAT I is administered at hundreds of schools in and out of the United States.

Q: HOW AND WHEN SHOULD I REGISTER?

A: A registration packet, complete with return envelope, is attached to the *Student Bulletin.* Mailing in these forms, plus the appropriate fees, completes the registration process. You should register about six weeks prior to the exam date.

Q: IS WALK-IN REGISTRATION PROVIDED?

A: Yes, on a limited basis. If you are unable to meet regular registration deadlines, you may attempt to register on the day of the test. (An additional fee is required.) You will be admitted only if space remains after preregistered students have been seated.

Q: CAN I GET MORE INFORMATION?
A: Yes. If you require information which is not available in this book, write or call one of these College Board regional offices.

Middle States: Suite 410, 3440 Market Street, Philadelphia, Pennsylvania 19104-3338. (215) 387-7600. Fax (215) 387-5805.
or
126 South Swan Street, Albany, New York 12210. (518) 472-1515. Fax (518) 472-1544.

Midwest: 1800 Sherman Avenue, Suite 401, Evanston, Illinois 60201-3715. (708) 866-1700. Fax (708) 866-9280.

New England: 470 Totten Pond Road, Waltham, Massachusetts 02154-1982. (617) 890-9150. Fax (617) 890-0693.

South: 2970 Clairmont Road, Suite 250, Atlanta, Georgia 30329-1639. (404) 636-9465. Fax (404) 633-3006.

Southwest: 701 Brazos Street, Suite 400, Austin, Texas 78701-3253. (512) 472-0231. Fax (512) 472-1401.

West: 2099 Gateway Place, Suite 480, San Jose, California 95110-1017. (408) 452-1400. Fax (408) 453-7396
or
4155 East Jewell Avenue, Suite 900, Denver, Colorado 80222-4510. (303) 759-1800. Fax (303) 756-8248.
or
Capitol Place, Suite 1200, 915 L Street, Sacramento, California 95814-3700. (916) 444-6262. Fax (916) 444-2868.

TAKING THE SAT I:
SUCCESSFUL OVERALL APPROACHES

I. The "Plus-Minus" System

Many who take the SAT I won't get their best possible score because they spend too much time on difficult questions, leaving insufficient time to answer the easy questions. Don't let this happen to you. Since every question within each section is worth the same amount, use the following system, *marking on your answer sheet:*

1. Answer easy questions immediately.
2. Place a "+" next to any problem that seems solvable but is too time consuming.
3. Place a "−" next to any problem that seems impossible. Act quickly; don't waste time deciding whether a problem is a "+" or a "−."

After working all the problems you can do immediately, go back and work your "+" problems. If you finish them, try your "−" problems (sometimes when you come back to a problem that seemed impossible, you will suddenly realize how to solve it).

Your answer sheet should look something like this after you finish working your easy questions:

```
 1. Ⓐ ● Ⓒ Ⓓ Ⓔ
+2. Ⓐ Ⓑ Ⓒ Ⓓ Ⓔ
 3. Ⓐ Ⓑ ● Ⓓ Ⓔ
−4. Ⓐ Ⓑ Ⓒ Ⓓ Ⓔ
+5. Ⓐ Ⓑ Ⓒ Ⓓ Ⓔ
```

Make sure to erase your "+" and "−" marks before your time is up. The scoring machine may count extraneous marks as wrong answers.

II. The Elimination Strategy

Take advantage of being allowed to mark in your testing booklet. As you eliminate an answer choice from consideration, *make sure to mark it out in your question booklet* as follows:

$$\cancel{(A)}$$
?(B)
$$\cancel{(C)}$$
$$\cancel{(D)}$$
?(E)

Notice that some choices are marked with question marks, signifying that they may be possible answers. This technique will help you avoid reconsidering those choices you have already eliminated and will help you narrow down your possible answers. *These marks in your testing booklet do not need to be erased.*

III. The "Avoiding Misreads" Method

Sometimes a question may have different answers depending upon what is asked. For example,

If $6y + 3x = 14$, what is the value of y?

The question may instead have asked, "what is the value of x?"

Or   If $3x + x = 20$, what is the value of $x + 2$?

Notice that this question doesn't ask for the value of x, but rather the value of $x + 2$.

Or   All of the following statements are true EXCEPT . . .

Or   Which of the expressions used in the first paragraph does NOT help develop the main idea?

Notice that the words EXCEPT and NOT change the above question significantly.

To avoid "misreading" a question (and therefore answering it incorrectly), simple *circle* what you must answer in the question. For example, do you have to find x or $x + 2$? Are you looking for what is true or the *exception* to what is true. To help you avoid misreads, mark the questions in your test booklet in this way:

If $6y + 3x = 14$, what is the value of ⓨ?

If $3x + x = 20 + 4$, what is the value of ⟨$x + 2$⟩?

All of the following statements are true ⟨EXCEPT⟩. . .

Which of the expressions used in the first paragraph does ⟨NOT help develop the main idea⟩?

And, once again, *these circles in your question booklet do not have to be erased.*

IV. The Multiple-Multiple-Choice Technique

Some math and verbal questions use a "multiple-multiple-choice" format. At first glance, these questions appear more confusing and more difficult than normal five-choice (A, B, C, D, E) multiple-choice problems. Actually, once you understand "multiple-multiple-choice" problem types and technique, they are often easier than a comparable standard multiple-choice question. For example,

If x is a positive integer, then which of the following must be true?

   I. $x > 0$
  II. $x = 0$
 III. $x < 1$

(A) I only   (D) I and II only
(B) II only   (E) I and III only
(C) III only

Since x is a positive integer, it must be a counting number. Note that possible values of x could be 1, or 2, or 3, or 4, and so on. Therefore, statement I, $x > 0$, is always true. So next to I on your question booklet, place a *T* for *true*.

T   I. $x > 0$
    II. $x = 0$
   III. $x < 1$

Now realize that the correct final answer choice (A, B, C, D, or E) *must* contain *true statement I*. This eliminates (B) and (C) as possible correct answer choices, as they do *not* contain true statement I. You should cross out (B) and (C) on your question booklet.

Statement II is *incorrect.* If x is positive, x cannot equal zero. Thus, next to II, you should place an *F* for *false*.

T   I. $x > 0$
F   II. $x = 0$
    III. $x < 1$

Knowing that II is false allows you to eliminate any answer choices that contain *false statement II*. Therefore, you should cross out (D), as it contains a false statement II. Only (A) and (E) are left as possible correct answers. Finally, you realize that statement III is also false, as x must be 1 or greater. So you place an *F* next to III, thus eliminating choice (E) and leaving (A), I only. This technique often saves some precious time and allows you to take a better educated guess should you not be able to complete all parts (I, II, III) of a multiple-multiple-choice question.

A Summary of General Strategies

1. **Set a goal.** Remember that an average score is about 50% right.
2. **Know the directions.**
3. Go into each section **looking for the questions you can do and should get right.**
4. **Don't get stuck** on any one question.
5. Be sure to **mark your answers in the right place.**
6. Be careful. **Watch out for careless mistakes.**
7. **Know when to skip a question.**
8. **Guess only if you can eliminate** one or more answers.
9. Don't be afraid to **fill in your answer or guess on grid-ins.**
10. **Practice** using the **"Plus-Minus" System,** the **Elimination Strategy,** the **"Avoiding Misreads" Method,** and the **Multiple-Multiple-Choice Technique.**
11. **Remember to erase** any extra marks on your answer sheet.

Part II: Analysis of Exam Areas

INTRODUCTION TO VERBAL REASONING

The Verbal Reasoning sections of the SAT I consist of three basic types of questions: sentence completions, analogies, and critical reading.

One Verbal Reasoning section is 30 minutes in length and contains 30 questions—sentence completions, analogies, and two critical reading passages. Another verbal section is 30 minutes in length and contains 35 questions—sentence completions, analogies, and one longer critical reading passage. And finally, a third verbal section is 15 minutes in length and contains 13 to 15 critical reading questions based on two related (paired) passages. Some questions concern one passage or the other, and some questions concern both passages.

Although the order of the sections and the number of questions may change, at this time the three sections total about 78 to 80 questions that count toward your score. These three sections generate a scaled verbal score that ranges from 200 to 800. About 50% right should generate an average score.

The questions within each of the sentence completion and analogy sections are arranged in slight graduation of difficulty from easier to more demanding questions. Basically, the first few questions are the easiest; the middle few are of average difficulty; and the last few are difficult. There is no such pattern for the critical reading passages or questions.

ANALOGIES

You will have approximately 10 analogy questions on each of two verbal sections on your exam, for a total of about 20 questions. In each section, the analogy questions are generally arranged in order from easier to more difficult.

Ability Tested

The analogy sections test your ability to understand logical relationships between pairs of words.

15

Basic Skills Necessary

The basic skills necessary for this section are a strong twelfth-grade vocabulary and the ability to distinguish relationships between words and ideas.

Directions

In each question below, you are given a related pair of words or phrases. Select the lettered pair that *best* expresses a relationship similar to that in the original pair of words.

Analysis of Directions

It is important that you focus on understanding the relationship between the original pair because this is really what you are trying to parallel. Notice that you are to select the *best* answer or most similar relationship. The use of the word *best* implies that there may be more than one good answer.

Suggested Approach with Samples

- **To begin with, make sure you know just what both words in the first pair mean. A simple word like *run* may be a noun or a verb. As a noun, it may mean the act of running, or a score in a baseball game, or a flaw in panty hose. As a verb, it may be intransitive (without an object) and mean to move rapidly—to run in a race. Or it may be transitive (taking an object) and mean to control or direct—to run a business.**

To determine what parts of speech the words in the original pair are, look at the five answer choices. All of the choices will be the same parts of speech as the original pair. So if you're not sure about a word in the first pair, the words in the choices will tell you what parts of speech are being used.

Sample

1. BOARDS : ROWBOAT ::
   - (A) disembarks : airplane
   - (B) enters : account book
   - (C) gets on : bus
   - (D) refuses : time
   - (E) hopes : fear

The word *boards* may be a verb meaning gets into or a noun describing the lumber from which *rowboats* are constructed. The best answer is (C). the choices make clear that *boards* is a verb. The relationship between *boards* and *rowboat* is the same as the relationship between *gets on* and *bus.*

- **To help determine the relationship between the original pair, construct a sentence explaining how the two words are related.**

Samples

2. SONNET : LITERATURE ::
   - (A) rhythm : poetry
   - (B) football : sport
   - (C) dancing : ballet
   - (D) research : biology
   - (E) acting : actor

The best answer is (B). In this case, you might say to yourself, "A *sonnet* is a type of *literature*" and therefore recognize that the relationship here is between an example and the larger category. Now, doing the same thing with the answer choices, you will find that the correct answer (B) shows the same relationship. *Football* is a type of *sport.* This sentence can be expressed as *"Sonnet* is to *literature* in the same way as *football* is to *sport."*

3. ANONYMOUS : NAME ::
   - (A) careful : measurement
   - (B) quick : importance
   - (C) formless : shape
   - (D) large : body
   - (E) colorful : hue

The best choice is (C). Your sentence should go something like this: "An *anonymous* person or thing is lacking a *name.*" Choice (C) is best because it correctly completes the sentence: "*Anonymous* describes the lack of a *name* in the same way as *formless* describes the lack of *shape.*"

Remember the standard analogy sentence: "A is to B in the same way as C is to D."

- **Try to make your sentence as precise as you can. Since some of the choices may be generally the same, a precise relationship may be required.**

Sample

4. HEART : HUMAN ::
   - (A) tail : dog
   - (B) hand : child
   - (C) kitchen : house
   - (D) brick : wall
   - (E) engine : car

The best choice is (E). While a *heart* is part of a *human,* a more precise relationship is that the *heart* is the essential, life-giving part of a *human.* Therefore, while every answer satisfies the part-whole relationship, (E) is the best answer, since the *engine* is the essential, life-giving part of the *car.*

- **Be sure to keep the order of the first pair like the order of your answer. Wrong answers may present a correct relationship but in the wrong order.**

Sample

5. SLEEPER : SMOKE ALARM ::
   - (A) snake : hiss
   - (B) air raid : siren
   - (C) car horn : driver
   - (D) sailor : lighthouse
   - (E) crossing : bell

The best choice is (D). Here a *sleeper* is warned by a *smoke alarm* in the same way as a *sailor* is warned by a *lighthouse.* Choice (C) is incorrect because the order is reversed.

- **Occasionally, you will need to consider not only the primary relationship between the original words, but also a secondary relationship.**

Sample

6. VANDALIZE : PROPERTY ::
   (A) judge : murderer
   (B) criticize : creativity
   (C) incinerate : combustibles
   (D) slander : reputation
   (E) courage : villainy

The best choice is (D). "To *vandalize* is to destroy *property.*" This sentence tells you that the original relationship is between an action and its object: *Property* is the object of vandalism. Beyond this primary relationship, there are secondary relationships to consider. First, notice that destruction is the object of vandalism. Second, notice that it is unlawful destruction. Scanning the choices, you see that to *judge* can destroy (condemn to death) a *murderer*; to *criticize* can destroy (by discouraging) *creativity*; and *courage* can (under certain conditions) destroy *villainy.* But in none of these choices— (A), (B), or (E)—is the relationship between the terms typically or necessarily one of destruction. In choice (C), to *incinerate* necessarily destroys *combustibles* (flammable objects); and in choice (D), *slander* typically destroys *reputation.* So both of these are possible choices. However, only one of them refers to a typically unlawful act as well, choice (D). Thus, taking the secondary relationships of the original pair fully into account, you should conclude that (D) is the best choice.

- **Remember that the second pair of words does not have to be from the same category, class, or type as the first pair of words.**

Sample

7. PUPPY : DOG ::
   - (A) sapling : tree
   - (B) canine : feline
   - (C) cat : lion
   - (D) poodle : terrier
   - (E) collie : mutt

The best choice is (A). Since in both pairs the first word is a youthful version of the second word, *sapling : tree* makes for a good analogy. It is not important that the first pair are animals and the second pair are plants. What is essential is the relationship.

Some Types of Relationships

The more practice you have working analogy problems, the more quickly you'll recognize some of the common relationships. Some relationships are given below. There are many other possibilities as well.

CLASSIFICATIONS: sorts, kinds, general to specific, specific to general, thing to quality or characteristic, opposites, degree, etc.

A broad category is paired with a narrower category
RODENT : SQUIRREL :: fish   : flounder
(broad   (narrower   (broad   (narrower
category)   category)   category)   category)

A person is paired with a characteristic
GIANT : BIGNESS :: baby : helplessness
(person)   (character-   (person) (character-
        istic)   istic)

The general is paired with the specific
PERSON : BOY :: vehicle : bus
(general)   (specific)   (general)   (specific)

A word is paired with a synonym of itself
VACUOUS : EMPTY :: seemly : fit
(word)   (synonym)   (word)   (synonym)

A word is paired with an antonym of itself
SLAVE : FREEMAN :: desolate : joyous
(word)   (antonym)   (word)   (antonym)

A word is paired with a definition of itself
ASSEVERATE : AFFIRM :: segregate : separate
(word)   (definition)   (word)   (definition)

A male is paired with a female
COLT : FILLY :: buck : doe
(male)   (female)   (male)   (female)

A family relationship is paired with a similar family relationship
FATHER : SON :: uncle :: nephew
(family relationship)   (family relationship)

A virtue is paired with a failing
FORTITUDE : COWARDICE :: honesty : dishonesty
(virtue)   (failing)   (virtue)   (failing)

An element is paired with a greater degree
WIND : TORNADO :: water : flood
(element)   (extreme)   (element)   (extreme)

A lesser degree is paired with a greater degree
HAPPY : ECSTATIC :: warm : hot
(lesser)   (greater)   (lesser)   (greater)

The plural is paired with the singular
WE : I   :: they : he
(plural) (singular) (plural) (singular)

STRUCTURALS: part to whole, whole to part, part to part, etc.

A part is paired with a whole
LEG : BODY :: wheel : car
(part)   (whole)   (part)   (whole)

A whole is paired with a part
TABLE : LEGS :: building : foundations
(whole)   (part)   (whole)   (part)

OPERATIONALS: time sequence, operations, stages, phases, beginning to ending, before to after, etc.

One element of time is paired with another element of time
DAY : NIGHT :: sunrise : sunset

(time element)   (time element)   (time element)   (time element)

A time sequence relationship is expressed
START : FINISH :: birth   : death

(beginning)   (ending)   (beginning)   (ending)

A complete operation is paired with a stage
FOOTBALL GAME : QUARTER :: baseball game : inning

(operation)   (stage)   (operation)   (stage)

OVERLAPPING: Many analogies will overlap into more than one of the above basic types and will have to be analyzed by their purpose, use, cause-effect relationship, etc.

A user is paired with his or her tool
FARMER : HOE :: dentist : drill

(user)   (tool)   (user)   (tool)

A creator is paired with a creation
ARTIST : PICTURE :: poet : poem

(creator)   (creation)   (creator)   (creation)

A cause is paired with its effect
CLOUD : RAIN :: sun   : heat

(cause)   (effect)   (cause)   (effect)

A person is paired with his or her profession
TEACHER : EDUCATION :: doctor : medicine

(person)   (profession)   (person)   (profession)

An instrument is paired with a function it performs
CAMERA : PHOTOGRAPHY :: yardstick : measurement

(instrument)   (function)   (instrument)   (function)

A symbol is paired with an institution
FLAG : GOVERNMENT :: cross : Christianity

(symbol)   (institution)   (symbol)   (institution)

A reward is paired with an action
MEDAL : BRAVERY :: trophy : championship

(reward)   (action)   (reward)   (action)

An object is paired with an obstacle that hinders it
AIRPLANE : FOG :: car : rut
(object)   (obstacle)   (object)   (obstacle)

Something is paired with a need that it satisfies
WATER : THIRST :: food : hunger
(thing)   (need)   (thing)   (need)

Something is paired with its natural medium
SHIP : WATER :: airplane : air
(thing)   (natural   (thing)   (natural
          medium)   medium)

Something is paired with something else that can operate it
DOOR : KEY :: safe : combination
(thing)   (operator)   (thing) (operator)

An object is paired with the material of which it is made
COAT : WOOL :: dress : cotton
(object)   (material)   (object)   (material)

Practice with Word Pairs

The following exercises are designed to increase your skill in determining the relationship between two words. This skill will help you predict the necessary relationship for a second pair of words in an analogy question.

For each item in this exercise, write a short sentence telling the relationship between the two words.

Example: PAW : CAT   A *paw* is part of a *cat.*

1. PAPER : WOOD *Paper is used to make wood.*

2. ROOF : HOUSE *A roof protects a house.*

3. DETAIN : RELEASE *Detain is an antonym of relese.*

4. SLITHER : SNAKE *To slither is an action of a snake.*

5. HEART : PUMP *An action of the heart is to pump.*

6. SPY : COVERT _____

7. OASIS : DESERT *antonyms* _____

8. COLD : SHIVER *Cold causes people to shiver.*

9. TYPEWRITER : RIBBON _____

10. MAGNET : IRON _____

11. TIRE : RUBBER _____

12. BINDERY : BOOKS _____

13. PEBBLE : BOULDER _____

14. METAL : ANVIL _____

15. DICTIONARY : MEANING _____

Possible Answers for Word Pairs

1. PAPER is made from WOOD.

2. The ROOF is the upper covering of a HOUSE.

3. DETAIN (hold up) is the opposite of RELEASE (let go).

4. SLITHER is the way a SNAKE travels.

5. The HEART performs the same function as a PUMP.

6. The activities of a SPY are COVERT.

7. An OASIS is a fertile area in a DESERT.

8. COLD makes people SHIVER.

9. A TYPEWRITER uses a RIBBON.

10. A MAGNET attracts IRON.

11. A TIRE is made mostly of RUBBER.

12. A BINDERY is a place where BOOKS are produced.

13. A PEBBLE is a very, very small BOULDER.

14. METAL is forged or shaped on an ANVIL.

15. A DICTIONARY is used to find the MEANING of words.

A Summary of Strategies for Analogy Questions

Make sure you know what both words mean. Check the choices to see if the words are being used as nouns, verbs, etc.

Construct a sentence explaining how the two words are related.

Try to make your sentence as precise as you can.

Be sure to keep the order of your answer like the order of the first pair.

Sometimes you will need to consider the secondary relationship between the words, not only the primary relationship.

Remember that the second pair of words does not have to be from the same category, class, or type as the first pair of words.

SENTENCE COMPLETION

You will have approximately 10 sentence completions on each of two verbal sections of the exam for a total of about 20 questions. In each section, the sentence completions will basically be arranged in order from easy to difficult.

Ability Tested

This section tests your ability to complete sentences with a word or words that retain the meaning of the sentence and are structurally and stylistically correct.

Basic Skills Necessary

Good reading comprehension skills help in this section, as does a good twelfth-grade vocabulary.

Directions

Each blank in the following sentences indicates that something has been omitted. Consider the lettered words beneath the sentence and choose the word or set of words that best fits the whole sentence.

Analysis of Directions

Note that you must choose the *best* word or words. In cases where several choices *might* fit, select the one that fits the meaning of the sentence most precisely. If the sentence contains two blanks, remember that *both* of the words corresponding to your choice must fit.

Suggested Approach with Samples

• *After* reading the sentence and *before* looking at the answer choices, think of words you would insert and look for synonyms of them.

Sample

1. Money _____ to a political campaign should be used for political purposes and nothing else.

How would you fill in the blank? Maybe with the word *given* or *donated*? Now look at the choices and find a synonym for *given* or *donated*.

(A) attracted
(B) forwarded
(C) contributed
(D) ascribed
(E) channeled

The best choice is (C) *contributed.* It is the nearest synonym of *given* or *donated* and makes good sense in the sentence.

• Look for signal words. Some signal words such as *however, although, on the other hand, but, instead, despite, regardless, rather than,* and *except* connect contrasting ideas.

Samples

2. Most candidates spend _____ they can raise on their campaigns, but others wind up on election day with a _____.
   (A) all . . . debt
   (B) whatever . . . liability
   (C) everything . . . surplus
   (D) every cent . . . deficit
   (E) nothing . . . war chest

The best choice is (C). *But* signals that the first half of the sentence *contrasts* with the second half. The fact that most candidates spend *everything* (and end up with nothing) contrasts with those who end up with a *surplus.*

3. Can public opinion be influenced so that it _____ rather than encourages the proliferation of the sale of firearms?
   (A) redoubles
   (B) advances
   (C) inverts
   (D) impedes
   (E) amplifies

The best choice is (D). The clue here is *rather than encourages.* You need a verb whose object is *proliferation* and which means the opposite of *encourages.* The best choice is *impedes,* which means obstructs or retards. To *invert* is to turn upside down.

4. The critic praised the scenery of the film enthusiastically, but _____ her enthusiasm when she discussed its plot and characterizations.
   (A) expanded
   (B) established
   (C) augmented
   (D) declined
   (E) tempered

The best choice is (E). The *but* signals that you need a verb denoting something different from the enthusiasm of the first part of the sentence. Choices (A), (B), and (C) contradict the *but.* The verb *tempered* (moderated, reduced in intensity) is both more suitable in meaning and more idiomatic than (D).

- **Other signal words such as** *in other words, besides, and, in addition, also, therefore, furthermore,* **and** *as* **often connect similar ideas or lead to a definition of the missing word.**

Samples

5. The tools found in the New Mexico excavation are _____, as a single implement might have several edges, each with a different use.
   (A) ancient
   (B) primitive
   (C) ferrous
   (D) versatile
   (E) reliable

The best choice is (D). The *tools* the sentence describes have *several edges* and several uses, and the missing adjective should fit these conditions. *Versatile* means capable of many things.

6. This treatise is concerned only with the process unique to the period in question; therefore, no attempt has been made to _____ phenomena _____ to that era.
   (A) include . . . unrelated
   (B) omit . . . irrelevant
   (C) re-create . . . germane
   (D) discuss . . . essential
   (E) evaluate . . . pertinent

The best choice is (A). The words in the first half of the sentence that are especially related to those to be filled in in the second half are *is concerned only* and *unique to the period*. The verb in the first blank is parallel to *is concerned* and describes the contents. Choices (A) *include,* (D) *discuss,* or possibly (E) *evaluate* are possible. The second blank needs an adjective that will make the phrase _____ *to that era* parallel to *unique to the period.* Choice (B) *irrelevant* would work, but only (A) has the correct first word.

• **Watch for contrasts between positive and negative words. Look for words like *not, never,* and *no.***

Samples

7. A virtuous person will not shout _____ in public; he or she will respect the _____ of other people.

The first blank is obviously a negative word, something that a good person would *not* shout; the second blank is a positive word, something that a good person *would* respect. Here are the choices:

    (A) obscenities . . . feelings
    (B) loudly . . . comfort
    (C) anywhere . . . presence
    (D) blessings . . . cynicism
    (E) insults . . . threat

The best choice is (A). Choice (B) is neutral-positive; (C) is neutral-neutral; (D) is positive-negative; (E) is negative-negative. Only choice (A) offers a negative-positive pair of words.

8. The chairperson was noted for not being obstinate; on the contrary, the members praised her _____.
    (A) resistance
    (B) experience
    (C) coherence
    (D) verbosity
    (E) flexibility

The best choice is (E). The correct answer must describe a praiseworthy quality opposite to obstinacy. Athough (B) and (C) are good qualities, only *flexibility* (E) means pliancy, the quality of being flexible.

- **Negative words can change the direction of the sentence, sometimes making the logic of the sentence more difficult to follow.**

Sample

9. Tamino's choice of the quest to rescue Pamina is _____, not accidental, and he undertakes it with _____ and steadfastness.
   (A) considered . . . trepidation
   (B) circumstantial . . . valor
   (C) intentional . . . reluctance
   (D) deliberate . . . courage
   (E) fortuitous . . . ardor

The best choice is (D). The adjective must be the opposite of *accidental.* The better choices are the synonyms of (A), (C), and (D)—*considered, intentional,* and *deliberate.* (B) and (E) do not fit this context. The second blank requires a noun that is like *steadfastness* or describes a sterling quality. Choice (A) *trepidation* means fear or hesitancy, and choice (C) *reluctance* means unwillingness. Neither will do, but (D) *courage* is what is needed.

- **Questions with two words missing should be attempted one word at a time.**

Sample

10. The _____ predictions of greatly decreased revenues next year have frightened lawmakers into _____ budget reductions.
    (A) encouraging . . . sizeable
    (B) convincing . . . minute
    (C) alarming . . . negligible
    (D) optimistic . . . huge
    (E) dire . . . drastic

The best choice is (E). Notice that trying the first word will help you eliminate answer choices (A), (B), and (D). If the predictions are of decreasing funds and frightening to lawmakers, the first adjective must be either *alarming* (C) or *dire* (E) (fearful, dreadful). Now try the second choice to get the correct answer. Since the lawmakers have been scared into action, you can infer that the reductions are *drastic* (E) rather than *negligible* (C).

• **Sometimes it is more efficient to work from the second blank first.**

Samples

11. Her parents were _____ when, despite losing the first three games, Sally _____ to win the set by a 6–3 score.
    (A) surprised . . . failed
    (B) relieved . . . came back
    (C) puzzled . . . refused
    (D) alarmed . . . attempted
    (E) delighted . . . was unable

The best answer is (B). There are no clues here to tell you which of the first words describes the reaction of the parents. Any of the five might work. But if you deal with the second blank first, you can see that the word *despite* makes it clear that Sally must win the set. Choice (B) *came back* looks like the best choice, although (D) is possible. That (B) is better is confirmed by the first word, as *relieved* is better than *alarmed*.

12. The merger will eliminate _____ and provide more _____ cross-training of staff.
    (A) profit . . . and more
    (B) paperwork . . . or less
    (C) duplication . . . effective
    (D) bosses . . . wasteful
    (E) competitors . . . aggressive

The best choice is (C). The second blank is something that is provided. Chances are that the something provided is a positive word, and *effective* seems like a good choice. Reading choice (C) into the sentence, you will find that it makes good sense and is stylistically and structurally correct.

• **If you don't spot any signal words or you don't know the meaning of some of the choices (or if you're just stumped), quickly read each answer choice in and see which sounds best. Sometimes this last method will help you at least eliminate some of the choices so that you can take an educated guess.**

Sample

13. The fertile and productive fields are located at the _____ of the Gila and the Arizona Rivers and are _____ by waters from both.
    (A) junction . . . desiccated
    (B) confluence . . . irrigated
    (C) bank . . . drained
    (D) source . . . submerged
    (E) end . . . inundated

The best choice is (B). The first word probably refers to the place where the rivers are close, since the fields are watered by both. Except for (C), any of the four nouns is possible. *Confluence* means a flowing together, the place where two waterways come together. The past participle must refer to the watering of these fertile lands. So *desiccated* (dried up) or *drained* can be eliminated. If the fields are productive, *irrigated* (supplied with water) makes better sense than *inundated* or *submerged*, which suggest destructive flooding.

A special reminder: Always read your answer into the sentence to make sure it makes sense. This will often help you avoid oversights or simple mistakes.

A Summary of Strategies for Sentence Completion Questions

After reading the sentence and before looking at the choices, think of words you would insert and look for synonyms of them.

Look for signal words like *however, although,* and *but* that connect contrasting ideas.

Look for signal words like *and, in other words,* and *therefore* that often connect similar ideas or lead to definitions of missing words.

Watch for contrasts between positive and negative words.

Negative words can change the direction of the sentence, sometimes making the logic of the sentence difficult to follow.

Questions with two words missing should be attempted one word at a time.

Sometimes it is more efficient to work from the second blank first.

If you're stumped, quickly read each answer choice into the sentence and see which sounds best.

Always read your answer into the sentence to make sure it makes sense.

CRITICAL READING

Critical reading appears in all three verbal sections—on two occasions, along with sentence completions and analogies as 30-minute sections and once alone as a complete 15-minute section. In one section, there are two passages—one 400 to 550 words in length, one 500 to 700 words in length—with from 5 to 9 questions following each passage. In another section, there is one longer passage, 750 to 850 words in length, followed by 12 or 13 questions. And in the 15-minute section, there are two related, or paired, passages—totaling about 750 to 900 words in length—with 13 to 15 questions following the "double passage." There are questions on each of the two passages and questions on both of the passages. In total, there are four sets of questions on five passages. Each exam will contain about 40 critical reading questions.

Ability Tested

This section tests your ability to understand, interpret, and analyze reading passages on a variety of topics. The passages on each exam will come from four content areas: humanities, social sciences, natural sciences, and narrative (fiction or nonfiction).

The common types of questions are those that ask you

- about the meaning of a word or phrase in the passage.
- about the main idea, main point, purpose, or even a possible title of the passage.
- about information that is directly stated in the passage.
- about information that is assumed, implied, suggested, or can be inferred.
- to recognize applications of the author's opinions or ideas.
- to evaluate how the author develops and presents the passage.
- to recognize the style or tone of the passage.

Basic Skills Necessary

Students who have read widely and know how to read and mark a passage actively and efficiently tend to do well on this section.

Directions

Questions follow each of the passages below. Using only the stated or implied information in each passage and in its introduction, if any, answer the questions.

Analysis of Directions

1. If you don't know the answer, take an educated guess or skip it.

2. Use only the information given or implied in a passage. Do not consider outside information, even if it seems more accurate than the given information.

Suggested Approaches with Sample Passages

- Base your answer on what you read in the passage, the introduction to the passage, or footnotes given following the passage. The passage must support your answer. All questions can and should be answered from information given or implied in the passage.

- Some good or true answers are not correct. Make sure that the answer you select is "what the question is asking for" according to the passage.

- Be sure to read all of the choices to make sure you have the best of the ones given. Some other choices may be good, but you're looking for the *best*. Watch out for "attractive distractors."

- Pace yourself. Don't get stuck on the passage or on any one question. If you have difficulty with one question, either take an educated guess by eliminating some choices or leave it blank and return to it briefly before you read the next passage (if there is more than one passage).

- When more than one reading passage is given, you may wish to first read the passage that is of more interest or familiarity to you and answer those questions before reading the next passage. But be careful if you skip a passage to mark your answers in the proper place on your answer sheet.

- You may wish to skim a few questions first, marking words which give you a clue about what to look for when you read the passage. This method can be especially helpful on unfamiliar passages. Try it on a variety of passages to see how it works for you.

- Read the passage actively, marking main points and other items you feel are important such as conclusions, names, definitions, places, and/or numbers. Make only a few such marks per paragraph. Remember, these marks are to help you understand the passage.

- On paired passages, the first questions will refer to Passage 1, the next group will refer to Passage 2, and the final group will refer to both passages as they relate to each other.

Sample Single Passage

Questions 1–5 are based on the following passage.

The following sample passage is the length of the shortest passage on the exam, 400 to 550 words.

Woodrow Wilson is usually ranked among the country's great presidents in spite of his failures to win Senate approval of the League of Nations. Wilson had yearned for a political career all his life; he won his first office in 1910
(5) when he was elected governor of New Jersey. Two years later he was elected president in one of the most rapid political rises in our history. For a while Wilson had practiced law but found it both boring and unprofitable; then he became a political scientist of great renown and
(10) finally president of Princeton University. He did an outstanding job at Princeton but lost out in a battle with Dean Andrew West for control of the graduate school. When he was asked by the Democratic boss of New Jersey, Jim Smith, to run for governor, Wilson readily accepted because his
(15) position at Princeton was becoming untenable.

Until 1910 Wilson seemed to be a conservative Democrat in the Grover Cleveland tradition. He had denounced Bryan in 1896 and had voted for the National Democratic candidate who supported gold. In fact, when the Democratic

(20) machine first pushed Wilson's nomination in 1912, the young New Jersey progressives wanted no part of him. Wilson later assured them that he would champion the progressive cause, and so they decided to work for his election. It is easy to accuse Wilson of political expediency,
(25) but it is entirely possible that by 1912 he had changed his views as had countless other Americans. While governor of New Jersey, he carried out his election pledges by enacting an impressive list of reforms.

Wilson secured the Democratic nomination on the forty-
(30) sixth ballot after a fierce battle with Champ Clark of Missouri and Oscar W. Underwood of Alabama. Clark actually had a majority of votes but was unable to attract the necessary two-thirds. In the campaign, Wilson emerged as the middle-of-the-road candidate—between the conserva-
(35) tive William H. Taft and the more radical Theodore Roosevelt. Wilson called his program the New Freedom, which he said was the restoration of free competition as it had existed before the growth of the trusts. In contrast, Theodore Roosevelt was advocating a New Nationalism,
(40) which seemed to call for massive federal intervention in the economic life of the nation. Wilson felt that the trusts should be destroyed, but he made a distinction between a trust and a legitimately successful big business. Theodore Roosevelt, on the other hand, accepted the trusts as
(45) inevitable but said that the government should regulate them by establishing a new regulatory agency. The former president also felt that a distinction should be made between the "good" trusts and the "bad" trusts.

1. The author's main purpose in writing this passage is to
   (A) argue that Wilson is one of the great U.S. presidents
   (B) survey the differences between Wilson, Taft, and Roosevelt
   (C) explain Wilson's concept of the New Freedom
   (D) discuss some major events of Wilson's career
   (E) suggest reasons that Wilson's presidency may have started World War I

The best choice is (D). Choices (A) and (E) are irrelevant to the information in the passage, and choices (B) and (C) mention secondary purposes rather than the primary one.

2. The author implies which of the following about the New Jersey progressives?
   (A) They did not support Wilson after he was governor.
   (B) They were not conservative Democrats.
   (C) They were more interested in political expediency.
   (D) Along with Wilson, they were supporters of Bryan in 1896.
   (E) They particularly admired Wilson's experience as president of Princeton University.

The best choice is (B). In the second paragraph. Wilson's decision to champion the progressive cause after 1912 is contrasted with his earlier career, when he seemed to be a conservative Democrat. Thus, it may be concluded that the progressives, whom Wilson finally joined, were not conservative Democrats, as was Wilson earlier in his career. Choices (A) and (D) contradict information in the paragraph, while choices (C) and (E) are not suggested by any information given in the passage.

3. The passage supports which of the following conclusions about the progress of Wilson's political career?
   (A) Few politicians have progressed so rapidly toward the attainment of higher office.
   (B) Failures late in his career caused him to be regarded as a president who regressed instead of progressed.
   (C) Wilson encountered little opposition once he determined to seek the presidency.
   (D) The League of Nations marked the end of Wilson's reputation as a strong leader.
   (E) Wilson's political progress was aided by Champ Clark and Oscar Underwood.

The best choice is (A). This choice is explicitly supported by the third sentence in the first paragraph in which we are told that Wilson *was elected president in one of the most rapid political rises in our history.*

4. At the end of the first paragraph in the phrase "his position at Princeton was becoming untenable" (lines 14–15), the meaning of "untenable" is which of the following?
   (A) Unlikely to last for ten years
   (B) Filled with considerably less tension
   (C) Difficult to maintain or continue
   (D) Filled with achievements that would appeal to voters
   (E) Something he did not have a tenacious desire to continue

The best choice is (C). Although choice (E) may attract your attention because *tenacious* looks similar to *tenable,* the correct choice is (C), which is the conventional definition of *untenable.*

5. From the passage, which of the following can be inferred about the presidential campaign of 1912?
   (A) Woodrow Wilson won the election by an overwhelming majority.
   (B) The inexperience of Theodore Roosevelt accounted for his radical position.
   (C) Wilson was unable to attract two-thirds of the votes but won anyway.
   (D) There were three nominated candidates for the presidency.
   (E) Wilson's New Freedom did not represent Democratic interests.

The best choice is (D). Choices (A), (B), and (C) contain information that is not addressed in the passage and can be eliminated as irrelevant. Choice (E) contradicts the fact that Wilson was a Democratic candidate. The discussion of Taft and Roosevelt as the candidates who finally ran against Wilson for the presidency supports choice (D).

Related, or Paired, Passages

Questions 1–13 are based on the following passages.

The following two passages, written in 1960 and 1980, discuss some limitations of television programs.

Passage 1

Despite all this increase in commercialization some—but not all—advertising men have wanted still greater control of the total content of the shows they sponsor. One producer, John E. Hasty, who had made shows for both Hollywood
(5) and television, was quoted as arguing that television could reach its full potential as an advertising medium only when advertising men produced the shows. "TV viewers cannot be regarded as an audience to be entertained," he said. "They are prospects . . . for what the sponsor has to sell.

(10) This fact constitutes the show's reason for being. . . . Thus in
a TV production the selling motive stands as the dominant
factor."

He granted that showmen from Broadway and Hollywood
might possess certain important skills that affect scripts,
(15) talent, music, and choreography and that they might be
generously endowed with skill and imagination. But, he
asked, "Does this overbalance a seasoned adman's experience in mass selling?"

Many sponsors tend to view their television vehicles as
(20) total advertisements. The Institute for Advertising Research has begun offering a new measuring technique called
Television Program Analysis which weights the total value
of a program as an ad for the company. And an advertising
trade journal in 1960 observed, "From all indications, a
(25) better tailoring of program type to advertiser, and commercial to program, is in the making. Taken together, commer-
cials and program in many cases accentuate the values of a
high-consumption economy."

Marketing consultant Victor Lebow summed up the
(30) powerful appeal television has as a selling medium when he
pointed out: "It creates a new set of conditions, impelling
toward a monopoly of the consumer's attention. For the first
time, almost the entire American consuming public has
become a captive audience. . . . Television actually sells the
(35) generalized idea of consumption." Cases in point to support
this theory that television sells "the generalized idea of
consumption" might be the squeals and ahs of television
audiences on panel shows when prizes such as stoves,
refrigerators, rotisseries, and matched luggage are unveiled
(40) amid fanfare.

One might speculate also on what it does to a people's
sense of values—especially to children's—when discussions
of significant events are followed on television by announc-
ers who in often louder and more solemn voices announce a
(45) great new discovery for a hair bleach. Or, to consider
another kind of juxtaposition, a broadcast appeal to aid
hungry children in mid-1960 was followed immediately by a
dog-food commercial.

Passage 2

A story's "newsworthiness" is often determined by geog-
(50) raphy. Journalist Thomas Griffith describes how he and his
colleagues used to argue over "how many people would
have to be killed where to make news—three people in an
auto wreck in your own town? Ten people drowning in a
shipwreck in the English channel; twenty-five in an ava-
(55) lanche in the Alps—and now the numbers increase sharply—
one hundred in an earthquake in Turkey; three hundred in
the collapse of a bridge in Bolivia; one thousand in a
typhoon off Calcutta; fifteen hundred in a fire in China?"
News, it appears, is what happens in your own backyard.
(60) This kind of reporting helps to magnify our provincialism.
The average American, asked to draw a map of the world,
would probably show the U.S.A. occupying half of the land
surface, with Europe and Russia and China and Africa
tucked off in some untidy, insignificant corner of the globe.
(65) Television news dissolves meaning in a wash of flashy
images. The takeover of Afghanistan is summed up with a
close-up view of a weeping widow, the problem of inflation
with an image of the interior of a supermarket with a tight
shot of the price of hamburger, the importance of gold price
(70) fluctuations with footage of gold traders frantically jostling
each other to get their orders in. A typical half-hour news
broadcast has fifteen to twenty stories. Allowing time for
commercial interruptions, that leaves an average of one
minute per story. Congressman Michael Synar says this
(75) makes for a simple-minded electorate: "When I go home I
have to deal with people, and all they know of a four-
hundred-page bill is one paragraph in the Sunday paper or a
thirty-second TV spot. Issues don't break that way, but
people just don't grasp the complexity."
(80) The criterion for how much time a story gets, or whether
it appears at all, is not its relative importance in world
affairs. "We like stories that have wiggle," one network
executive says. "Sexy stories. Iran has wiggle. Defectors
from the Bolshoi have wiggle. Stories about government
(85) agencies have *no wiggle.*"

In the mind of many network news executives, the difference between a good news story and Marilyn Monroe's posterior is undetectable. Reporters are told to go after the human interest angle to a story—the "people factor"—
(90) rather than to explore the how or why of a particular event. Researcher David Altheide once accompanied a reporter assigned to do a story on proposed alternatives to achieve racial integration. As they left the studio, the reporter explained how he planned to do the story: "Just barely give
(95) a background as to what these alternatives are. Explain the story over film of kids, bless their little hearts, who have no say in the matter whatsoever, caught in a game of politics between their parents and the school board." The dramatic peg for the story was thus determined before the reporter
(100) had even arrived at the scene!

Notice that the line numbers of the passages continue from the first to the second passage. The first group of questions are typically about Passage 1.

1. Which of the following best fulfills the ideal of the producer quoted in the first two paragraphs of Passage 1?
   (A) Music television
   (B) Educational television
   (C) Home-shopping television
   (D) Twenty-four hour television news
   (E) Situation comedy

The best answer is (C). Since the producer believes that selling is the real reason for television and sees the audience only as buyers, his ideal would be realized by home-shopping television where there is no pretense about buying and selling.

2. In line 17, "seasoned" means
   (A) improved in quality
   (B) experienced
   (C) softened
   (D) flavored
   (E) changed in ability

The best choice is (B). Although a dictionary would list all five of these definitions of *seasoned,* here it means experienced or mature.

3. According to Passage 1, television programs may be expected to become
   (A) increasingly dependent on comedy and games
   (B) more carefully crafted to sell a product
   (C) more dependent on Broadway and Hollywood directors
   (D) less dependent on depicting sex and violence
   (E) more carefully edited to suit children's viewing

The best choice is (B). The third paragraph speaks of *a better tailoring of program type to advertiser, and commercial to program.*

4. The sentence "Television actually sells the generalized idea of consumption" (lines 34–35) is best understood to mean that
   (A) the more people watch television, the more likely they are to buy an advertised product
   (B) television is by and large indifferent to the ecological needs of the modern world
   (C) television, more than any other medium, is suited to the selling of products to a mass audience
   (D) game and panel programs which feature costly prizes pander to the greed of the audience
   (E) by reflecting the consumer values of society, television encourages its viewer to consume more

The best choice is (E). Although some of the statements here may be true or may express ideas that the passage is in sympathy with, only (E) specifically paraphrases or interprets the quotation of the question. By showing consumer products and luxury, television programs make the idea of owning more attractive to viewers.

5. In line 46, the word "juxtaposition" means
    (A) placing side by side
    (B) sequence of events
    (C) misunderstanding
    (D) unintentional joke
    (E) inappropriate comparison

The best choice is (A). A *juxtaposition* is a placing side by side.

The next group of questions is usually about Passage 2.

6. Which of the following best answers the question of the first paragraph of Passage 2, "how many people would have to be killed where to make news" (lines 51–52)?
    (A) A small number of deaths will not make news.
    (B) The number killed in an earthquake must be at least four times greater than the number killed in an avalanche.
    (C) Local accidents are not news.
    (D) The smaller the number of deaths, the closer to home they must be.
    (E) Ten deaths in an air crash in East Africa would be more likely to make news than ten deaths in an explosion in West Africa.

The best choice is (D). The question asks both *how many* and *where.* The passage makes clear that news, on television, is *what happens in your own backyard,* so a small number of local deaths would make news, but in distant areas, the size and spectacle would have to be much greater.

7. In the second paragraph of Passage 2, the point of describing the world map an average American would draw is to show that
   (A) Americans know less about geography than the citizens of other countries
   (B) the United States occupies half of the world's land surface
   (C) Americans have a false notion of the importance of the United States
   (D) Americans are usually unable to identify the capital cities of other nations
   (E) Americans' knowledge of geography has improved since television became popular

The best choice is (C). The paragraph is about the *provincialism,* that is, the narrowness of outlook, of most Americans, and the map most Americans would draw reveals how little they know about the rest of the world and how much they overestimate their own importance. The passage does not tell us whether or not people elsewhere are more or less provincial.

8. In Passage 2 (line 77), the word "bill" means
   (A) a statement of charges for services or goods
   (B) any written document with a seal
   (C) a list of things offered
   (D) a draft of a law
   (E) a bank note

The best choice is (D). As it is used here, *bill* means the draft of a law. The speaker is a congressman speaking of his constituents' ignorance of legislation in congress.

9. The phrase to "have wiggle" used in the fourth paragraph of Passage 2 is best taken to mean to
   (A) have popular appeal
   (B) have overt sexual interest
   (C) involve stars of film or theater
   (D) move sinuously
   (E) have serious implications

The best choice is (A). As it is used here, *wiggle* is figurative, not literal, since *Iran has wiggle*. It stands for what has popular appeal.

10. Of the following aspects of television mentioned in Passage 2, which does the author believe should be foremost in news broadcasting?
    (A) "flashy images" (lines 65–66)
    (B) "wiggle" (line 82)
    (C) "the human interest angle" (lines 88–89)
    (D) "the 'people factor' " (line 89)
    (E) "the how or why of a particular event" (line 90)

The best choice is (E). The author would favor television news that deals with *the how or why* of events, although television programmers have preferred the four other options.

11. From Passage 2, it can be inferred that a news story on which of the following topics would be least likely to appear on television news broadcasts?
    (A) The computer systems of the Internal Revenue Service
    (B) A local woman's entry in the Miss America contest
    (C) The marriage of a rock star and a soap opera actress
    (D) The effect of flooding on the Mississippi
    (E) Espionage in New York City

The best choice is (A). The computers of the IRS have little drama, human interest, or local appeal, so they are less likely to be considered *newsworthy*.

The last group of questions usually relies on both passages, comparing and contrasting general ideas and specific points.

12. Unlike Passage 2, Passage 1 is an attack upon television chiefly for its
    (A) parochialism
    (B) materialism
    (C) superficiality
    (D) anti-intellectualism
    (E) lack of objectivity

The best choice is (B). The focus of Passage 1 is on materialism, television as a vehicle for selling. Passage 2 attacks the parochialism, superficiality, and anti-intellectualism of television news broadcasts.

13. Which of the following best describes the primary difference between the two passages?
    (A) Passage 1 is serious in tone, while Passage 2 is comic and colloquial.
    (B) Passage 1, on the whole, approves of television programming, while Passage 2 is harshly critical.
    (C) Passage 1 is concerned with the way that television harms the moral values of all viewers, while Passage 2 is concerned with the failure to report world events accurately.
    (D) Passage 1 is chiefly concerned with the influence of advertisers on television, while Passage 2 is chiefly concerned with the superficiality of television news programs.
    (E) Passage 1 is concerned with the audience of television programs, while Passage 2 is concerned with the programs.

The best choice is (D). Passage 2, though colloquial, is very serious in tone. Neither passage approves of television as it is. Passage 1 mentions value in only one paragraph. Both passages are concerned with audience and programs. Choice (D) is a reasonable summary of the two passages.

A Summary of Strategies for Critical Reading Questions

Base your answer on what you read in the passage, the introduction to the passage, or footnotes given following the passage.

The passage must support your answer.

Some good or true answers are not correct. Make sure the answer you select is "what the question is asking for."

Be sure to read all of the choices to make sure you have the best of the ones given.

Pace yourself. Don't get stuck on the passage or any one question.

When more than one reading passage is given, you may wish to first read the passage that is of more interest or familiarity to you and answer those questions first. When skipping, be extra careful to mark your answers in the proper place on your answer sheet.

You may wish to skim a few questions first, marking words which give you a clue about the passage before you read the passage.

Read the passage actively, marking main points and other items you feel are important.

On paired passages, the first questions will refer to Passage 1, the next group of questions to Passage 2, and the final group to both passages as they relate to each other.

INTRODUCTION TO MATHEMATICAL REASONING

The Mathematical Reasoning sections of the SAT I consist of three basic types of questions: regular multiple-choice questions, quantitative comparisons, and grid-ins.

One Mathematical Reasoning section is 30 minutes in length and contains 25 multiple-choice questions. Another math section is 30 minutes in length and contains 15 quantitative comparisons and 10 grid-ins (25 total questions). And finally, a third math section is 15 minutes in length and contains 10 multiple-choice questions. Although the order of the sections and the number of questions may change, at this time, the three sections total 60 math questions that count toward your score. These three sections generate a scaled math score that ranges from 200 to 800. About 50% right should generate an average score.

The math sections are slightly graduated in difficulty. That is, the easiest questions are basically at the beginning and the more difficult ones at the end. If a section has two types of questions, usually each type starts with easier problems. For example, a section starts with easy quantitative comparisons, and the last few quantitative comparisons become difficult before you start grid-ins. The grid-ins start with easy questions and move toward the more difficult ones at the end.

- You will be given reference information preceding each Mathematical Reasoning section. You should be familiar with this information.

- You may use a calculator on the new SAT I. Bring a calculator you are familiar with.

USING YOUR CALCULATOR

The new SAT I allows the use of calculators, and the College Board (the people who sponsor the exam) recommends that each test taker take a calculator to the test. Even though no question will require the use of a calculator—that is, each question can be answered without a calculator—in some instances, using a calculator will save you valuable time.

You should

- Bring your own calculator, since you can't borrow one during the exam.
- Bring a calculator even if you don't think you'll use it.
- Make sure that you are familiar with the use of your calculator.
- Make sure that your calculator has new, fresh batteries and is in good working order.
- Practice using your calculator on some of the problems to see when and where it will be helpful.
- Check for a shortcut to any problem that seems to involve much computation. But use your calculator if it will be time effective. If there appears to be too much computation or the problem seems impossible without the calculator, you're probably doing something wrong.
- Before doing an operation, check the number that you keyed in on the display to make sure that you keyed in the right number. You may wish to check each number as you key it in.
- Before using your calculator, set up the problem and/or steps on your paper. Write the numbers on paper as you perform each step on your calculator. (It is generally safer not to use the memory function on your calculator.)
- Be sure to carefully clear the calculator before beginning new calculations.

Be careful that you

- Don't rush out and buy a sophisticated calculator for the test.
- Don't bring a calculator that you're unfamiliar with.
- Don't bring a pocket organizer, handheld mini-computer, laptop computer, or calculator with a typewriter-type keypad or paper tape.
- Don't bring a calculator that requires an outlet or any other external power source.
- Don't bring a calculator that makes noise.
- Don't try to share a calculator.
- Don't try to use a calculator on every problem.
- Don't become dependent on your calculator.

Take advantage of being allowed to use a calculator on the test. Learn to use a calculator efficiently by practicing. As you approach a problem, first focus on how to solve that problem, and then decide if the calculator will be helpful. Remember, a calculator can save you time on some problems, but also remember that each problem can be solved without a calculator. Also remember that a calculator will not solve a problem for you by itself. You must understand the problem first.

BASIC SKILLS AND CONCEPTS YOU SHOULD BE FAMILIAR WITH

ARITHMETIC

Operations with fractions
Applying addition, subtraction, multiplication, and division to
  problem solving
Arithmetic mean (average), mode, and median
Ratio and proportion
Number properties: positive and negative integers, odd and even
  numbers, prime numbers, factors and multiples, divisibility
Word problems, solving for: percents, averages, rate, time, distance,
  interest, price per item
Number line: order, consecutive numbers, fractions, betweenness

ALGEBRA

Operations with signed numbers
Substitution for variables
Working with algebraic expressions
Word problems
Solving equations
Solving inequalities
Basic factoring
Working with positive exponents
Working with positive roots
Elementary quadratic equations

GEOMETRY

Vertical angles
Angles in figures
Perpendicular and parallel lines
Perimeter, area, angle measure of polygons
Circumference, area, radius, diameter
Triangles: right, isosceles, equilateral, angle measure, similarity
Special triangles: $30° - 60° - 90°$, $45° - 45° - 90°$
Pythagorean theorem
Volume and surface area of solids
Coordinate geometry: coordinates, slope

OTHER TOPICS

Interpreting graphs, charts, and tables
Sequence problems
Probability
Special symbols or false operations
Reasoning problems

The Mathematical Reasoning sections do NOT include:

Time-consuming and tedious computations
Fractional exponents
Use of quadratic formula
Complicated roots and radicals
Geometric proofs

MULTIPLE-CHOICE QUESTIONS

You should have a total of about 35 multiple-choice questions—25 in one 30-minute section and 10 in a 15-minute section.

Ability Tested

The Mathematical Reasoning multiple-choice section tests your ability to solve mathematical problems involving arithmetic, algebra, geometry, and word problems by using problem-solving insight, logic, and the application of basic skills.

Basic Skills Necessary

The basic skills necessary to do well on this section include first-year high school algebra and intuitive geometry. No formal trigonometry or calculus is necessary. Logical insight into problem-solving situations is also necessary.

Directions

Solve each problem in this section by using the information given and your own mathematical calculations, insights, and problem-solving skills. Then select the one correct answer of the five choices given and mark the corresponding circle on your answer sheet. Use the available space on the page for your scratchwork.

Notes

(1) All numbers used are real numbers.
(2) Calculators may be used.
(3) Some problems may be accompanied by figures or diagrams. These figures are drawn as accurately as possible EXCEPT when it is stated in a specific problem that a figure is not drawn to scale. The figures and diagrams are meant to provide information useful in solving the problem or problems. Unless otherwise stated, all figures and diagrams lie in a plane.

A list of data that may be used for reference is included.

Analysis of Directions

All scratchwork is to be done in the test booklet; get used to doing this because no scratch paper is allowed into the testing area.

You are looking for the *one* correct answer; therefore, although other answers may be close, there is never more than one right answer.

Suggested Approach with Samples

- **Take advantage of being allowed to mark on the test booklet by always underlining or circling what you are looking for. This will ensure that you are answering the right question.**

Samples

1. If $x + 6 = 9$, then $3x + 1 =$
   (A) 3   (B) 9   (C) 10   (D) 34   (E) 46

You should first circle or underline $3x + 1$ because this is what you are solving for. Solving for x leaves $x - 3$, and then substituting into $3x + 1$ gives $3(3) + 1$, or 10. The most common mistake is to solve for x, which is 3, and *mistakenly choose* (A) as your answer. But remember, you are solving for $3x + 1$, not just x. You should also notice that most of the other choices would all be possible answers if you made common or simple mistakes. The correct answer is (C). *Make sure that you are answering the right question.*

2. Together, a hat and coat costs $125. The coat costs $25 more than the hat. What is the cost of the coat?
   (A) $25   (B) $50   (C) $75   (D) $100   (E) $125

The key words here are *cost of the coat,* so circle those words. To solve algebraically,

$$x = \text{hat}$$
$$x + 25 = \text{coat (cost \$25 more than the hat)}$$

Together they cost $125.

$$(x + 25) + x = 125$$
$$2x + 25 = 125$$
$$2x = 100$$
$$x = 50$$

But this is the cost of the *hat*. Notice that $50 is one of the answer choices, (B). Since $x = 50$, then $x + 25 = 75$. Therefore, the coat costs $75, which is choice (C). *Always answer the question that is being asked.* Circling the key word or words will help you do that.

- **Substituting numbers for variables can often be an aid to understanding a problem. Remember to substitute simple numbers, since *you* have to do the work.**

Samples

3. If $x > 1$, which of the following decreases as x decreases?

I. $x + x^2$

II. $2x^2 - x$

III. $\dfrac{1}{x + 1}$

(A) I only   (D) I and II only
(B) II only   (E) II and III only
(C) III only

This problem is most easily solved by taking each situation and substituting simple numbers. However, in the first situation (I. $x + x^2$), you should recognize that this expression will decrease as x decreases. Trying $x = 2$ gives $2 + (2)^2 = 6$. Now, trying $x = 3$ gives $3 + (3)^2 = 12$. Notice that choices (B), (C), and (E) are already eliminated because they do not contain I. You should also realize that now you need to try only the values in II. Since III is not paired with I as a possible choice, III cannot be one of the answers.

Trying $x = 2$ in the expression $2x^2 - x$ gives $2(2)^2 - 2$, or $2(4) - 2 = 6$. Now, trying $x = 3$ gives $2(3)^2 - 3$, or $2(9) - 3 = 15$. This expression also decreases as x decreases. Therefore, the correct answer is (D). Once again, notice that III was not even attempted because it was not one of the possible choices. Be sure to make logical substitutions. Use a positive number, a negative number, or zero when applicable to get the full picture.

4. If x is a positive integer in the equation $12x = q$, then q must be
   (A) a positive even integer
   (B) a negative even integer
   (C) zero
   (D) a positive odd integer
   (E) a negative odd integer

At first glance, this problem appears quite complex. But let's plug in some numbers, and see what happens. For instance, first plug in 1 (the simplest positive integer) for x.

$$12x = q$$
$$12(1) = q$$
$$12 = q$$

Now try 2.

$$12x = q$$
$$12(2) = q$$
$$24 = q$$

Try it again. No matter what positive integer is plugged in for x, q will always be positive and even. Therefore, the answer is (A).

Trying simple numbers in word problems can also be effective. Remember to select numbers that are easy to work with such as 1, 2, 10, or 100.

5. A corporation triples its annual bonus to 50 of its employees. What percent of the employees' new bonus is the increase?
   (A) 50%   (D) 200%
   (B) 66⅔%   (E) 300%
   (C) 100%

The correct answer is (B). Let's use $100 for the normal bonus. If the annual bonus was normally $100, tripled it would now be $300. Therefore, the increase ($200) is ⅔ of the new bonus ($300). Two-thirds is 66⅔%.

- **Sometimes you will immediately recognize the proper formula or method to solve a problem. If this is not the situation, try a reasonable approach and then work from the answers.**

Samples

6. Barney can mow the lawn in 5 hours, and Fred can mow the lawn in 4 hours. How long will it take them to mow the lawn together?
   - (A) 5 hours
   - (B) 4½ hours
   - (C) 4 hours
   - (D) 2⅔ hours
   - (E) 1 hour

Suppose that you are unfamiliar with the type of equation for this problem. Try the "reasonable" method. Since Fred can mow the lawn in 4 hours by himself, it will take less than 4 hours if Barney helps him. Therefore, choices (A), (B) and (C) are ridiculous. Taking this method a little further, suppose that Barney could also mow the lawn in 4 hours. Then, together it would take Barney and Fred 2 hours. But since Barney is a little slower than this, the total time should be a little more than 2 hours. The correct answer is (D), 2⅔ hours.

Using the equation for this problem would give the following calculations:

$$\frac{1}{5} + \frac{1}{4} = \frac{1}{x}$$

In 1 hour, Barney could do ⅕ of the job, and in 1 hour, Fred could do ¼ of the job. Unknown $\frac{1}{x}$ is that part of the job they could do together in one hour. Now solving, you calculate as follows:

$$\frac{4}{20} + \frac{5}{20} = \frac{1}{x}$$

$$\frac{9}{20} = \frac{1}{x}$$

Cross multiplying gives $9x = 20$

Therefore, $x = {}^{20}\!/_{9}$ or 2⅔

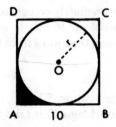

7. Circle O is inscribed in square ABCD as shown above. The area of the shaded region is approximately
   (A) 10   (B) 25   (C) 30   (D) 50   (E) 75

The correct answer is (A). Using a reasonable approach, you would first find the area of the square: $10 \times 10 = 100$. Then divide the square into four equal sections as follows:

Since a quarter of the square is 25, then the shaded region must be much less than 25. The only possible answer is choice (A) 10.

Another approach to this problem would be to first find the area of the square: $10 \times 10 = 100$. Then subtract the approximate area of the circle: $A = \pi(r^2) \cong 3(5^2) = 3(25) = 75$. Therefore, the total area inside the square but outside the circle is approximately 25. One quarter of that area is shaded. Therefore, $25/4$ is approximately the shaded area. The closest answer is (A) 10.

- **"Pulling" information out of the word problem structure can often give you a better look at what you are working with; therefore, you gain additional insight into the problem.**

Samples

8. If a mixture is ³⁄₇ alcohol by volume and ⁴⁄₇ water by volume, what is the ratio of the volume of alcohol to the volume of water in this mixture?
   (A) ³⁄₇   (B) ⁴⁄₇   (C) ¾   (D) ⁴⁄₃   (E)⁷⁄₄

The first bit of information that should be pulled out should be what you are looking for: "ratio of the volume of alcohol to the volume of water." Rewrite it as $A{:}W$ and then into its working form: A/W. Next, you should pull out the volumes of each: $A = ³⁄₇$ and $W = ⁴⁄₇$.

Now the answer can be easily figured by inspection or substitution. Using $(³⁄₇)/(⁴⁄₇)$, invert the bottom fraction and multiply to get $³⁄₇ × ⁷⁄₄ = ¾$. The ratio of the volume of alcohol to the volume of water is 3 to 4. The correct answer is (C).

When pulling out information, actually write out the numbers and/or letters to the side of the problem, putting them into some helpful form and eliminating some of the wording.

9. Bill is ten years older than his sister. If Bill was twenty-five years of age in 1983, in what year could he have been born?
   (A) 1948   (D) 1963
   (B) 1953   (E) 1968
   (C) 1958

The key words here are *in what year* and *could he have been born.* Thus the solution is simple: $1983 - 25 = 1958$, answer (C). Notice that you pulled out the information *twenty-five years of age* and *in 1983.* The fact about Bill's age in comparison to his sister's age was not needed, however, and was not pulled out.

- **Sketching diagrams or simple pictures can also be very helpful in problem solving because the diagram may tip off either a simple solution or a method for solving the problem.**

Samples

10. If all sides of a square are halved, the area of that square is
    - (A) halved
    - (B) divided by 3
    - (C) divided by 4
    - (D) divided by 8
    - (E) divided by 16

One way to solve this problem is to draw a square and then halve all its sides. Then compare the two areas.

Your first diagram   Halving every side

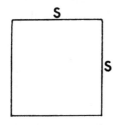   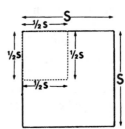

Notice that the total area of the new square will now be one-fourth the original square. The correct answer is (C).

11. If P lies on $\widehat{ON}$ such that $\widehat{OP} = 2\widehat{PN}$ and Q lies on $\widehat{OP}$ such that $\widehat{OQ} = \widehat{QP}$, what is the relationship of $\widehat{OQ}$ to $\widehat{PN}$?
    - (A) ⅓   (B) ½   (C) 1   (D) ²⁄₁   (E) ³⁄₁

A sketch would look like this:

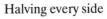

It is evident that $\widehat{OQ} = \widehat{PN}$, so the ratio is 1/1, or 1. Or you could assign values on $\widehat{ON}$ such that $\widehat{OP} = 2\widehat{PN}$: $\widehat{OP}$ could equal 2, and $\widehat{PN}$ could equal 1. If Q lies on $\widehat{OP}$ such that $\widehat{OQ} = \widehat{QP}$, then $\widehat{OP}$ (2) is divided in half. So $\widehat{OQ} = 1$, and $\widehat{QP} = 1$. So the relationship of $\widehat{OQ}$ to $\widehat{PN}$ is 1 to 1. The correct answer is (C).

8 × 3 × 2 = 48

12. What is the maximum number of milk cartons, each 2″ wide by 3″ long by 4″ tall, that can fit into a cardboard box with inside dimensions of 16″ wide by 9″ long by 8″ tall?

(A) 12   (B) 18   (C) 20   (D) 24   (E) 48

The correct answer is (E). Drawing a diagram, as shown below, may be helpful in envisioning the process of fitting the cartons into the box. Notice that 8 cartons will fit across the box, 3 cartons deep, and two "stacks" high:

$$8 \times 3 \times 2 = 48 \text{ cartons}$$

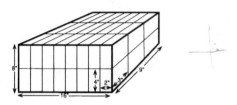

13. If point P(1, 1) and Q(1, 0) lie on the same coordinate graph, which must be true?

   I. P and Q are equidistant from the origin.
  II. P is farther from the origin that P is from Q.
 III. Q is farther from the origin than Q is from P.

(A) I only   (D) I and II only
(B) II only   (E) I and III only
(C) III only

First draw the coordinate graph and then plot the points as follows:

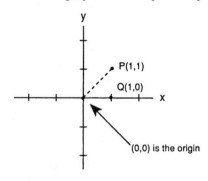

The correct answer is (B). Only II is true. P is farther from the origin than P is from Q.

- **Marking in diagrams as you read the questions can save you valuable time. Marking can also give you insight into how to solve a problem because you will have the complete picture clearly in front of you.**

Samples

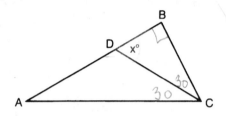

14. In the triangle above, CD is an angle bisector, angle ACD is 30°, and angle ABC is a right angle. What is the measurement of angle *x* in degrees?

    (A) 30°   (B) 45°   (C) 60°   (D) 75°   (E) 80°

You should have read the problem and marked as follows: In the triangle above, CD is an angle bisector (*Stop and mark in the drawing*), angle ACD is 30° (*Stop and mark in the drawing*), and angle ABC is a right angle (*Stop and mark in the drawing*). What is the measurement of angle *x* in degrees? (*Stop and mark in or circle what you are looking for in the drawing*).

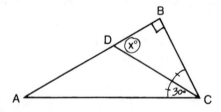

   Now, with the drawing marked in, it is evident that, since angle ACD is 30°, then angle BCD is also 30° because they are formed by an angle bisector (divides an angle into two equal parts). Since angle ABC is 90° (right angle) and angle BCD is 30°, then angle *x* is 60° because there are 180° in a triangle.

$$180 - (90 + 30) = 60$$

The correct answer is (C). *Always mark in diagrams as you read descriptions and information about them. This includes what you are looking for.*

15. If each square in the figure
    has a side of length 3,
    what is the perimeter?
    (A) 12
    (B) 14
    (C) 21
    (D) 30
    (E) 36

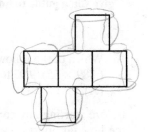

Mark the known facts.

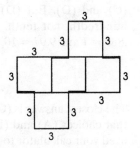

We now have a calculation for the perimeter: 30 *plus* the darkened parts. Now look carefully at the top two darkened parts. They will add up to 3. (Notice how the top square may slide over to illustrate that fact.)

The same is true for the bottom
darkened parts. They will add to 3.

Thus, the total perimeter is
30 + 6 = 36, choice (E).

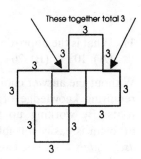

- **If it appears that extensive calculations are going to be necessary to solve a problem, check to see how far apart the choices are and then approximate. The reason for checking the answers first is to give you a guide to how freely you can approximate.**

Sample

16. Which of the following is the best approximation of
    (.889 × 55)/9.97 to the nearest tenth?
    (A) 49.1   (B) 7.7   (C) 4.9   (D) 4.63   (E) .5

Before starting any computations, take a glance at the answers to see how far apart they are. Notice that the only close answers are (C) and (D). But (D) is not possible, since it is to the nearest hundredth, not tenth. Now, making some quick approximations, .889 = 1 and 9.97 = 10, which leaves the problem in this form:

$$\frac{1 \times 55}{10} = \frac{55}{10} = 5.5$$

The closest answer is (C). Therefore, it is the correct answer. Notice that choices (A) and (E) are not reasonable. You could also have used your calculator to obtain an exact answer and then rounded to the nearest tenth.

- **In some instances, it will be easier to work from the answers. Do not disregard this method because it will at least eliminate some of the choices and could give you the correct answer.**

Sample

17. What is the approximate value of $\sqrt{1596}$?
    (A) 10   (B) 20   (C) 30   (D) 40   (E) 50

Without the answer choices, this would be a very difficult problem, requiring knowledge of a special procedure to calculate square roots. By working up from the answer choices, however, the problem is easily solvable. Since $\sqrt{1596}$ means *what number times itself equals 1596,* you can take any answer choice and multiple it by itself. As soon as you find the answer choice that when multiplied by itself approximates 1596, you've got the correct answer. You may wish to start working from the middle choice, since the answers are usually in increasing or decreasing order. In the problem above, start with choice (C) 30. Since $30 \times 30 = 900$, which is too small, you could now eliminate (A), (B), and (C) as too small. If your calculator computes square roots, you could have used it and then rounded off.

$$\frac{x}{4} = 20 \qquad x = 80$$

18. If $(x/4) + 2 = 22$, what is the value of x?

 (A) 40   (B) 80   (C) 100   (D) 120   (E) 160

If you cannot solve this algebraically, you may use the *work up from your choices* strategy. But start with (C) 100. What if $x = 100$?

$$(x/4) + 2 = 22$$
$$(100/4) + 2 \stackrel{?}{=} 22$$
$$25 + 2 \stackrel{?}{=} 22$$
$$27 \neq 22$$

Note that since 27 is too large, choices (D) and (E) will also be too large. Therefore, try (A). If (A) is too small, then you know the answer is (B). If (A) works, the answer is (A).

$$(x/4) + 2 = 22$$
$$(40/4) + 2 \stackrel{?}{=} 22$$
$$10 + 2 \stackrel{?}{=} 22$$
$$12 \neq 22$$

Since (A) is too small, the answer must be (B).

19. What is the greatest common factor of the numbers 18, 24, and 30?

 (A) 2   (B) 3   (C) 4   (D) 6   (E) 12

The correct answer is (D). The largest number which divides evenly into 18, 24, and 30 is 6. You could have worked from the answers. But here you should start with the largest answer choice, since you're looking for the *greatest* common factor.

- **Some questions will need to be completely worked out. If you don't see a fast method but do know that you could compute the answer, use your calculator.**

Samples

20. What is the final cost of a watch that sells for $49.00 if the sales tax is 7%?
    - (A) $49.07
    - (B) $49.70
    - (C) $52.00
    - (D) $52.43
    - (E) $56.00

The correct answer is (D). Since the sales tax is 7% of $49.00,

$$7\% \text{ of } \$49.00 = (.07)(\$49.00)$$
$$= \$3.43$$

The total cost of the watch is therefore

$$\$49.00 + \$3.43 = \$52.43$$

Your calculator might have helped with these calculations.

Price List

Top sirloin............................	$2.99 per pound or 2 pounds for $5.00
Filet mignon.........................	$4.00 per pound
London broil	$1.79 per pound or 3 pounds for $5.00

21. Randy owns and manages Randy's Steakhouse. He needs to buy the following meats in order to have enough for the weekend business: 9 pounds of top sirloin, 8 pounds of filet mignon, and 7 pounds of London broil. What is the least amount Randy can spend to buy the meat he needs for the weekend business?
    - (A) $97.00
    - (B) $71.44
    - (C) $66.78
    - (D) $54.99
    - (E) $34.78

The correct answer is (C).

top sirloin:	8 pounds + 1 pound
	= (4 × $5.00) + $2.99 (note: 2 pounds for $5.00)
	= $20.00 + $2.99
	= $22.99

filet mignon:	8 pounds
	= 8 × $4.00
	= $32.00

London broil:	6 pounds + 1 pound
	= (2 × $5.00) + $1.79 (note: 3 pounds for $5.00)
	= $10.00 + $1.79
	= $11.79

Add to find the total: $22.99 + $32.00 + $11.79 = $66.78

- **Some problems may ask you to identify a sequence of either numbers or figures. If numbers are given, look for an obvious pattern (odd numbers then even numbers, increasing, decreasing, etc.) You may wish to first check for a common difference between the numbers.**

Sample

$$1, 3, 6, 10, 15 \ldots$$

22. Which of the following is the next number in the series given above?
    (A) 20   (B) 21   (C) 25   (D) 26   (E) 30

Notice that the pattern here is based on the difference between the numbers:

$$+2 \qquad +3 \qquad +4 \qquad +5 \qquad +6$$

$$1, \quad 3, \quad 6, \quad 10, \quad 15, \quad -$$

Therefore, the answer is (B) 21.

- **Some questions will involve probability and possible combinations. If you don't know a formal method, try some possibilities. Set up what could happen. But set up only as much as you need to.**

Samples

23. What is the probability of throwing two dice in one toss so that they total 11?

    (A) ⅙   (B) ¹⁄₁₁   (C) ¹⁄₁₈   (D) ¹⁄₂₀   (E) ¹⁄₃₆

You should simply list all the possible combinations resulting in 11 (5 + 6 and 6 + 5) and realize that the total possibilities are 36 (6 × 6). Thus the probability equals

$$\frac{\text{possibilities totaling 11}}{\text{total possibilities}} = \frac{2}{36} = \frac{1}{18}$$

Answer (C) is correct.

24. What is the probability of tossing a penny twice so that both times it lands heads up?

    (A) ⅛   (B) ¼   (C) ⅓   (D) ½   (E) ⅔

The correct answer is (B). The probability of throwing a head in one throw is

$$\frac{\text{chances of a head}}{\text{total chances (1 head + 1 tail)}} = \frac{1}{2}$$

Since you trying to throw a head *twice,* multiply the probability for the first toss (½) times the probability for the second toss (again ½). Thus, ½ × ½ = ¼, and ¼ is the probability of throwing heads twice in two tosses. Another way of approaching this problem is to look at the total number of possible outcomes:

	First Toss	*Second Toss*
1.	H	H
2.	H	T
3.	T	H
4.	T	T

Thus, there are four different possible outcomes. There is only one way to throw two heads in two tosses. Thus, the probability of tossing two heads in two tosses is 1 out of 4 total outcomes, or ¼.

25. How many combinations are possible if a person has 4 sports jackets, 5 shirts, and 3 pairs of slacks?
    (A) 4   (B) 5   (C) 12   (D) 60   (E) 120

The correct answer is (D). Since each of the 4 sports jackets may be worn with 5 different shirts, there are 20 possible combinations. These may be worn with each of the 3 pairs of slacks for a total of 60 possible combinations. Stated simply, $5 \cdot 4 \cdot 3 = 60$ possible combinations.

- **Some problems may not ask you to solve for a numerical answer or even an answer including variables. Rather, you may be asked to set up the equation or expression without doing any solving. A quick glance at the answer choices will help you know what is expected.**

Samples

26. Which equation can be used to find the perimeter, P, of a rectangle that has a length of 18 feet and a width of 15 feet?
    (A) $P = (18)(15)$ (D) $P = (2)15 + 18$
    (B) $P = 18 + 15$ (E) $P = 2(15 + 18)$
    (C) $P = 2(15)(18)$

The correct answer is (E). The perimeter of a rectangle can be found by adding the length to the width and doubling this sum. $P = 2(15 + 18)$.

> Harold's age is 3 years less than half Sue's age
> If Harold is 9 years old, how old is Sue?

27. Suppose S represents Sue's age. Which of the following equations can be used to find Sue's age?
    (A) $9 = (½)(S) - 3$ (D) $3 - 9 = (½)(S)$
    (B) $9 - 3 = (½)(S)$ (E) $(½)(9) = S - 3$
    (C) $9 = 3 - (½)(S)$

$$9 = \frac{1}{2}S - 3$$

The correct answer is (A). Changing the word sentence into a number sentence (equation):

Harold's age is 3 years less than half Sue's age.

$$9 \quad = \quad \tfrac{1}{2}S - 3$$

28. Rick is three times as old as Maria, and Maria is four years older than Leah. If Leah is z years old, what is Rick's age in terms of z?
    (A) $3z + 4$
    (B) $3z - 12$
    (C) $3z + 12$
    (D) $(z + 4)/3$
    (E) $(z - 4)/3$

The correct answer is (C). Since

$$z = \text{Leah's age}$$
$$z + 4 = \text{Maria's age}$$
$$3(z + 4) = \text{Rick's age}$$

or

$$3z + 12 = \text{Rick's age}$$

- **In some problems, you may be given special symbols that you are unfamiliar with. Don't let these special symbols alarm you. They typically represent an operation or combination of operations that you are familiar with. Look for the definition of the special symbol or how it is used.**

Sample

29. If $\odot$ is a binary operation such that $a \odot b$ is defined as $\dfrac{a^2 - b^2}{a^2 + b^2}$, then what is the value of $3 \odot 2$?
    (A) $-\frac{5}{13}$ (B) $\frac{1}{13}$ (C) $\frac{1}{5}$ (D) $\frac{5}{13}$ (E) 1

The correct answer is (D). The value of $a \odot b =$

$$\frac{a^2 - b^2}{a^2 + b^2}$$

Simply replacing a with 3 and b with 2 gives

$$\frac{3^2 - 2^2}{3^2 + 2^2} = \frac{9 - 4}{9 + 4} = \frac{5}{13}$$

A Summary of Strategies for Multiple-Choice Math Questions

Underline or circle what you are looking for.

Substitute in simple numbers.

Use a reasonable approach.

Pull out information.

Draw or sketch diagrams and figures.

Mark in or label diagrams.

Approximate.

Work from the answers.

Use your calculator.

Look for obvious patterns in a series.

Try some possible outcomes.

Check the answer choices for procedure-type problems.

Look for definitions in special-symbol problems.

Finally, don't get stuck on any one problem!

QUANTITATIVE COMPARISON

You should have a total of about 15 quantitative comparison questions. They will typically appear as the first 15 questions in a 30-minute section which also includes about 10 grid-in questions.

Ability Tested

Quantitative comparisons test your ability to use mathematical insight, approximation, simple calculations, or common sense to quickly compare two given quantities.

Basic Skills Necessary

This section requires twelfth-grade competence in high school arithmetic, algebra, and intuitive geometry. Skills in approximating, comparing, and evaluating are also necessary. No advanced mathematics is necessary.

Directions

In this section, you will be given two quantities, one in column A and one in column B. You are to determine a relationship between the two quantities and mark—

- (A) if the quantity in column A is greater than the quantity in column B.
- (B) if the quantity in column B is greater than the quantity in column A.
- (C) if the quantities are equal.
- (D) if the comparison cannot be determined from the information that is given.

AN (E) RESPONSE WILL NOT BE SCORED.

Notes

- (1) Sometimes, information concerning one or both of the quantities to be compared is given. This information is not boxed and is centered above the two columns.
- (2) All numbers used are real numbers. Letters such as a, b, m and x represent real numbers.

(3) In a given question, if the same symbol is used in column A and column B, that symbol stands for the same value in each column.

Analysis of Directions

The purpose here is to make a comparison. Therefore, exact answers are not always necessary. (Remember that you can tell whether you are taller than someone in many cases without knowing that person's height. Comparisons such as this can be made with only partial information—just enough to compare.) (D) is not a possible answer if there are values in each column because you can always compare values.

If you get different relationships, depending on the values you choose for variables, then the answer is always (D). Notice that there are only four possible choices here. *Never* mark (E) on your answer sheet for quantitative comparison.

Note that you can add, subtract, multiply, and divide both columns by the same value and the relationship between them will not change. **Exception**—You should not multiply or divide both columns by negative numbers because then the relationship reverses. Squaring both columns is permissible as long as each side is positive. Memorize the directions to save time in answering the questions.

Suggested Approach with Samples

- **This section emphasizes shortcuts, insight, and quick techniques. Long and/or involved mathematical computation is unnecessary and is contrary to the purpose of this section.**

Sample

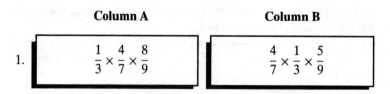

	Column A	Column B
1.	$\dfrac{1}{3} \times \dfrac{4}{7} \times \dfrac{8}{9}$	$\dfrac{4}{7} \times \dfrac{1}{3} \times \dfrac{5}{9}$

Cancel each side as follows:

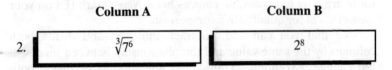

This leaves

$$\frac{8}{9} \qquad\qquad \frac{5}{9}$$

Since $\frac{8}{9}$ is greater than $\frac{5}{9}$, the correct answer is (A).

- **Always keep the columns in perspective before starting any calculations. Take a good look at the value in each column before starting to work on one column.**

Samples

Column A	Column B

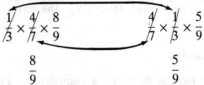

2. $\sqrt[3]{7^6}$ 2^8

After looking at each column (note that the answer could not be (D) because there are values in each column), compute the value on the left. Since you are taking a cube root, simply divide the power of 7 by 3 leaving 7^2, or 49. There is no need to take 2 out to the 8th power; just do as little as necessary:

$$2^2 = 4$$
$$2^3 = 8$$
$$2^4 = 16$$
$$2^5 = 32$$

STOP

It is evident that 2^8 is much greater than 49; the correct answer is (B). Approximating can also be valuable while remembering to keep the columns in perspective.

3.

Column A	Column B
$(.18)^{100}$	$(1.8)^{10}$

In column A, a fractional value (a value less than one) is multiplied by itself many times. So its value becomes increasingly smaller. (For example, $\frac{1}{2} \times \frac{1}{2} = \frac{1}{4}$; $\frac{1}{4} \times \frac{1}{2} = \frac{1}{8}$, and so forth). In column B, a number greater than 1 is multiplied by itself; its value grows larger. So column B is greater. Even a calculator wouldn't have helped here.

As you keep the columns in perspective, notice if the signs $(+, -)$ in each column are different. If they are, you don't need to work out the problem.

4.

Column A	Column B
$(-3)^4$	-3^4

Since $(-3)^4$ is to an even power, column A has a positive answer. Column B really means $-(3^4)$, which will give you a negative answer. Therefore, column A is greater.

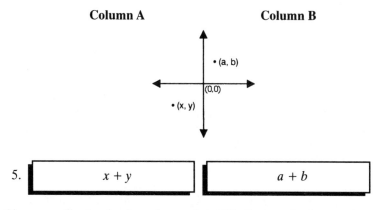

5.

Column A	Column B
$x + y$	$a + b$

Since coordinates (x, y) are in quadrant III, they are both negative, so their sum is negative. Since coordinates (a, b) are in quadrant I, they are both positive, so their sum is positive. Therefore, column B is greater than column A.

- **Often, simplifying one or both columns can make an answer evident.**

Sample

Column A	**Column B**
a, b, c, all greater than 0	

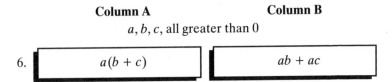

6. $a(b + c)$ | $ab + ac$

Using the distributive property on column A to simplify gives ab and ac. Therefore, the columns are equal.

- **If a problem involves variables (without an equation), substitute in the numbers 0, 1, and −1. Then try ½ and 2 if necessary. Using 0, 1, and −1 will often tip off the answer.**

Samples

Column A	**Column B**

7. $a + b$ | ab

Substituting 0 for a and 0 for b gives:

$0 + 0$		$0(0)$
Therefore, 0	$=$	0

Using these values for a and b gives the answer (C). But anytime you multiply two numbers, it is not the same as when you add them, so try some other values. Substituting 1 for a and −1 for b gives

$1 + (-1)$		$1(-1)$
Therefore, 0	$>$	−1

and the answer is now (A).

Anytime you get more than one comparison (different relationships) depending on the values chosen, the correct answer must be (D), the relationship cannot be determined. Notice that if you had substituted the values $a = 4, b = 5$; or $a = 6, b = 7$; or $a = 7, b = 9$; and so on, you would repeatedly have gotten the answer (B) and might have chosen the incorrect answer.

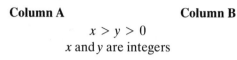

Column A   **Column B**

$$x > y > 0$$
x and y are integers

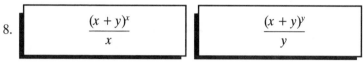

8.

$$\frac{(x + y)^x}{x} \qquad\qquad \frac{(x + y)^y}{y}$$

Plug in values for x and y such that $x > y > 0$. For example, let $y = 1$ and $x = 2$. This gives

$$\frac{(2 + 1)^2}{2} \qquad\qquad\qquad \frac{(1 + 2)^1}{1}$$

$$\frac{(3)^2}{2} \qquad\qquad\qquad \frac{(3)^1}{1}$$

$$\frac{9}{2} \qquad > \qquad \frac{3}{1}$$

Using these values, $\frac{9}{2}$ or $4\frac{1}{2}$, is greater than 3, so column A is greater. Using other values such that $x > y > 0$ will always give the same relationship. Column A is greater.

- **The use of partial comparisons can be valuable in giving you insight into finding a comparison. If you cannot simply make a complete comparison, look at each column part by part.**

Sample

Column A   **Column B**

9.

$$\frac{1}{57} - \frac{1}{65} \qquad\qquad \frac{1}{58} - \frac{1}{63}$$

Since finding a common denominator would be too time consuming, you should first compare the first fraction in each column (partial comparison). Notice that $\frac{1}{57}$ is greater than $\frac{1}{58}$. Now compare the second fractions and notice that $\frac{1}{65}$ is less than $\frac{1}{63}$. Using some common sense and insight, if you start with a larger number and subtract a smaller number, it must be greater than starting with a smaller number and subtracting a larger number, as pointed out below.

The correct answer is (A).

- **Sometimes you can solve for a column directly, in one step, without solving and substituting. If you have to solve an equation or equations to give the columns values, take a second and see if there is a very simple way to get an answer before going through all of the steps.**

Sample

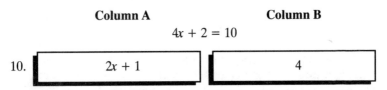

Hopefully, you would spot that the easiest way to solve for $2x + 1$ is directly by dividing $4x + 2 = 10$ by 2, leaving $2x + 1 = 5$. Therefore,

$$5 \qquad > \qquad 4$$

Solving for x first in the equation and then substituting would also have worked but would have been more time consuming. The correct answer is (A).

- **Marking diagrams can be very helpful for giving insight into a problem. Remember that figures and diagrams are drawn as accurately as possible, but just because something "looks" larger is not enough reason to choose an answer.**

Sample

Column A	Column B

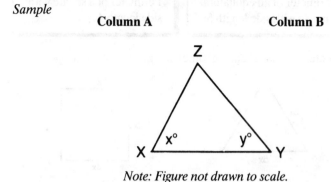

Note: Figure not drawn to scale.

$$XZ = YZ$$

11.

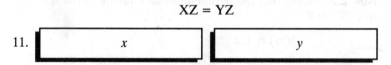

Even though x appears larger, this is not enough. Mark in the diagram as shown.

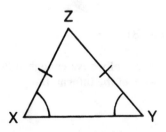

Notice that you should mark things of equal measure with the same markings, and since angles opposite equal sides in a triangle are equal, $x = y$. The correct answer is (C).

- **Drawing diagrams can be helpful in giving you insight into a problem or tipping off a simple solution. If you are given a description of a diagram or a geometry problem without a diagram, you may wish to make a sketch.**

Sample

Column A	Column B
12.	Perimeter of an equilateral triangle with side length $5x$	Perimeter of a square with side length $4x$

Simply sketch and label each geometric figure as follows:

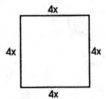

Now it is evident that the perimeter of an equilateral triangle with side $5x$ is

$$3(5x) = 15x$$

The perimeter of a square with side $4x$ is $4(4x) = 16x$

Since $4x$ and $5x$ represent lengths of sides, x must be a positive number. Therefore,

$$15x \qquad < \qquad 16x$$

The correct answer is (B).

- **Check to see if you actually have enough information to make a comparison. Be aware of the information you are given and what you need.**

Samples

Column A	Column B
13.	Distance traveled by an airplane going 200 miles per hour	Distance traveled by an airplane going 190 miles per hour

Since no information is given for the amount of time each of the airplanes was traveling, no determination can be made about their distances traveled. You cannot assume that each airplane traveled the same amount of time. The correct answer is (D).

	Column A	Column B
14.	Volume of right circular cylinder with diameter x	Volume of right circular cylinder with diameter $x + 1$

The correct answer is (D). Since the height of each right circular cylinder is necessary to obtain the volume, no comparison can be made.

Column A   **Column B**

Houses sold in one year

Age	Number
1–2	1200
3–4	1570
5–6	1630
7–8	1440
9–10	1520

	Column A	Column B
15.	Number of houses sold from 5 to 10 years old	Number of houses sold from 4 to 8 years old

The correct answer is (D). Since the chart does not distinguish how many houses are 3 years old or 4 years old, the numbers cannot be determined, so no comparison can be made.

- **If you are given information that is unfamiliar to you and difficult to work with, change the number slightly (but remember what you've changed) to something easier to work with.**

Sample

Column A   **Column B**

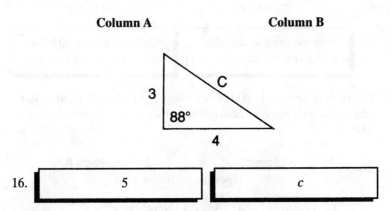

16.   5 c

Since the 88° shown in the figure is unfamiliar to work with, change it to 90° for now so that you may use the Pythagorean theorem to solve for c.

$$a^2 + b^2 = c^2$$

Solve for c as follows:

$$(3)^2 + (4)^2 = c^2$$
$$9 + 16 = c^2$$
$$25 = c^2$$

Therefore, $5 = c$

But since you used 90° instead of 88°, you should realize that the side opposite the 88° will be slightly smaller, or less than 5. The correct answer is then (A), $5 > c$. (Some students may have noticed the 3:4:5 triangle relationship and not have needed the Pythagorean theorem.)

- **If you are given symbols that are unfamiliar to you, don't be alarmed. These new symbols typically represent an operation or some operations that you are familiar with. Look for the definition of the new symbol or how the symbol is used.**

Sample

	Column A	**Column B**

For all real numbers, $p \mathbin{\#} q = p^2/q$

17.

Column A	**Column B**
Value of $p \mathbin{\#} q$ if $p = -q$	q

This new symbol $\#$ is defined as

$$p \mathbin{\#} q = \frac{p^2}{q}$$

Now, since $p = -q$, simply plug in $-q$ in place of p.

$$p \mathbin{\#} q = \frac{(-q)^2}{q} = \frac{q^2}{q} = q$$

Both columns are equal. The correct answer is (C).

- **On occasion, you will actually have to solve information centered between the columns or information in the columns. You should be able to work these quickly.** *Remember, if it takes too long, you're probably doing it wrong.*

Samples

Column A	**Column B**

18.

Column A	**Column B**
The value of $5x - 9$ when $x = 6$	The value of $9 - 5x$ when $x = -6$

Quickly plug in the values given.

$5x - 9$		$9 - 5x$
$5(6) - 9$		$9 - 5(-6)$
$30 - 9$		$9 + 30$
21	$<$	39

Therefore, (B) is the correct answer.

Column A   **Column B**

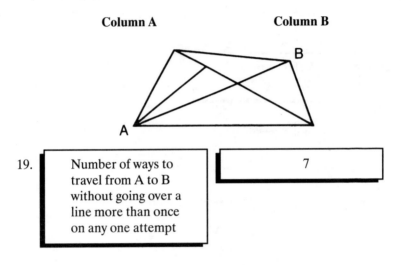

19.
Number of ways to travel from A to B without going over a line more than once on any one attempt	7

The following diagrams show eight ways of going from A to B, and there are more.

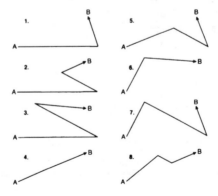

The correct answer is (A).

- **Since quantitative comparison is designed for speed and short-cuts, long computation is normally not required. but if you don't see the fast method or if you need to do any involved calculations, remember that you can use a calculator on the test.**

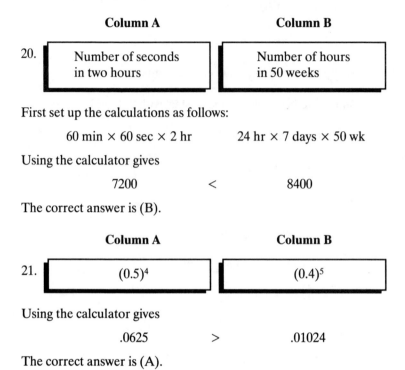

	Column A	Column B
20.	Number of seconds in two hours	Number of hours in 50 weeks

First set up the calculations as follows:

$$60 \text{ min} \times 60 \text{ sec} \times 2 \text{ hr} \qquad 24 \text{ hr} \times 7 \text{ days} \times 50 \text{ wk}$$

Using the calculator gives

$$7200 \qquad < \qquad 8400$$

The correct answer is (B).

	Column A	Column B
21.	$(0.5)^4$	$(0.4)^5$

Using the calculator gives

$$.0625 \qquad > \qquad .01024$$

The correct answer is (A).

A Summary of Strategies for Quantitative Comparisons

Use speed and shortcuts.

Check each column before working.

Watch the signs $(+, -)$ in each column.

Substitute in simple numbers (start with 0, 1, and -1).

Simplify columns if possible.

Compare part by part.

Solve directly.

Mark in or label diagrams.

Draw or sketch diagrams or figures.

Check the information given.

Change the numbers slightly while working.

· Look for definitions in special-symbol problems.

Do the work quickly.

If no shortcut is evident, use a calculator if necessary.

Don't get stuck on any one problem. If it takes too long, you're probably doing it wrong!

Remember:　Never choose (D) if there are values in each column.

Always choose (D) if you get different comparisons depending on the values you use.

When in doubt, plug in numbers.

GRID-IN QUESTIONS

The SAT I has introduced a new and unfamiliar math question type—the grid-in question. This question type is very similar to the familiar multiple-choice question except that you will now solve the problem and enter your answer by carefully marking the circles on a special grid. You will not be selecting from a group of possible answers.

Since you will not be selecting from a group of possible answers, you should be extra careful in checking and double checking your answer. Your calculator can be useful in checking answers. Also, keep in mind that answers to grid-in questions are given either full credit or no credit. There is no partial credit. No points are deducted for incorrect answers in this section. That is, there is no penalty for guessing or attempting a grid-in, so at least take a guess.

Ability Tested

The grid-in section tests your ability to solve mathematical problems involving arithmetic, algebra, geometry, and word problems by using problem-solving insight, logic, and application of basic skills.

Basic Skills Necessary

The basic skills necessary to do well on this section include high school algebra and intuitive geometry. No formal trigonometry or calculus is necessary. Skills in arithmetic and basic algebra, along with some logical insight into problem-solving situations, are also necessary. Understanding the rules and procedures for gridding in answers is important.

Before you begin working grid-in questions, it is important that you become familiar with the grid-in rules and procedures and learn to grid accurately. Let's start explaining the rules and procedures by analyzing the directions.

Directions with Analysis

The following questions require you to solve the problem and enter your answer by carefully marking the circles on the special grid. Examples of the appropriate way to mark the grid follow. (Comments in parentheses have been added to help you understand how to grid properly.)

Answer: 3.7

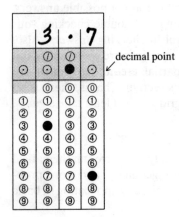

decimal point

(Notice that the decimal point is located in the shaded row, just above the numbers. Also notice that the answer has been written in above the gridding. You should always write in your answer, but the filled-in circles are most important because they are the ones scored.)

Answer: 1/2

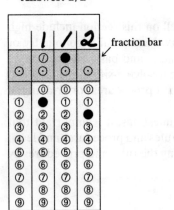

fraction bar

(Notice that the slash mark (/) indicates a fraction bar. This fraction bar is located in the shaded row and just above the decimal point in the two middle columns. Obviously, a fraction bar cannot be in the first or last column.)

Answer: 1½

Do not grid in mixed numbers in the form of mixed numbers. **Always** change mixed numbers to improper fractions or decimals.

Change to 1.5   or   **Change to 3/2**

(Either an improper fraction or a decimal is acceptable. Never grid in a mixed number because it will always be misread. For example, 1½ will be read by the computer doing the scoring as 11/2.)

Answer: 123

Space permitting, answers may start in any column. Each grid-in answer below is correct.

(You should try to grid your answers from right to left, learning to be consistent as you practice. But space permitting, you may start in any column.)

Note: Circles must be filled in correctly to receive credit. Mark only one circle in each column. No credit will be given if more than one circle in a column is marked. Example:

Answer: 258
No credit!!!!

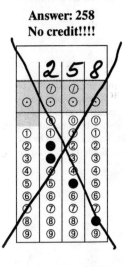

(Filling in more than one circle in a column is equivalent to selecting more than one answer in multiple choice. This type of answer fill-in will never receive any credit. Be careful to avoid this mistake.)

Answer: 8/9

Accuracy of decimals: Always enter the most accurate decimal value that the grid will accommodate. For example: An answer such as .8888 . . . can be gridded as .888 or .889. Gridding this value as .8, .88, or .89 is considered inaccurate and therefore **not acceptable.** The acceptable grid-ins of 8/9 are:

8/9   .888   .889

(Review "accuracy of decimals" a second time. Notice that you must be as accurate as the grid allows.)

Be sure to write your answers in the boxes at the top of the circles before doing your gridding. Although writing out the answers above the columns is not required, it is very important to insure accuracy. Even though some problems may have more than one correct answer, grid only **one answer**. Grid-in questions contain no negative answers.

(Fractions can be reduced to lowest terms, but it is not required as long as they will fit in the grid. You are not required to grid a zero before a fraction. For example, either .2 or 0.2 is acceptable. If your answer is zero, you are required only to grid a zero in one column. **Important:** If you decide to change an answer, be sure to erase the old gridded answer completely.)

PRACTICE GRID-INS

The following practice exercises will help you become familiar with the gridding process. Properly filled in grids are given following each exercise. Hand write and grid in the answers given.

Exercise 1

Answer: 4.5   **Answer: .7**   **Answer: 22.7**

Answer: 1/3

4

Answer: 4/7

5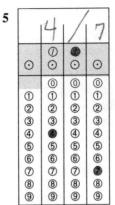

Answer: 9/2

6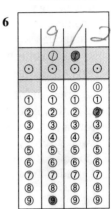

Answer: 3¼

7

Answer: 4½

8

Answer: 9¹⁄₇

9

Answers to Exercise 1

Answer: 4.5

1

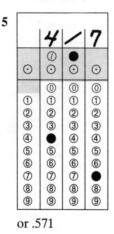

or 9/2

Answer: .7

2

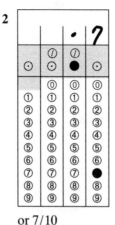

or 7/10

Answer: 22.7

3

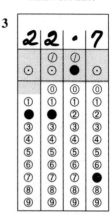

Answer: 1/3

4

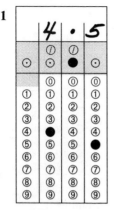

or .333

Answer: 4/7

5

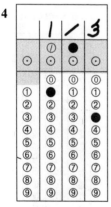

or .571

Answer: 9/2

6

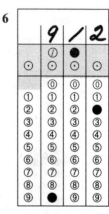

or 4.5

Answer: 3¼

Answer: 4½

Answer: 9¹⁄₇

7

8

9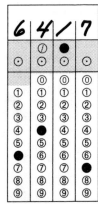

3¼ must be changed to 13/4 or 3.25

4½ must be changed to 9/2 or 4.5

9¹⁄₇ must be changed to 64/7 or 9.14

Exercise 2

Answer: 0

Answer: 39

Answer: 1,542

1

2

3

Answer: 7⅓

Answer: 1

Answer: 685

4   2 2 / 3

5   1

6   6 8 5

Answer: .7272

Answer: .666 . . .

Answer: .222 . . .

7   . 7 2 7

8   . 6 6 7

9   . 2 2 2

Answers to Exercise 2

Answer: 0   **Answer: 39**   **Answer: 1,542**

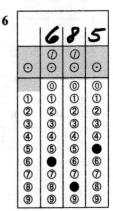

Disregard the
comma (,)

Answer: 7⅓   **Answer: 1**   **Answer: 685**

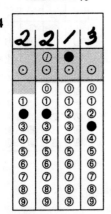

7⅓ must be
changed to 22/3
or 7.33

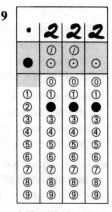

Answer: .7272   **Answer: .666 . . .**   **Answer: .222 . . .**

.72 or .73 will **not** be correct

.666 will also be correct or 2/3 (.66, .67, .7, or .6 will **not** be correct)

2/9 will also be correct (.2 or .22 will **not** be correct)

Suggested Approaches with Samples

Most of the following strategies, described and suggested in the multiple-choice section, will also work on grid-in questions.

- Circle or underline what you are looking for.
- Substitute numbers for variables to understand a problem.
- Try simple numbers to solve a problem.
- Pull information out of word problems.
- Draw/sketch diagrams or simple figures.
- Mark in diagrams.
- Use your calculator when appropriate to solve a problem.

You should also

- Make sure that your answer is reasonable.
- Jot down your scratch work or calculations in the space provided in your test booklet.
- Approximate or use your calculator to check your answers if time permits.

There are some specific items and strategies that should be noted for grid-in questions:

- **There is no penalty for guessing on grid-in questions. Although it may be difficult to get an answer correct by simply writing in a wild guess, you should not be afraid to fill in your answer—even if you think it's wrong.**

- **Make sure to answer what is being asked. If the question asks for percent and you get an answer of 57%, grid in 57, *not* .57. Or if a question asks for dollars and you get an answer of 75 cents, remember that 75 cents is .75 dollar. Grid in .75, *not* 75.**

- **In some questions, more than one answer is possible. Grid-in only one answer. If you work out a question and get the answer $x > 5$, grid in 6, or 7, or 8 but *not more than one* of them.**

- **Some questions will have a note in parentheses (   ) that says, "Disregard the % sign when gridding your answer" or "Disregard the $ sign when gridding your answer." Follow the directions. If your answer is 68%, grid in 68, or if it's $95, grid in 95.**

- **Answers that are mixed numbers such as $3\frac{1}{2}$ or $7\frac{1}{4}$ must be changed to improper fractions ($3\frac{1}{2} = \frac{7}{2}$, $7\frac{1}{4} = \frac{29}{4}$) or decimals ($3\frac{1}{2} = 3.5$, $7\frac{1}{4} = 7.25$) before being gridded. Improper fractions or decimals can be gridded. Mixed numbers cannot. The scoring system cannot distinguish between $3\frac{1}{2}$ and $31/2$.**

- **Since you cannot work from answer choices that are given or eliminate given choices, you will have to actually work out each answer. The use of your calculator on some problems in this section could enhance the speed and accuracy of your work.**

- **Writing in your answer in the space provided at the top of the grid is for your benefit only. It's wise to always write in your answer, but remember, the grid-in answer is the only one scored. Be sure to grid accurately and properly.**

Following are some sample grid-in questions. Consider for each how you would grid in the answer in the proper places on the answer sheet. Also consider when it would be appropriate to use a calculator to help you work out problems and to check the accuracy of your work.

- **Fraction and decimal forms are acceptable.**

Sample

1. If $\frac{1}{3}z - \frac{1}{4} = \frac{1}{2}$, then $z =$

The correct answer is $\frac{9}{4}$ or 2.25 (Either answer will receive full credit.) To solve for z you could multiply both sides of the equation by the lowest common denominator of 12 to get rid of the fractions as follows:

$$12(\tfrac{1}{3}z - \tfrac{1}{4}) = 12(\tfrac{1}{2})$$
$$4z - 3 = 6$$
$$4z = 9$$
$$z = \tfrac{9}{4} = 2.25$$

- **Your gridding is what counts. Your written-in answer is for your benefit. Be accurate.**

Sample

2. Acme Taxi lists the following rates on its door:

$1.20 for the first $\frac{1}{4}$ mile
$0.90 for each additional $\frac{1}{4}$ mile
$6.00 per hour for waiting

At these rates, if there was a 15-minute wait at the bank, how much will a 1.5-mile taxi trip cost? (Disregard the $ sign when gridding your answer.)

The correct answer is $7.20, gridded as 7.20. (You would **not** get credit for gridding 7.00, 7, 72, or 720, even if you had written the right answer above the grid circles.) You should solve the problem as follows:

At $6.00 per hour, a 15-minute ($\frac{1}{4}$ hour) wait will cost $1.50. The first $\frac{1}{4}$ mile will cost $1.20. The remaining $1\frac{1}{4}$, or $\frac{5}{4}$ miles will cost $5(.90) = \$4.50$. The total bill will be the sum.

$$\$1.50 + \$1.20 + \$4.50 = \$7.20$$

- **Make sure you answer the question. Your answer must be in the units asked for.**

$$\frac{2}{3} \cdot n = 12 \cdot \frac{3}{2} \quad \frac{3 \cdot}{2}$$
$$n = 18$$

Sample

3. If Gina completed ⅔ of her project in 12 days, how many days are needed to do the entire project?

The correct answer is 18. To solve, let n = number of days to complete the project. Then

$$\frac{2}{3} \cdot n = 12$$
$$n = 12 \div \frac{2}{3}$$
$$= \frac{12}{1} \cdot \frac{3}{2}$$
$$= 36/2$$
$$= 18$$

The questions asks for the number of *days* to complete the project. Therefore, 432 hours or 2⁴⁄₇ weeks would **not** be correct.

- **Even if there is more than one possible answer, grid in only one answer.**

$$\frac{-4x}{-4} > \frac{-4}{-4} \quad x < 1$$

Sample

4. If $-4x + 12 > -16$, and $x > 0$, then what is one possible integer value for x?

The correct answer is 1, 2, 3, 4, 5, or 6. (Any of these answers would give you full credit. But do not grid more than one of them.) You could solve the problem as follows:

$$-4x + 12 > -16$$

Add -12 to each side $-4x + 12 + (-12) > -16 + (-12)$
leaving $-4x > -28$

Dividing each side by (-4) gives

$$x < 7$$

(Note: The inequality is reversed.)

- **Fractions do not have to be reduced as long as they fit into the grid. (You should probably be in the habit of reducing them anyway, but it's not required here.)**

Sample

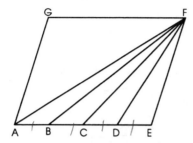

5. In the parallelogram above, if AB = BC = CD = DE, what is the ratio of the area of triangle ABF + triangle BCF to the area of triangle CDF + triangle DEF?

The correct answer is 1/1. (2/2 would also be acceptable, since you don't have to reduce fractions.) You could mark the diagram and solve the problem as follows:

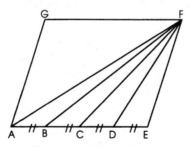

In parallelogram AEFG, if all of the triangles marked have the same base and they all meet at F (giving them all the same height, since the formula for area of a triangle is ½ × base × height), then they all have equal areas. Therefore, the ratio of the area of triangle ABF + triangle BCF to the area of triangle CDF + triangle DEF is 2/2.

- **Follow directions when you're told to disregard the sign.**

Sample

6. A basketball is fully inflated to 24 pounds per square inch. A football is fully inflated to 16 pounds per square inch. The air pressure in the basketball is what percentage of the air pressure in the football? (Disregard the % sign when gridding your answer.)

The correct answer is 150%, which is gridded as <u>150</u>. You could have worked the problem as follows. To compute percentage simply plug into the formula

$$\frac{\text{is number}}{\text{of number}} = \text{percentage}$$

Note that the question reads: The *air pressure in the basketball is* what percentage *of the air pressure in the football*? Thus,

$$\frac{\text{air pressure in basketball}}{\text{air pressure in football}} = \frac{24}{16} = 1.50 = 150\%$$

- **Change your answer into a form to fit the grid if necessary.**

Sample

7. A collection of coins consists of 19 quarters, 21 dimes, and 16 nickels. What percent of the coins are dimes? (Disregard the % sign when gridding your answer.)

The correct answer is 37.5. (Even though your answer could have been 37½, this could not have been placed in the grid.) You could solve the problem as follows. There is a total of 56 coins, of which 21 are dimes. The percent of dimes (*d*) is

Set up a ratio. $\dfrac{d}{100} = \dfrac{21}{56}$

Reduce one side. $\dfrac{d}{100} = \dfrac{3}{8}$

Cross multiply. $8d = (3)(100)$
    $8d = 300$

Divide by 8. $$d = \frac{300}{8} = 37\%$$

$$d = 37\frac{1}{2} = 37.5$$

- **Use the calculator to your advantage.**

Samples

8. A speed of 75 miles per hour is approximately equivalent to how many feet per second?

The correct answer is 110. You could solve this problem as follows:

$$75 \text{ miles per hour} = \frac{75 \text{ miles}}{1 \text{ hour}}$$

Since 1 mile = 5280 feet and 1 hour = 60 minutes = 3600 seconds,

$$\frac{75 \text{ miles}}{1 \text{ hour}} = \frac{75 \times 5280 \text{ feet}}{1 \times 3600 \text{ seconds}}$$

$$= 110 \text{ feet per second}$$

9. What is ¾% of 540?

The correct answer is 4.05. You could solve as follows:

$$\begin{aligned} \text{¾\% of } 540 &= (\text{¾\%})(540) \\ &= (0.75\%)(540) \\ &= (0.0075)(540) \\ &= 4.05 \end{aligned}$$

Bowler	Score
1	148
2	163
3	157
4	148
5	181
6	164
7	157
8	131
9	182

10. The chart above shows how each of nine bowlers scored in the first game of a bowling tournament. Their average score was how much greater than their median score?

The correct answer is 2. To find the mean, simply total all of the scores and divide by 9. This would give you $1431 \div 9 = 159$. To find the median, you must put the scores in order and count to the middle (the fifth spot).

131, 148, 148, 157, 157, 163, 164, 181, 182

The mean is 157. $159 - 157 = 2$

A Summary of Strategies for Grid-in Questions

Realize that there is no penalty for guessing.

Know the grid-in rules and procedures.

Change mixed numbers to improper fractions or decimals.

Understand that fractions and decimal forms are acceptable.

Write in your answer at the top, but remember that the grid-in part is scored.

Grid accurately and properly.

Be sure to answer the question being asked.

Grid in only one answer, even if more than one are possible.

Know that fractions do not have to be reduced if they fit.

Follow directions carefully.

Change your answer to fit the grid.

Use your calculator.

Draw figures.

Mark in diagrams.

Make sure your answer is reasonable.

Jot down scratch work in the test booklet.

Check your answers.

Don't get stuck on any one problem!

CHARTS, TABLES, AND GRAPHS

The Mathematical Reasoning sections of the SAT I will also include some questions about charts, tables, and graphs. You should know how to (1) read and understand information given, (2) calculate, analyze and apply the information given, and (3) spot trends and predict some future trends. When you encounter a chart, table, or graph, you should:

- Focus on understanding the important information given.
- Not memorize the information, but refer to it when you need to.
- Review any additional information given with a graph (headings, scale factors, legends, etc.)
- Read the question and possible choices, noticing key words.
- Look for obvious large changes, high points, low points, trends, etc. Obvious information often leads to an answer.

CHARTS AND TABLES

Charts and tables are often used to give an organized picture of information, or data. Be sure that you understand *what is given*. Column headings and line items give the important information. These titles give the numbers meaning.

Questions 1–2 are based on the following chart.

BURGER SALES FOR THE WEEK OF AUGUST 8 TO AUGUST 14

Day	Hamburgers	Cheeseburgers
Sunday	120	92
Monday	85	80
Tuesday	77	70
Wednesday	74	71
Thursday	75	72
Friday	91	88
Saturday	111	112

1. On which day were the most burgers sold (hamburgers and cheeseburgers)?
   (A) Saturday   (D) Friday
   (B) Monday   (E) Sunday
   (C) Thursday

The answer is (A). Working from the answers is probably the easiest method of answering this question.

(A) Saturday 111 + 112 = <u>223</u>
(B) Monday   85 + 80 = 165
(C) Thursday 75 + 72 = 147
(D) Friday   91 + 88 = 179
(E) Sunday   120 + 92 = 212

Another method is to *approximate* the answers.

2. On how many days were more hamburgers sold than cheesburgers?
   (A) 7   (B) 6   (C) 5   (D) 4   (E) 3

The correct answer is (B). Hamburgers outsold cheeseburgers every day except Saturday.

GRAPHS

Information may be displayed in many ways. The three basic types of graphs you should know are *bar graphs, line graphs,* and *pie graphs* (or *pie charts*).

Bar Graphs

Bar graphs convert the information in a chart into separate bars or columns. Some graphs list numbers along one edge and places, dates, people, or things (individual categories) along another edge. Always try to determine the *relationship* between the columns in a graph or chart.

Number of Delegates Committed to Each Candidate

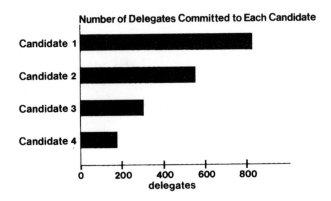

3. The bar graph above shows that Candidate 1 has how many more delegates committed than Candidate 2?
   (A) 150   (B) 200   (C) 250   (D) 400   (E) 550

The correct answer is (C). Notice that the graph shows the "Number of Delegates Committed to Each Candidate," with the numbers given along the bottom of the graph in increases of 200. The names are listed along the left side. Candidate 1 has approximately 800 delegates (possibly a few more). The bar graph for Candidate 2 stops about three quarters of the way between 400 and 600. Now, consider that halfway between 400 and 600 would be 500. So Candidate 2 is at about 550. 800 − 550 = 250.

Line Graphs

Line graphs convert data into points on a grid. These points are then connected to show a relationship among the items, dates, times, etc. Notice the slopes of the lines connecting the points. These lines will show increases and decreases. The sharper the slope *upward,* the greater the *increase.* The sharper the slope *downward,* the greater the *decrease.* Line graphs can show trends, or changes, in data over a period of time.

Questions 4–5 are based on the following graph.

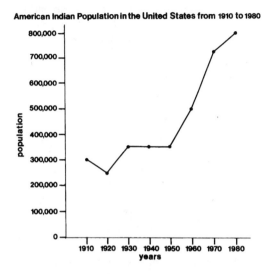

American Indian Population in the United States from 1910 to 1980

4. In which of the following years were there about 500,000 American Indians?
   (A) 1930   (D) 1960
   (B) 1940   (E) 1970
   (C) 1950

The correct answer is (D). The information along the left side of the graph shows the number of Indians in increases of 100,000. The bottom of the graph shows the years from 1910 to 1980. You will notice that in 1960 there were about 500,000 American Indians in the United States. Using the edge of a sheet of paper as a ruler will help you see that the dot in the 1960 column lines up with 500,000 on the left.

5. During which of the following time periods was there a decrease in the American Indian population?
   (A) 1910 to 1920   (D) 1960 to 1970
   (B) 1920 to 1930   (E) 1970 to 1980
   (C) 1930 to 1940

The correct answer is (A). Since the slope of the line goes *down* from 1910 to 1920, there must have been a decrease. If you read the actual numbers, you will notice a decrease from 300,000 to 250,000.

Circle Graphs, or Pie Charts

A circle graph, or pie chart, shows the relationship between the whole circle (100%) and the various slices that represent portions of that 100%. The larger the slice, the higher the percentage.

Questions 6–7 are based on the following circle graph.

How John Spends His Monthly Paycheck

6. If John receives $100 on this month's paycheck, how much will he put in the bank?
   (A) $2   (B) $20   (C) $35   (D) $60   (E) $80

The correct answer is (B). John puts 20% of his income in the bank. 20% of $100 is $20. So he will put $20 in the bank.

7. What is the ratio of the amount of money John spends on his hobby to the amount he puts in the bank?
   (A) 1/6   (B) 1/2   (C) 5/8   (D) 5/7   (E) 3/4

The correct answer is (E). To answer this question, you must use the information in the graph to make a ratio.

$$\frac{\text{his hobby}}{\text{in the bank}} = \frac{15\%}{20\%} = \frac{15}{20} = \frac{3}{4}$$

Notice that the ratio 15%/20% reduces to 3/4.

A Summary of Strategies for Charts, Tables, and Graphs

Examine the entire graph, noticing labels and headings.

Focus on the information given.

Look for major changes—high points, low points, and trends.

Don't memorize the chart, table, or graph; refer to it.

Skimming questions can be helpful.

Circle or underline important words in the question.

Pay special attention to which part of the chart, table, or graph the question is referring to.

If you don't understand the graph, reread the labels and headings.

Don't get stuck on any one question!

Part III: Practice-Review-Analyze-Practice

Three Full-Length Practice Tests

   This section contains three full-length practice simulation SAT I tests. The practice tests are followed by complete answers, explanations, and analysis techniques. The format, levels of difficulty, question structure, and number of questions are similar to those on the actual SAT I. The actual SAT I is copyrighted and may not be duplicated and these questions are not taken directly from the actual tests.

   When taking these exams, try to simulate the test conditions by following the time allotments carefully.

PRACTICE TEST 1

ANSWER SHEET FOR PRACTICE TEST 1
(Remove This Sheet and Use It to Mark Your Answers)

SECTION 1

1 Ⓐ Ⓑ Ⓒ Ⓓ Ⓔ
2 Ⓐ Ⓑ Ⓒ Ⓓ Ⓔ
3 Ⓐ Ⓑ Ⓒ Ⓓ Ⓔ
4 Ⓐ Ⓑ Ⓒ Ⓓ Ⓔ
5 Ⓐ Ⓑ Ⓒ Ⓓ Ⓔ

6 Ⓐ Ⓑ Ⓒ Ⓓ Ⓔ
7 Ⓐ Ⓑ Ⓒ Ⓓ Ⓔ
8 Ⓐ Ⓑ Ⓒ Ⓓ Ⓔ
9 Ⓐ Ⓑ Ⓒ Ⓓ Ⓔ
10 Ⓐ Ⓑ Ⓒ Ⓓ Ⓔ

11 Ⓐ Ⓑ Ⓒ Ⓓ Ⓔ
12 Ⓐ Ⓑ Ⓒ Ⓓ Ⓔ
13 Ⓐ Ⓑ Ⓒ Ⓓ Ⓔ
14 Ⓐ Ⓑ Ⓒ Ⓓ Ⓔ
15 Ⓐ Ⓑ Ⓒ Ⓓ Ⓔ

16 Ⓐ Ⓑ Ⓒ Ⓓ Ⓔ
17 Ⓐ Ⓑ Ⓒ Ⓓ Ⓔ
18 Ⓐ Ⓑ Ⓒ Ⓓ Ⓔ
19 Ⓐ Ⓑ Ⓒ Ⓓ Ⓔ
20 Ⓐ Ⓑ Ⓒ Ⓓ Ⓔ

21 Ⓐ Ⓑ Ⓒ Ⓓ Ⓔ
22 Ⓐ Ⓑ Ⓒ Ⓓ Ⓔ
23 Ⓐ Ⓑ Ⓒ Ⓓ Ⓔ
24 Ⓐ Ⓑ Ⓒ Ⓓ Ⓔ
25 Ⓐ Ⓑ Ⓒ Ⓓ Ⓔ

26 Ⓐ Ⓑ Ⓒ Ⓓ Ⓔ
27 Ⓐ Ⓑ Ⓒ Ⓓ Ⓔ
28 Ⓐ Ⓑ Ⓒ Ⓓ Ⓔ
29 Ⓐ Ⓑ Ⓒ Ⓓ Ⓔ
30 Ⓐ Ⓑ Ⓒ Ⓓ Ⓔ

SECTION 2

1 Ⓐ Ⓑ Ⓒ Ⓓ Ⓔ
2 Ⓐ Ⓑ Ⓒ Ⓓ Ⓔ
3 Ⓐ Ⓑ Ⓒ Ⓓ Ⓔ
4 Ⓐ Ⓑ Ⓒ Ⓓ Ⓔ
5 Ⓐ Ⓑ Ⓒ Ⓓ Ⓔ

6 Ⓐ Ⓑ Ⓒ Ⓓ Ⓔ
7 Ⓐ Ⓑ Ⓒ Ⓓ Ⓔ
8 Ⓐ Ⓑ Ⓒ Ⓓ Ⓔ
9 Ⓐ Ⓑ Ⓒ Ⓓ Ⓔ
10 Ⓐ Ⓑ Ⓒ Ⓓ Ⓔ

11 Ⓐ Ⓑ Ⓒ Ⓓ Ⓔ
12 Ⓐ Ⓑ Ⓒ Ⓓ Ⓔ
13 Ⓐ Ⓑ Ⓒ Ⓓ Ⓔ
14 Ⓐ Ⓑ Ⓒ Ⓓ Ⓔ
15 Ⓐ Ⓑ Ⓒ Ⓓ Ⓔ

16 Ⓐ Ⓑ Ⓒ Ⓓ Ⓔ
17 Ⓐ Ⓑ Ⓒ Ⓓ Ⓔ
18 Ⓐ Ⓑ Ⓒ Ⓓ Ⓔ
19 Ⓐ Ⓑ Ⓒ Ⓓ Ⓔ
20 Ⓐ Ⓑ Ⓒ Ⓓ Ⓔ

21 Ⓐ Ⓑ Ⓒ Ⓓ Ⓔ
22 Ⓐ Ⓑ Ⓒ Ⓓ Ⓔ
23 Ⓐ Ⓑ Ⓒ Ⓓ Ⓔ
24 Ⓐ Ⓑ Ⓒ Ⓓ Ⓔ
25 Ⓐ Ⓑ Ⓒ Ⓓ Ⓔ

SECTION 3

1 Ⓐ Ⓑ Ⓒ Ⓓ Ⓔ
2 Ⓐ Ⓑ Ⓒ Ⓓ Ⓔ
3 Ⓐ Ⓑ Ⓒ Ⓓ Ⓔ
4 Ⓐ Ⓑ Ⓒ Ⓓ Ⓔ
5 Ⓐ Ⓑ Ⓒ Ⓓ Ⓔ

6 Ⓐ Ⓑ Ⓒ Ⓓ Ⓔ
7 Ⓐ Ⓑ Ⓒ Ⓓ Ⓔ
8 Ⓐ Ⓑ Ⓒ Ⓓ Ⓔ
9 Ⓐ Ⓑ Ⓒ Ⓓ Ⓔ
10 Ⓐ Ⓑ Ⓒ Ⓓ Ⓔ

11 Ⓐ Ⓑ Ⓒ Ⓓ Ⓔ
12 Ⓐ Ⓑ Ⓒ Ⓓ Ⓔ
13 Ⓐ Ⓑ Ⓒ Ⓓ Ⓔ
14 Ⓐ Ⓑ Ⓒ Ⓓ Ⓔ
15 Ⓐ Ⓑ Ⓒ Ⓓ Ⓔ

16 Ⓐ Ⓑ Ⓒ Ⓓ Ⓔ
17 Ⓐ Ⓑ Ⓒ Ⓓ Ⓔ
18 Ⓐ Ⓑ Ⓒ Ⓓ Ⓔ
19 Ⓐ Ⓑ Ⓒ Ⓓ Ⓔ
20 Ⓐ Ⓑ Ⓒ Ⓓ Ⓔ

21 Ⓐ Ⓑ Ⓒ Ⓓ Ⓔ
22 Ⓐ Ⓑ Ⓒ Ⓓ Ⓔ
23 Ⓐ Ⓑ Ⓒ Ⓓ Ⓔ
24 Ⓐ Ⓑ Ⓒ Ⓓ Ⓔ
25 Ⓐ Ⓑ Ⓒ Ⓓ Ⓔ

26 Ⓐ Ⓑ Ⓒ Ⓓ Ⓔ
27 Ⓐ Ⓑ Ⓒ Ⓓ Ⓔ
28 Ⓐ Ⓑ Ⓒ Ⓓ Ⓔ
29 Ⓐ Ⓑ Ⓒ Ⓓ Ⓔ
30 Ⓐ Ⓑ Ⓒ Ⓓ Ⓔ

31 Ⓐ Ⓑ Ⓒ Ⓓ Ⓔ
32 Ⓐ Ⓑ Ⓒ Ⓓ Ⓔ
33 Ⓐ Ⓑ Ⓒ Ⓓ Ⓔ
34 Ⓐ Ⓑ Ⓒ Ⓓ Ⓔ
35 Ⓐ Ⓑ Ⓒ Ⓓ Ⓔ

CUT HERE

ANSWER SHEET FOR PRACTICE TEST 1
(Remove This Sheet and Use It to Mark Your Answers)

SECTION 4

1 Ⓐ Ⓑ Ⓒ Ⓓ Ⓔ
2 Ⓐ Ⓑ Ⓒ Ⓓ Ⓔ
3 Ⓐ Ⓑ Ⓒ Ⓓ Ⓔ
4 Ⓐ Ⓑ Ⓒ Ⓓ Ⓔ
5 Ⓐ Ⓑ Ⓒ Ⓓ Ⓔ

6 Ⓐ Ⓑ Ⓒ Ⓓ Ⓔ
7 Ⓐ Ⓑ Ⓒ Ⓓ Ⓔ
8 Ⓐ Ⓑ Ⓒ Ⓓ Ⓔ
9 Ⓐ Ⓑ Ⓒ Ⓓ Ⓔ
10 Ⓐ Ⓑ Ⓒ Ⓓ Ⓔ

11 Ⓐ Ⓑ Ⓒ Ⓓ Ⓔ
12 Ⓐ Ⓑ Ⓒ Ⓓ Ⓔ
13 Ⓐ Ⓑ Ⓒ Ⓓ Ⓔ
14 Ⓐ Ⓑ Ⓒ Ⓓ Ⓔ
15 Ⓐ Ⓑ Ⓒ Ⓓ Ⓔ

16
17
18
19
20
21

CUT HERE

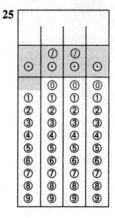

22

	⊘	⊘	
⊙	⊙	⊙	⊙
	⓪	⓪	⓪
①	①	①	①
②	②	②	②
③	③	③	③
④	④	④	④
⑤	⑤	⑤	⑤
⑥	⑥	⑥	⑥
⑦	⑦	⑦	⑦
⑧	⑧	⑧	⑧
⑨	⑨	⑨	⑨

23

	⊘	⊘	
⊙	⊙	⊙	⊙
	⓪	⓪	⓪
①	①	①	①
②	②	②	②
③	③	③	③
④	④	④	④
⑤	⑤	⑤	⑤
⑥	⑥	⑥	⑥
⑦	⑦	⑦	⑦
⑧	⑧	⑧	⑧
⑨	⑨	⑨	⑨

24

	⊘	⊘	
⊙	⊙	⊙	⊙
	⓪	⓪	⓪
①	①	①	①
②	②	②	②
③	③	③	③
④	④	④	④
⑤	⑤	⑤	⑤
⑥	⑥	⑥	⑥
⑦	⑦	⑦	⑦
⑧	⑧	⑧	⑧
⑨	⑨	⑨	⑨

25

	⊘	⊘	
⊙	⊙	⊙	⊙
	⓪	⓪	⓪
①	①	①	①
②	②	②	②
③	③	③	③
④	④	④	④
⑤	⑤	⑤	⑤
⑥	⑥	⑥	⑥
⑦	⑦	⑦	⑦
⑧	⑧	⑧	⑧
⑨	⑨	⑨	⑨

ANSWER SHEET FOR PRACTICE TEST 1
(Remove This Sheet and Use It to Mark Your Answers)

SECTION 5	SECTION 6	SECTION 7

SECTION 5

1 Ⓐ Ⓑ Ⓒ Ⓓ Ⓔ
2 Ⓐ Ⓑ Ⓒ Ⓓ Ⓔ
3 Ⓐ Ⓑ Ⓒ Ⓓ Ⓔ
4 Ⓐ Ⓑ Ⓒ Ⓓ Ⓔ
5 Ⓐ Ⓑ Ⓒ Ⓓ Ⓔ

6 Ⓐ Ⓑ Ⓒ Ⓓ Ⓔ
7 Ⓐ Ⓑ Ⓒ Ⓓ Ⓔ
8 Ⓐ Ⓑ Ⓒ Ⓓ Ⓔ
9 Ⓐ Ⓑ Ⓒ Ⓓ Ⓔ
10 Ⓐ Ⓑ Ⓒ Ⓓ Ⓔ

11 Ⓐ Ⓑ Ⓒ Ⓓ Ⓔ
12 Ⓐ Ⓑ Ⓒ Ⓓ Ⓔ
13 Ⓐ Ⓑ Ⓒ Ⓓ Ⓔ
14 Ⓐ Ⓑ Ⓒ Ⓓ Ⓔ
15 Ⓐ Ⓑ Ⓒ Ⓓ Ⓔ

SECTION 6

1 Ⓐ Ⓑ Ⓒ Ⓓ Ⓔ
2 Ⓐ Ⓑ Ⓒ Ⓓ Ⓔ
3 Ⓐ Ⓑ Ⓒ Ⓓ Ⓔ
4 Ⓐ Ⓑ Ⓒ Ⓓ Ⓔ
5 Ⓐ Ⓑ Ⓒ Ⓓ Ⓔ

6 Ⓐ Ⓑ Ⓒ Ⓓ Ⓔ
7 Ⓐ Ⓑ Ⓒ Ⓓ Ⓔ
8 Ⓐ Ⓑ Ⓒ Ⓓ Ⓔ
9 Ⓐ Ⓑ Ⓒ Ⓓ Ⓔ
10 Ⓐ Ⓑ Ⓒ Ⓓ Ⓔ

SECTION 7

1 Ⓐ Ⓑ Ⓒ Ⓓ Ⓔ
2 Ⓐ Ⓑ Ⓒ Ⓓ Ⓔ
3 Ⓐ Ⓑ Ⓒ Ⓓ Ⓔ
4 Ⓐ Ⓑ Ⓒ Ⓓ Ⓔ
5 Ⓐ Ⓑ Ⓒ Ⓓ Ⓔ

6 Ⓐ Ⓑ Ⓒ Ⓓ Ⓔ
7 Ⓐ Ⓑ Ⓒ Ⓓ Ⓔ
8 Ⓐ Ⓑ Ⓒ Ⓓ Ⓔ
9 Ⓐ Ⓑ Ⓒ Ⓓ Ⓔ
10 Ⓐ Ⓑ Ⓒ Ⓓ Ⓔ

11 Ⓐ Ⓑ Ⓒ Ⓓ Ⓔ
12 Ⓐ Ⓑ Ⓒ Ⓓ Ⓔ
13 Ⓐ Ⓑ Ⓒ Ⓓ Ⓔ
14 Ⓐ Ⓑ Ⓒ Ⓓ Ⓔ
15 Ⓐ Ⓑ Ⓒ Ⓓ Ⓔ

16 Ⓐ Ⓑ Ⓒ Ⓓ Ⓔ
17 Ⓐ Ⓑ Ⓒ Ⓓ Ⓔ
18 Ⓐ Ⓑ Ⓒ Ⓓ Ⓔ
19 Ⓐ Ⓑ Ⓒ Ⓓ Ⓔ
20 Ⓐ Ⓑ Ⓒ Ⓓ Ⓔ

21 Ⓐ Ⓑ Ⓒ Ⓓ Ⓔ
22 Ⓐ Ⓑ Ⓒ Ⓓ Ⓔ
23 Ⓐ Ⓑ Ⓒ Ⓓ Ⓔ
24 Ⓐ Ⓑ Ⓒ Ⓓ Ⓔ
25 Ⓐ Ⓑ Ⓒ Ⓓ Ⓔ

SECTION 1: VERBAL REASONING

Time: 30 Minutes
30 Questions

In this section, choose the best answer for each question and blacken the corresponding space on the answer sheet.

Sentence Completion

DIRECTIONS

Each blank in the following sentences indicates that something has been omitted. Consider the lettered words beneath the sentence and choose the word or set of words that best fits the whole sentence.

1. Loved and hated by thousands, Dr. Lucy Bertram may well be the most _____ physician ever to become surgeon general.
    (A) controversial
    (B) popular
    (C) successful
    (D) well-trained
    (E) professional

2. Over thousands of years, organisms have _____ many strategies to conserve water.
    (A) administered
    (B) evolved
    (C) organized
    (D) questioned
    (E) considered

3. My cat is a creature of contradictions: _____ yet affectionate, _____ yet alert.
    (A) aloof . . . dreamy
    (B) cruel . . . shrewd
    (C) quiet . . . lively
    (D) selfish . . . nimble
    (E) loving . . . sly

4. _____ for talking too much, the teacher _____ his reputa-
tion by keeping the class thirty minutes longer than the scheduled class
time.
   (A) Famous ... evinced
   (B) Renowned ... overturned
   (C) Notorious ... verified
   (D) Illustrious ... rebutted
   (E) Eminent ... established

5. If Senator Montana runs for reelection next year, she will have the
money-raising advantage of the _____.
   (A) campaigner
   (B) favorite
   (C) underdog
   (D) incumbent
   (E) candidate

6. Using his own home as _____, Marlowe obtained a private loan
that enabled him to _____ his financial obligations to the other
partners and emerge free of debt.
   (A) pledge ... increase
   (B) surety ... augment
   (C) collateral ... discharge
   (D) profit ... eliminate
   (E) deposit ... endorse

7. The absurdist as opposed to the heroic treatment of war reached
maturity in *Catch-22,* and the Vietnam War made this approach, which
seemed so _____ and shocking, the only way to write about that
conflict.
   (A) banal
   (B) radical
   (C) plausible
   (D) cozy
   (E) familiar

8. Since the issue is so insignificant, it was surprising that the disagree-
ment among city council members was so _____.
   (A) tepid
   (B) slovenly
   (C) trivial
   (D) acrimonious
   (E) genial

9. Many thought Billy Eckstine's band _____, because its musicians were young, avant-garde jazzmen, while its lead singer crooned _____ popular ballads.
   (A) progressive . . . romantic
   (B) old-fashioned . . . unique
   (C) inconsistent . . . conservative
   (D) unmusical . . . familiar
   (E) predictable . . . melodic

Analogies

DIRECTIONS

In each question below, you are given a related pair of words or phrases. Select the lettered pair that *best* expresses a relationship similar to that in the original pair of words.

10. HORSE : BRIDLE ::
    (A) canary : cage
    (B) ox : plough
    (C) dog : leash
    (D) beaver : dam
    (E) silver fox : trap

11. HUNTER : DECOY ::
    (A) mouse : mousetrap
    (B) angler : lure
    (C) language : code
    (D) treasure : map
    (E) predator : prey

12. HERB : OREGANO ::
    (A) poem : ballad
    (B) drama : actor
    (C) music : score
    (D) grocer : vegetable
    (E) automobile : truck

13. CHOREOGRAPHER : DANCE ::
    (A) conductor : symphony
    (B) artist : model
    (C) director : actor
    (D) ingredient : recipe
    (E) playwright : play

14. FESTER : RANKLE ::
    (A) dislike : tolerate
    (B) approve : question
    (C) adore : worship
    (D) conjugate : spell
    (E) inhibit : inhere

15. DISINTERESTED : PREJUDICE ::
    (A) naive : sophistication
    (B) inattentive : tedium
    (C) enthusiastic : alacrity
    (D) secure : confidence
    (E) narrow-minded : bias

Critical Reading

DIRECTIONS

Questions follow each of the passages below. Using only the stated or implied information in each passage and in its introduction, if any, answer the questions.

Questions 16–21 are based on the following passage.

The following passage is from a book about Paul Gauguin, the late nineteenth-century artist who left France to live and paint on the Pacific island of Tahiti.

Gauguin decided to settle in Mataiea, some forty-five kilometres from Papeete, probably on the advice of a Tahitian chief whom he had befriended. There he rented a native-style oval bamboo hut, roofed with pandanu leaves. Once settled, he was in a position to
(5) begin work in earnest and to tackle serious figure studies. It was probably soon after this that he painted *Vahine no te tiare,* his first portrait of a Tahitian model.

By the late summer of 1892 the completed canvas was back in Paris, hanging in the Goupil gallery. From the many subsequent
(10) references to this image in his correspondence, it is clear that Gauguin set considerable store by his "Tahitienne" and, by sending her on ahead to Paris, wanted her to serve as an ambassadress for the further images of Tahitian women he would be bringing back with him on his return. He pressed his male
(15) friends for their reactions to the girl, rather than to the picture, anxious to know whether they, like him, would be responsive to the beauty of her face: "And her forehead," he later wrote, "with the

majesty of upsweeping lines, reminded me of that saying of Poe's, 'There is no perfect beauty without a certain singularity in the
(20) proportions.' " No one, it seems, was quite attuned to his emotional perception: while Aurier was enthusiastic, excited by the picture's rarity value, Schuffenecker was somewhat taken aback by the painting's lack of Symbolist character. Indeed, apart from the imaginary floral background which harked back to Gauguin's 1888
(25) *Self-Portrait,* the image is a relatively straightforward one. Recent anthropological work, backed by the use of photography, had scientifically characterized the physical distinctions between the different races, distinctions that in the past had been imperfectly understood. Generally speaking, artists before Gauguin's time had
(30) represented Tahitians as idealized types, adjusting their features and proportions to accord with European taste. This meant that hitherto the Tahitian in Western art could scarcely be distinguished from his African or Asian counterpart. Unfortunately, Charles Giraud's paintings have disappeared so we cannot com-
(35) pare them with Gauguin's, but this first image by Gauguin suggests a desire to portray the Tahitian physiognomy naturalistically, without the blinkers of preconceived rules of beauty laid down by a classical culture. Naturalism as an artistic creed, though, was anathema to Gauguin; it made the artist a lackey of science and
(40) knowledge rather than a god-like creator. He wanted to go beyond empirical observation of this kind, to find a way of painting Tahiti that would accord with his Symbolist aspirations, that would embody the feelings he had about the place and the poetic image he carried with him of the island's mysterious past.

16. In line 10, the word "correspondence" means
    (A) correlation
    (B) agreement
    (C) conformity
    (D) similarity
    (E) letters

17. Gauguin found the faces of Tahitian women beautiful because of their
    (A) elegant coloration
    (B) unusual proportions
    (C) refusal to wear make-up
    (D) dark hair covering the forehead
    (E) openness and innocence

18. The passage suggests that a painter depicting a Tahitian in a period
    some time before Gauguin would probably
    (A) rely upon photographs for models
    (B) make an image that was not in accord with European ideals of
        female beauty
    (C) paint a picture that employed a symbolic landscape as background
    (D) fail to differentiate a Tahitian from the inhabitants of Asian
        countries
    (E) paint only models who were fully clothed in Western-style costume

19. It can be inferred that the author would like to see the lost paintings of
    Charles Giraud in order to
    (A) determine whether or not they presented the Tahitians realisti-
        cally
    (B) determine whether or not they were better paintings than Gauguin's
    (C) determine if they deserve their high reputation
    (D) compare the symbolism of these paintings with that of Gauguin's
    (E) discover what subjects Giraud chose to paint

20. Of the following phrases, which does the author use to refer to that
    aspect of Gauguin's art which attempts to depict the real world
    accurately?
      I. "the image is a relatively straightforward one" (line 25)
     II. "desire to portray the Tahitian physiognomy naturalistically" (line
         36)
    III. "a way of painting Tahiti that would accord with his Symbolist
         aspirations" (lines 41–42)

    (A) II only
    (B) III only
    (C) I and II only
    (D) I and III only
    (E) I, II, and III

21. The passage suggests that an important problem that Gauguin would
    have to deal with in his paintings of Tahiti was how to
    (A) reconcile his naturalistic and symbolistic impulses
    (B) make Europeans understand the beauty of Tahiti
    (C) find the necessary supplies in a remote location
    (D) earn enough money to support himself by selling his paintings in
        Paris
    (E) make artistic use of the new advances in photography

Questions 22–30 are based on the following passage.

Jim Hansen, a climatologist at NASA's Goddard Space Institute, is convinced that the earth's temperature is rising and places the blame on the buildup of green-house gases in the atmosphere. Unconvinced, John Sununu, former White House chief of staff, (5) doubts that the warming will be great enough to produce a serious threat and fears that measures to reduce the emissions would throw a wrench into the gears that drive the United States' troubled economy. The stakes in this debate are extremely high, for it pits society's short-term well-being against the future of all the planet's (10) inhabitants. Our past transgressions have altered major portions of the earth's surface, but the effects have been limited. Now we can foresee the possibility that to satisfy the energy needs of an expanding human population, we will rapidly change the climate of the entire planet, with consequences for even the most remote and (15) unspoiled regions of the globe.

The notion that certain gases could warm the planet is not new. In 1896 Svante Arrhenius, a Swedish chemist, resolved the long-standing question of how the earth's atmosphere could maintain the planet's relatively warm temperature when the oxygen and (20) nitrogen that make up 99 percent of the atmosphere do not absorb any of the heat escaping as infrared radiation from the earth's surface into space. He discovered that even the small amounts of carbon dioxide in the atmosphere could absorb large amounts of heat. Furthermore, he reasoned that the burning of coal, oil, and (25) natural gas could eventually release enough carbon dioxide to warm the earth.

Hansen and most other climatologists agree that enough green-house gases have accumulated in the atmosphere to make Arrhenius's prediction come true. Burning fossil fuels is not the (30) only problem; a fifth of our emissions of carbon dioxide now come from clearing and burning forests. Scientists are also tracking a host of other greenhouse gases that emanate from a variety of human activities; the warming effect of methane, chlorofluorocarbons, and nitrous oxide combined equals that of carbon dioxide. (35) Although the current warming from these gases may be difficult to detect against the background noise of natural climate variation, most climatologists are certain that as the gases continue to accumulate, increases in the earth's temperature will become evident even to skeptics.

(40)   The battle lines for this particular skirmish are surprisingly well balanced. Those with concerns about global warming point to the recent report from the United Nations Intergovernmental Plan on Climate Change, which suggests that with "business as usual," emissions of carbon dioxide by the year 2025 will be 25 percent

(45) greater than previously estimated. On the other side, the George C. Marshall Institute, a conservative think tank, published a report warning that without greenhouse gases to warm things up, the world would become cool in the next century. Stephen Schneider, a leading computer modeler of future climate change, accused

(50) Sununu of "brandishing the [Marshall] report as if he were holding a crucifix to repel a vampire."

If the reality of global warming were put on trial, each side would have trouble making its case. Jim Hansen's side could not prove beyond a reasonable doubt that carbon dioxide and the other

(55) greenhouse gases have warmed the planet. But neither could John Sununu's side prove beyond a reasonable doubt that the warming expected from greenhouse gases has not occurred.

22. The purpose of the first paragraph (lines 1–15) of the passage is to
    (A) argue for the reduction of greenhouse gases in the atmosphere
    (B) defend on economic grounds the reduction of greenhouse gases
    (C) present two opposing positions on the subject of the earth's rising temperature
    (D) lessen the concern of the public about the alleged buildup of greenhouse gases
    (E) introduce the two most important spokesmen for and against ecological reforms

23. In the first paragraph in line 8, the word "pits" means
    (A) removes the core of
    (B) sets in competition
    (C) depresses
    (D) marks with small scars
    (E) hardens

24. From the information in the second paragraph of the passage, it can be inferred that a planet
    (A) whose atmosphere was made up entirely of oxygen would be warmer than a planet equally distant from the sun with an atmosphere made up entirely of nitrogen
    (B) whose atmosphere was made up entirely of nitrogen would be warmer than a planet equally distant from the sun with an atmosphere made up entirely of oxygen
    (C) with a larger amount of carbon dioxide in its atmosphere, other factors being equal, will be warmer than a planet with less carbon dioxide
    (D) with a small amount of carbon dioxide in its atmosphere cannot increase this amount
    (E) with little infrared radiation escaping from its surface is likely to be extremely cold

25. The passage implies that a greenhouse gas is one that
    I. forms a large part of the earth's atmosphere
    II. absorbs heat escaping from the earth's surface
    III. can be formed by the clearing and burning of forests

    (A) III only
    (B) I and II only
    (C) I and III only
    (D) II and III only
    (E) I, II, and III

26. From the passage, it can be inferred that all of the following are greenhouse gases EXCEPT
    (A) nitrogen
    (B) carbon dioxide
    (C) methane
    (D) chlorofluorocarbons
    (E) nitrous oxide

27. Which of the following, if true, would call into question the argument of the Marshall report?

    I. Since the earth's climate did not grow colder in the five hundred years since 1400 when the amount of greenhouse gases released by humans was small, there is no reason to expect a decrease in temperature when the amounts of gas released are now much larger.

    II. The radical reduction of the emission of greenhouse gases will result in massive unemployment throughout the industrial world.

    III. Some scientific studies have shown that the temperature of the earth is unaffected by the presence of oxygen in the atmosphere.

    (A) I only
    (B) II only
    (C) I and II only
    (D) I and III only
    (E) I, II, and III

28. The word "skeptics" in line 39 most nearly means
    (A) scientists
    (B) ecologists
    (C) opponents
    (D) doubters
    (E) politicians

29. Stephen Schneider probably referred to Sununu's "brandishing the [Marshall] report as if he were holding a crucifix to repel a vampire" in order to

    I. amuse his audience
    II. suggest that Sununu's claims are melodramatic
    III. imply that the idea that greenhouse gases are dangerous is as imaginary as a vampire

    (A) III only
    (B) I and II only
    (C) I and III only
    (D) II and III only
    (E) I, II, and III

30. The effect of the final paragraph of the passage is to
    (A) stress the superiority of Jim Hansen's case
    (B) undermine Sununu's argument
    (C) support the conclusions of the Marshall report
    (D) call Arrhenius's theories into question
    (E) leave the debate about global warming unresolved

STOP. IF YOU FINISH BEFORE TIME IS CALLED, CHECK YOUR WORK ON THIS SECTION ONLY. DO NOT WORK ON ANY OTHER SECTION IN THE TEST.

SECTION 2: MATHEMATICAL REASONING

Time: 30 Minutes
25 Questions

DIRECTIONS

Solve each problem in this section by using the information given and your own mathematical calculations, insights, and problem-solving skills. Then select the one correct answer of the five choices given and mark the corresponding circle on your answer sheet. Use the available space on the page for your scratchwork.

Notes

(1) All numbers used are real numbers.
(2) Calculators may be used.
(3) Some problems may be accompanied by figures or diagrams. These figures are drawn as accurately as possible EXCEPT when it is stated in a specific problem that a figure is not drawn to scale. The figures and diagrams are meant to provide information useful in solving the problem or problems. Unless otherwise stated, all figures and diagrams lie in a plane.

Data That May Be Used for Reference

Area

rectangle
$A = lw$

triangle
$A = \frac{1}{2} bh$

circle
$A = \pi r^2$

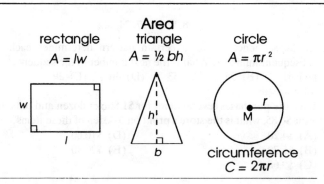

circumference
$C = 2\pi r$

Volume

rectangular solid
$V = lwh$

right circular cylinder
$V = \pi r^2 h$

Pythagorean Relationship

$a^2 + b^2 = c^2$

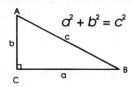

Special Triangles

30° – 60° – 90°

45° – 45° – 90°

A circle is composed of 360°
A straight angle measures 180°
The sum of the angles of a triangle is 180°

1. If ⅕ of a number is 2, what is ½ of the number?
   (A) 10   (B) 5   (C) 3   (D) 2   (E) 1

$$8, 9, 12, 17, 24, \ldots$$

2. In the sequence above, a certain pattern determines each of the subsequent numbers. What is the next number in the sequence?
   (A) 41   (B) 35   (C) 33   (D) 30   (E) 29

3. If a store purchases several items for $1.80 per dozen and sells them at 3 for $0.85, what is the store's profit on 6 dozen of these items?
   (A) $4.20   (D) $10.60
   (B) $5.70   (E) $20.40
   (C) $9.60

4. If $x = -1$, then $x^4 + x^3 + x^2 + x - 3 =$
   (A) −13   (B) −7   (C) −3   (D) −2   (E) 1

5. Which of the following numbers is divisible by 15?
   (A) 15,815   (D) 46,335
   (B) 16,428   (E) 55,555
   (C) 28,145

The product of two numbers is equal to
twice the difference of the two numbers.

6. Which equation best represents the above situation?
   (A) $x + y = 2(x - y)$ (D) $(x)(y) = 2(x - y)$
   (B) $x + y = 2(x \div y)$ (E) $(x)(y) = 2(x + y)$
   (C) $(x)(y) = 2(x \div y)$

7. Which of the following is equal to $(5x + 2)(3x - 4) - (2x - 3)(x + 2)$?
   (A) $13x^2 - 14$ (D) $13x^2 - 13x - 2$
   (B) $13x^2 + 2$ (E) $13x^2 - 15x - 2$
   (C) $13x^2 - 13x - 14$

8. If D is between A and B on $\overleftrightarrow{AB}$, which of the following must be true?
   (A) $AD = DB$ (D) $DB = AD + AB$
   (B) $DB = AB - AD$ (E) $AB = AD = BD$
   (C) $AD = AB + DB$

9. The symbol $\otimes$ represents a binary operation defined as $a \otimes b = a^3 + b^2$.
What is the value of $(-2) \otimes (-3)$?
   (A) 17   (B) 1   (C) 0   (D) −1   (E) −17

$-2^3 + -3^2$

$+ 9$

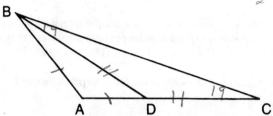

Note: Figure not drawn to scale.

10. In the figure above, AB = AD and BD = CD. If $\angle C$ measures 19°, what
is the measure of $\angle A$ in degrees?
    (A) 75   (B) 94   (C) 104   (D) 114   (E) 142

11. Angela has nickels and dimes in her pocket. She has twice as many
    dimes as nickels. What is the best expression of the amount of money
    she has in cents if x equals the number of nickels she has?
    (A) 25x   (D) 5(3x)
    (B) 10x + 5(2x)   (E) 20(x + 5)
    (C) x + 2x

12. If $x - 4 = y$, what must $(y - x)^3$ equal?
    (A) −64   (B) −12   (C) 12   (D) 64   (E) 128

13. The length of a rectangle is 3x, and its perimeter is 10x + 8. What is the
    width of the rectangle?
    (A) 2x + 4   (D) 4x + 4
    (B) 2x + 8   (E) 5x + 4
    (C) 4x + 8

14. If $\dfrac{3}{7} = \dfrac{10}{x-4}$, then $x =$

$3(x-4) = 70$
$3x - 12 = 70$
$3x = 82$

(A) 8²⁄₇   (B) 11   (C) 19⅓   (D) 24⅔   (E) 27⅓

15. A car travels 140 miles in 4 hours, while the return trip takes 3½ hours. What is the average speed in miles per hour for the entire trip?

$\dfrac{140}{4}$

$35\,mph$

(A) 35   (B) 37⅓   (C) 37½   (D) 40   (E) 75

16. If $a > b$, and $ab > 0$, which of the following must be true?

   I. $a > 0$ -1 -2 $\dfrac{-1}{-3}$ $\dfrac{1}{2}$
   II. $b > 0$
   III. $a/b > 0$

   (A) I only   (D) I and II only
   (B) II only   (E) I and III only
   (C) III only

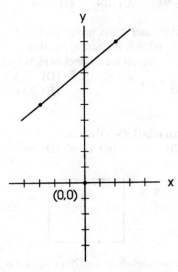

(0,0)

17. What is the slope of the line passing through the points $(-3c, 5c)$ and $(2c, 9c)$?

(A) -4 (B) $-\dfrac{5}{4}$ (C) $-\dfrac{4}{5}$ (D) $\dfrac{4}{5}$ (E) $\dfrac{5}{4}$

$\dfrac{9c - 5c}{2c - -3c}$

$\dfrac{4c}{5c}$

18. Today is Lucy's fourteenth birthday. Last year she was three years older than twice Charlie's age at that time. Using *C* for Charlie's age now, which of the following can be used to determined Charlie's age now?
    (A) $13 - 3 = 2(C - 1)$ (D) $13 + 3 = 2C$
    (B) $14 - 3 = 2C$ (E) $13 + 3 = 2(C - 1)$
    (C) $13 - 3 = 2C$

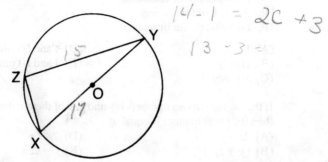

$14 - 1 = 2C + 3$

$13 - 3 =$

19. In circle O above, XY is a diameter, OX = 8.5, and YZ = 15. What is the area of △XYZ in square units?
    (A) 40   (B) 60   (C) 120   (D) 127.5   (E) 180

20. A bag contains 20 gumballs. If there are 8 red, 7 white, and 5 green, what is the minimum number of gumballs one must pick from the bag to be assured of one of each color?
    (A) 16   (B) 9   (C) 8   (D) 6   (E) 3

21. If the five vowels are repeated continuously in the pattern $a, e, i, o, u, a,$ $e, i, o, u,$ and so on, what vowel will the 327th letter be?
    (A) *a*   (B) *e*   (C) *i*   (D) *o*   (E) *u*

22. The base of an isosceles triangle exceeds each of the equal sides by 8 feet. If the perimeter is 89 feet, what is the length of the base in feet?
    (A) 27   (B) 29⅔   (C) 35   (D) 54   (E) 70

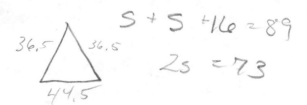

$S + S + 16 = 89$

$2s = 73$

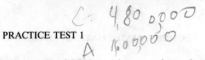

23. A random poll of 2500 moviegoers throughout New York found that 1500 preferred comedies, 500 preferred adventure films, and 500 preferred dramas. Of the 8,000,000 moviegoers in New York, which of the following is (are) the most reasonable estimate(s) drawn from the poll?

   I. 1,500,000 prefer comedies.
   II. 500,000 prefer dramas.
   III. 1,600,000 prefer dramas.

(A) I only   (D) I and II only
(B) II only   (E) I and III only
(C) III only

24. If the average of two numbers is y and one of the numbers is equal to z, then the other number is equal to
(A) $2z - y$ (D) $2y - z$
(B) $(y + z)/2$ (E) $y - 2z$
(C) $z - y$

25. What is the area of a rhombus with a perimeter of 40 and a diagonal of 10?
(A) $50\sqrt{3}$ (B) 100   (C) $100\sqrt{3}$ (D) 200   (E) 400

STOP. IF YOU FINISH BEFORE TIME IS CALLED, CHECK YOUR WORK ON THIS SECTION ONLY. DO NOT WORK ON ANY OTHER SECTION IN THE TEST.

SECTION 3: VERBAL REASONING

Time: 30 Minutes
35 Questions

In this section, choose the best answer for each question and blacken the corresponding space on the answer sheet.

Sentence Completion

DIRECTIONS

Each blank in the following sentences indicates that something has been omitted. Consider the lettered words beneath the sentence and choose the word or set of words that best fits the whole sentence.

1. It is _____ to assume that if aspirin can prevent second heart attacks, it can also _____ an attack in the first place.
   (A) fanciful ... eliminate
   (B) logical ... ward off
   (C) sensible ... encourage
   (D) reasonable ... foment
   (E) idle ... defend against

2. Cigars are not a safe _____ to cigarettes because, though cigar smokers do not inhale, they are still _____ higher rates of lung and mouth cancers than nonsmokers.
   (A) answer ... responsible for
   (B) preference ... free from
   (C) alternative ... subject to
   (D) rejoinder ... involved in
   (E) accent ... victimized by

3. Justices Marshall and Brennan opposed the death penalty on the grounds that it failed to _____ crimes, since all the available evidence made it clear that far more murders per capita were committed in states or countries with capital punishment than in those without it.
   (A) explain
   (B) augment
   (C) foster
   (D) deter
   (E) exculpate

141

4. After the smoke and _____ of the city, Mr. Fitzgerald was glad to return to the _____ air and peace of the mountains.
   (A) hubbub ... turbid
   (B) grime ... murky
   (C) tranquility ... effulgent
   (D) composure ... brisk
   (E) hustle-bustle ... exhilarating

5. A strike by Ford workers in Mexico poses a(n) _____ for the ruling party, which must choose between alienating its union ally or undermining its fight against inflation.
   (A) enigma
   (B) dilemma
   (C) problem
   (D) option
   (E) riddle

6. By combining an American cartoon character with Japanese traditions, the popular comic by Stan Sakai presents as hero a samurai rabbit, a unique _____ of East and West.
   (A) fusion
   (B) division
   (C) rejection
   (D) exclusion
   (E) query

7. A _____ that allowed voters to decide on the legality of casino gambling was passed by a(n) _____ nine-to-one margin.
   (A) statute ... meager
   (B) referendum ... overwhelming
   (C) prohibition ... huge
   (D) bill ... narrow
   (E) ban ... sizeable

8. The _____ upon which this fine novel is developed with great _____ and intelligence is that no males live beyond the age of eighteen.
   (A) theory ... fatuity
   (B) plot ... understanding
   (C) idea ... recalcitrance
   (D) premise ... subtlety
   (E) solution ... cleverness

9. The _____ use of washing machines and automobiles in the Middle Ages is part of the comedy of this high-spirited film.
   (A) untimely
   (B) anachronistic
   (C) unconvincing
   (D) archaic
   (E) supposed

10. Hoping to escape detection, Minnie _____ placed an ace in her sleeve while Rance shuffled the cards.
    (A) brazenly
    (B) overtly
    (C) furtively
    (D) hopefully
    (E) eagerly

Analogies

DIRECTIONS

In each question below, you are given a related pair of words or phrases. Select the lettered pair that *best* expresses a relationship similar to that in the original pair of words.

11. CLOTHES : LUGGAGE ::
    (A) baggage car : train
    (B) package : post office
    (C) documents : briefcase
    (D) airmail : mail carrier
    (E) plant : flowerpot

12. CYMBAL : BRASS ::
    (A) timpani : percussion
    (B) conductor : baton
    (C) viola : bow
    (D) clarinet : woodwind
    (E) violin : wood

13. DECADE : CENTURY ::
    (A) month : year
    (B) dime : dollar
    (C) yard : mile
    (D) gram : kilogram
    (E) minute : hour

14. JURY : EVIDENCE ::
    (A) lawyer : trial
    (B) diner : table
    (C) team : rules
    (D) doctor : symptoms
    (E) eyeglasses : reader

15. EARN : FILCH ::
    (A) create : plagiarize
    (B) injure : maim
    (C) plant : bury
    (D) lurk : sneak
    (E) lie : perjure

16. DISLIKE : LOATHE ::
    (A) praise : extol
    (B) yearn : desire
    (C) insure : rely
    (D) stuff : cram
    (E) hurry : run

17. CONSTELLATION : STAR ::
    (A) quasar : comet
    (B) sun : Milky Way
    (C) asteroid : planet
    (D) telescope : astronomer
    (E) solar system : planet

18. FOLLOW : STALK ::
    (A) dissipate : waste
    (B) glower : scowl
    (C) mature : ripen
    (D) light : illuminate
    (E) inquire : snoop

19. BACTERIUM : AGAR ::
    (A) plant : potting soil
    (B) host : parasite
    (C) meadow : mountainside
    (D) trout : lake
    (E) library : book

20. SLANDER : LIBEL ::
    (A) magazine : book
    (B) love : admiration
    (C) dance : song
    (D) speech : essay
    (E) felony : misdemeanor

21. CREDULOUS : DOUBT ::
    (A) naive : sorrow
    (B) avaricious : money
    (C) complacent : modesty
    (D) arduous : task
    (E) industrious : employment

22. SUPINE : PRONE ::
    (A) lying : reclining
    (B) dark : light
    (C) straight : narrow
    (D) open : overt
    (E) pensive : thoughtful

23. SURFEIT : DEARTH ::
    (A) reign : election
    (B) flood : drought
    (C) top : bottom
    (D) teacher : pupil
    (E) hand : finger

Critical Reading

DIRECTIONS

Questions follow the passage below. Using only the stated or implied information in the passage and in its introduction, if any, answer the questions.

Questions 24–35 are based on the following passage.

Early in the day Dorothea had returned from the infant school which she had set going in the village, and was taking her usual place in the pretty sitting-room which divided the bedrooms of the sisters, bent on finishing a plan for some buildings (a kind of work
(5) which she delighted in), when Celia, who had been watching her with a hesitating desire to propose something, said—

"Dorothea dear, if you don't mind—if you are not very busy—
suppose we looked at mamma's jewels to-day, and divided them? It
is exactly six months to-day since uncle gave them to you, and you
(10) have not looked at them yet."

Celia's face had the shadow of a pouting expression in it, the full
presence of the pout being kept back by an habitual awe of
Dorothea. To her relief, Dorothea's eyes were full of laughter as
she looked up.

(15)   "What a wonderful little almanac you are, Celia! Is it six
calendar or six lunar months?"

"It is the last day of September now, and it was the first of April
when uncle gave them to you. You know, he said that he had
forgotten them till then. I believe you have never thought of them
(20) since you locked them up in the cabinet here."

"Well, dear, we should never wear them, you know." Dorothea
spoke in a full cordial tone, half caressing, half explanatory. She had her
pencil in her hand, and was making tiny side-plans on a margin.

Celia coloured, and looked very grave. "I think, dear, we are
(25) wanting in respect to mamma's memory, to put them by and take
no notice of them. And," she added, after hesitating a little,
"necklaces are quite usual now; and Madame Poinçon, who was
stricter in some things even than you are, used to wear ornaments.
And Christians generally—surely there are women in heaven now
(30) who wore jewels." Celia was conscious of some mental strength
when she really applied herself to argument.

"You would like to wear them?" exclaimed Dorothea, an air of
astonished discovery animating her whole person. "Of course,
then, let us have them out. Why did you not tell me before? But the
(35) keys, the keys!" She pressed her hands against the sides of her
head and seemed to despair of her memory. "They are here," said
Celia, with whom this explanation had been long meditated and
prearranged.

The casket was soon open before them, and the various jewels
(40) spread out on the table. It was no great collection, but a few of the
ornaments were really of remarkable beauty, the finest that was
obvious at first being a necklace of purple amethysts set in exquisite
gold work, and a pearl cross with five brilliants in it. Dorothea
immediately took up the necklace and fastened it round her sister's
(45) neck, where it fitted almost as closely as a bracelet; but the circle
suited the style of Celia's head and neck, and she could see that it
did, in the pier-glass opposite.

"There, Celia! you can wear that with your Indian muslin. But this cross you must wear with your dark dresses."

(50)   Celia was trying not to smile with pleasure. "O Dodo, you must keep the cross yourself."

"No, no, dear, no," said Dorothea, putting up her hand with careless deprecation.

"Yes, indeed you must; it would suit you—in your black dress,
(55) now," said Celia, insistingly. "You *might* wear that."

"Not for the world, not for the world. A cross is the last thing I would wear as a trinket." Dorothea shuddered slightly.

"Then you will think it wicked in me to wear it," said Celia, uneasily.

(60)   "No, dear, no," said Dorothea, stroking her sister's cheek. "Souls have complexions too: what will suit one will not suit another."

"But you might like to keep it for mamma's sake."

"No, I have other things of mamma's—her sandal-wood box
(65) which I am so fond of—plenty of things. In fact, they are all yours, dear. We need discuss them no longer. There—take away your property."

Celia felt a little hurt. There was a strong assumption of superiority in this Puritanic toleration, hardly less trying to the
(70) blond flesh of an unenthusiastic sister than a Puritanic persecution.

24. From the details of the passage, it can be learned or inferred that

    I. Dorothea and Celia are sisters
   II. Dorothea and Celia may be orphans
  III. Dorothea and Celia are temperamentally very alike

  (A) III only
  (B) I and II only
  (C) I and III only
  (D) II and III only
  (E) I, II, and, III

25. The first paragraph of the passage refers to the "infant school" and "plan for some buildings" in order to suggest that Dorothea is
  (A) prying and interfering
  (B) rich and idle
  (C) self-centered and ambitious
  (D) active and unselfish
  (E) philanthropic and ineffectual

26. In lines 15–16, Dorothea asks Celia whether it is "six calendar or six lunar months" because she
    (A) wishes to know exactly how many days have passed
    (B) is good-humoredly teasing Celia
    (C) had hoped to keep the jewels from Celia
    (D) wishes to demonstrate the scientific precision of her mind
    (E) has forgotten what the current month is

27. In line 25, the phrase "wanting in respect" can be best understood to mean
    (A) obliged to be more deferential
    (B) desirous to esteem
    (C) lewd in regard
    (D) deficient in regard
    (E) eager for consideration

28. The "argument" to which Celia has "really applied herself" (line 31) is intended to convince Dorothea to
    (A) show greater respect for their dead mother
    (B) give all of the jewels to her
    (C) give the most valuable of the jewels to her
    (D) agree to sharing and wearing the jewels
    (E) examine the jewels and lock them up again

29. Although in line 21 Dorothea has said, "we should never wear them, you know," she changes her opinion because she
    (A) is moved by Celia's appeal to the memory of their mother
    (B) is convinced by Celia's reference to Madame Poinçon
    (C) realizes that Celia wants to wear the jewels
    (D) sees how becoming the jewels are to Celia
    (E) can appear superior to Celia by refusing to wear them herself

30. In line 53, the word "deprecation" means
    (A) protest
    (B) lessening
    (C) indifference
    (D) removal
    (E) agreement

31. The word "trying" in line 69 means
    (A) irksome
    (B) attempting
    (C) effortful
    (D) experimental
    (E) determining

32. In line 69, "Puritanic toleration" is a reference to
    (A) Celia's awe of Dorothea
    (B) Celia's acceptance of Dorothea's foibles
    (C) Celia's love of jewels and finery
    (D) Dorothea's hypocritical indifference to finery
    (E) Dorothea's self-denial and generosity

33. In the last line of the passage, the word "unenthusiastic" refers to
    (A) Dorothea's refusal to wear jewels
    (B) Dorothea's giving her permission for Celia to wear jewels
    (C) Celia's attitude toward self-denial
    (D) Celia's attitude toward wearing jewels
    (E) the author's attitude toward Dorothea

34. The inconsistency in Dorothea's reasoning that the passage reveals is her
    (A) forgetting about when the jewels were given to her
    (B) losing the keys to the cabinet holding the jewels
    (C) insistence that Christians cannot wear jewels
    (D) wanting Celia to wear jewels but refusing to wear them herself
    (E) deceitful claim that she honors the memory of her mother

35. The purpose of the passage as a whole is to
    (A) reveal the likeness of Celia and Dorothea
    (B) expose the submerged ill feelings between Celia and Dorothea
    (C) reveal the differences in the natures of Celia and Dorothea
    (D) demonstrate the dangers of materialism
    (E) satirize the hypocrisy of the two young women

STOP. IF YOU FINISH BEFORE TIME IS CALLED, CHECK YOUR WORK ON THIS SECTION ONLY. DO NOT WORK ON ANY OTHER SECTION IN THE TEST.

SECTION 4: MATHEMATICAL REASONING

Time: 30 Minutes
25 Questions

DIRECTIONS

This section is composed of two types of questions. Use the 30 minutes allotted to answer both question types. Your scratchwork should be done on any available space in the section.

Notes

(1) All numbers used are real numbers.
(2) Calculators may be used.
(3) Some problems may be accompanied by figures or diagrams. These figures are drawn as accurately as possible EXCEPT when it is stated in a specific problem that a figure is not drawn to scale. The figures and diagrams are meant to provide information useful in solving the problem or problems. Unless otherwise stated, all figures and diagrams lie in a plane.

Data That May Be Used for Reference

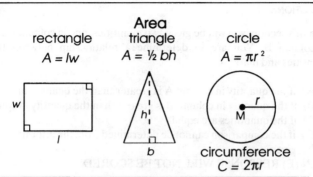

Area

rectangle	triangle	circle
$A = lw$	$A = \tfrac{1}{2}bh$	$A = \pi r^2$

circumference
$C = 2\pi r$

Volume

rectangular solid	right circular cylinder
$V = lwh$	$V = \pi r^2 h$

Pythagorean Relationship

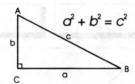

$$a^2 + b^2 = c^2$$

Special Triangles

30° – 60° – 90°   45° – 45° – 90°

A circle is composed of 360°
A straight angle measures 180°
The sum of the angles of a triangle is 180°

Quantitative Comparison

DIRECTIONS

In this section, you will be given two quantities, one in column A and one in column B. You are to determine a relationship between the two quantities and mark—

(A) if the quantity in column A is greater than the quantity in column B.
(B) if the quantity in column B is greater than the quantity in column A.
(C) if the quantities are equal.
(D) if the comparison cannot be determined from the information that is given.

AN (E) RESPONSE WILL NOT BE SCORED.

Notes

(1) Sometimes, information concerning one or both of the quantities to be compared is given. This information is not boxed and is centered above the two columns.
(2) All numbers used are real numbers. Letters such as a, b, m, and x represent real numbers.
(3) In a given question, if the same symbol is used in column A and column B, that symbol stands for the same value in each column.

	Column A	**Column B**
1.	$3^2 + 4 \times 10^2 - 4^2$	$3^2 - 4 \times 10^2 - 4^2$

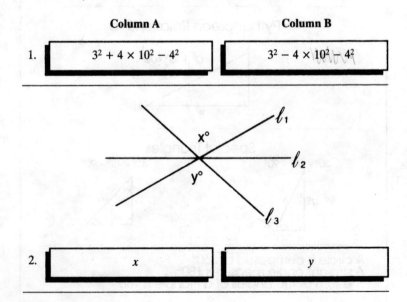

	Column A	**Column B**
2.	x	y

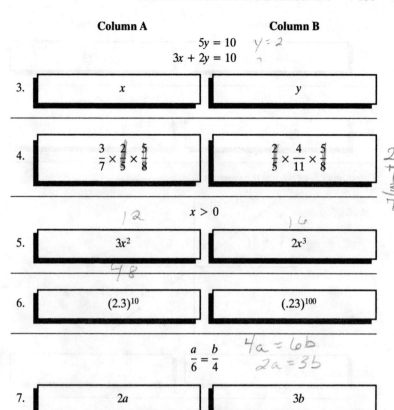

	Column A	Column B

$$5y = 10 \quad y = 2$$
$$3x + 2y = 10 \quad 2$$

3. x | y

4. $\dfrac{3}{7} \times \dfrac{2}{5} \times \dfrac{5}{8}$ | $\dfrac{2}{5} \times \dfrac{4}{11} \times \dfrac{5}{8}$

$\begin{array}{c} 28 \\ 77 \\ \frac{3}{77} \end{array}$

$x > 0$

5. $3x^2$ | $2x^3$

6. $(2.3)^{10}$ | $(.23)^{100}$

$$\dfrac{a}{6} = \dfrac{b}{4} \qquad \begin{array}{c} 4a = 6b \\ 2a = 3b \end{array}$$

7. $2a$ | $3b$

Questions 8–9 refer to the diagram.

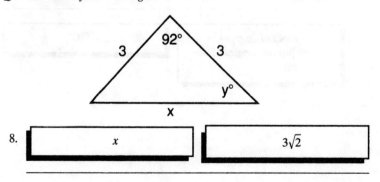

8. x | $3\sqrt{2}$

	Column A	**Column B**
9.	y	43°

$$0 < y < 1$$

| 10. | $4y^2 - 4y + 1$ | $(2y + 1)^2$ |

Questions 11–12 refer to the diagram.

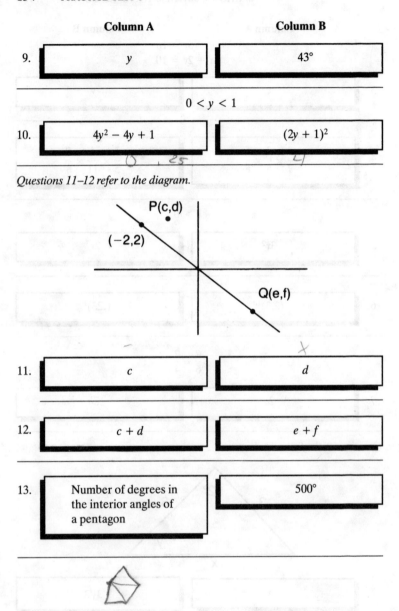

11.	c	d

12.	$c + d$	$e + f$

13.	Number of degrees in the interior angles of a pentagon	500°

Column A	**Column B**

$$n \neq 0$$
$$n \neq -\tfrac{1}{2}$$
$$n \neq -1$$

14.

$\dfrac{1}{1 + \dfrac{1}{1 + 1/n}}$	$\dfrac{n+1}{2n+1}$

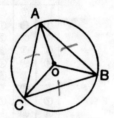

Equilateral $\triangle ABC$
is inscribed in circle O

$$AB = AC = CB = 8\sqrt{3}$$

15.

$OA + OB + OC$	24

Grid-in Questions

DIRECTIONS

Questions 16–25 require you to solve the problem and enter your answer by carefully marking the circles on the special grid. Examples of the appropriate way to mark the grid follow.

Answer: 3.7   **Answer: 1/2**

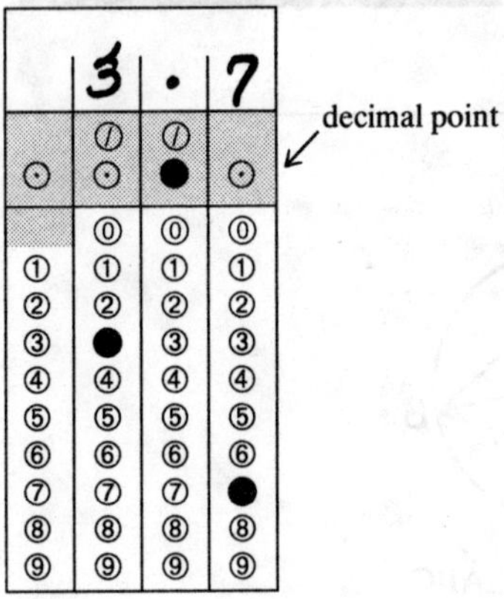

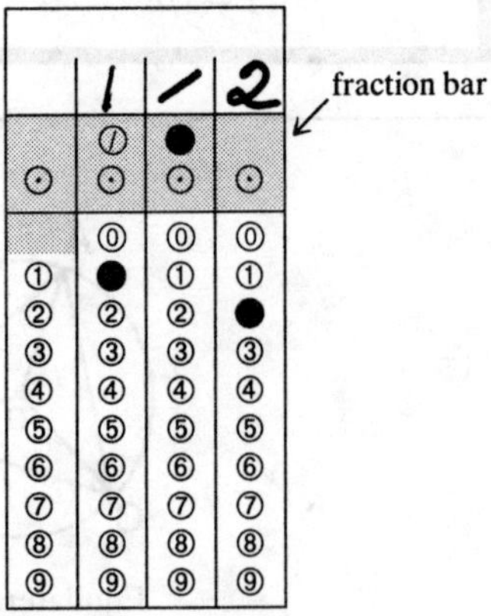

decimal point

fraction bar

Answer: 1½

Do not grid in mixed numbers in the form of mixed numbers. **Always** change mixed numbers to improper fractions or decimals.

Change to 1.5   or   Change to 3/2

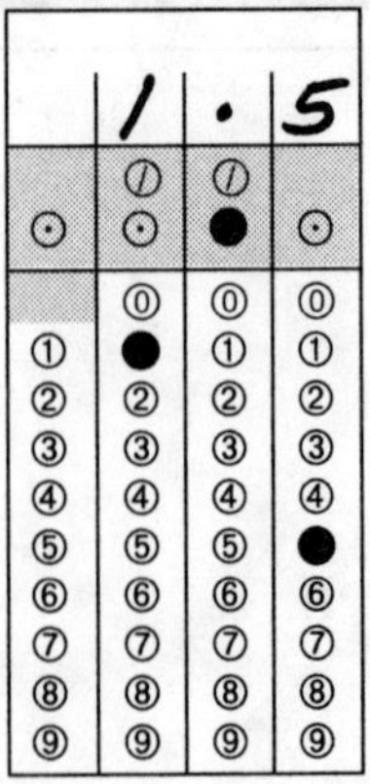

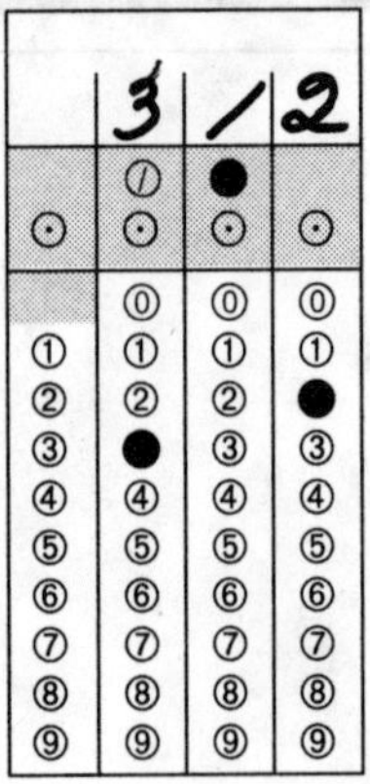

Answer: 123

Space permitting, answers may start in any column. Each grid-in answer below is correct.

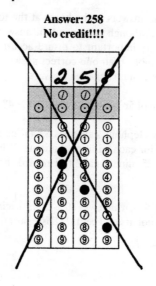

Note: Circles must be filled in correctly to receive credit. Mark only one circle in each column. No credit will be given if more than one circle in a column is marked. Example:

Answer: 258
No credit!!!!

Answer: 8/9

Accuracy of decimals: Always enter the most accurate decimal value that the grid will accommodate. For example: An answer such as .8888 . . . can be gridded as .888 or .889. Gridding this value as .8, .88, or .89 is considered inaccurate and therefore **not acceptable.** The acceptable grid-ins of 8/9 are:

8/9   .888   .889

Be sure to write your answers in the boxes at the top of the circles before doing your gridding. Although writing out the answers above the columns is not required, it is very important to insure accuracy. Even though some problems may have more than one correct answer, grid only **one answer.** Grid-in questions contain no negative answers.

16. What is the value of $5x^2 - 3x + 2$ when $x = -4$?

17. A long-distance telephone call costs $2.45 for the first 3 minutes and $.32 per minute for each additional minute. What is the cost in dollars and cents for a 25-minute call? (Disregard the $ sign when gridding your answer.)

18. A jacket sold for $56, which was 80% of its original price. What was the original price in dollars and cents? (Disregard the $ sign when gridding your answer.)

19. What is the length of the side of a cube whose volume is 64 cubic units?

> **BILL FOR PURCHASES**
>
> | | |
> |---|---:|
> | Science Textbooks | $840 |
> | Lab Equipment | $460 |
> | Formaldehyde | $320 |
> | Teacher's Manuals | $120 |
> | TOTAL | $2220 |

20. Scholastic Supplies, Inc., sends the bill above to Zither Junior High School. Although the bill includes the cost of science lab workbooks, Scholastic Supplies forgot to list them on the bill. How much did the science lab workbooks cost Zither Junior High? (Disregard the $ sign when gridding your answer.)

21. If the numerator of a fraction is tripled, and the denominator of a fraction is doubled, the resulting fraction will reflect an increase of what percent? (Disregard the % sign when gridding your answer.)

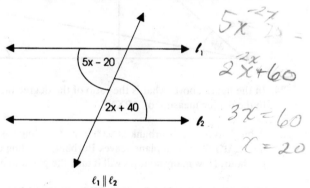

$\ell_1 \parallel \ell_2$

22. In the figure above, what is the value of x?

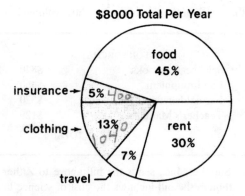

$8000 Total Per Year

food 45%

insurance → 5% 400

clothing → 13% 0
1040

rent 30%

7%

travel

23. Based on the chart above, how much more money was spent on clothing than on insurance?

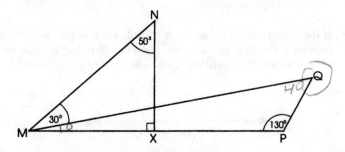

24. In the figure above, what is the ratio of the degree measure of ∠MQP to the degree measure of ∠PXN?

40 : 90 4/9

25. A bus leaves from Burbank at 9:00 A.M., traveling east at 50 miles per hour. At 1:00 P.M., a plane leaves Burbank traveling east at 300 miles per hour. How many minutes will it take the plane to overtake the bus?

STOP: IF YOU FINISH BEFORE TIME IS CALLED, CHECK YOUR WORK ON THIS SECTION ONLY. DO NOT WORK ON ANY OTHER SECTION IN THE TEST.

4 2/3   5 mph

SECTION 5: VERBAL REASONING

Time: 15 Minutes
15 Questions

In this section, choose the best answer for each question and blacken the corresponding space on the answer sheet.

Critical Reading

DIRECTIONS

Questions follow the two passages below. Using only the stated or implied information in each passage and in its introduction, if any, answer the questions.

Questions 1–15 are based on the following passages.

The two passages that follow are taken from recent historical studies of Christopher Columbus.

Passage 1

In his history published in 1552, Francisco López de Gomara wrote: "The greatest event since the creation of the world (excluding the incarnation and death of Him who created it) is the discovery of the Indies." On the strength of this realization,
(5) Columbus emerged from the shadows, reincarnated not so much as a man and historical figure as he was as a myth and symbol. He came to epitomize the explorer and discoverer, the man of vision and audacity, the hero who overcame opposition and adversity to change history. By the end of the sixteenth century, English
(10) explorers and writers acknowledged the primacy and inspiration of Columbus. He was celebrated in poetry and plays, especially by the Italians. Even Spain was coming around. In a popular play, Lope de Vega in 1614 portrayed Columbus as a dreamer up against the stolid forces of entrenched tradition, a man of singular purpose
(15) who triumphed, the embodiment of that spirit driving humans to explore and discover.

Historians cannot control the popularizers of history, myth-makers, or propagandists, and in post-Revolutionary America the few historians who studied Columbus were probably not disposed
(20) to try. Even if they had been, there was little information available on which to assess the real Columbus and distinguish the man from

161

the myth. With the discovery and publication of new Columbus documents by Martin Fernández de Navarrete in 1825, this was less of an excuse, and yet the material only provided more
(25) ammunition to those who would embellish the symbolic Columbus through the nineteenth century.

Washington Irving mined the new documents to create a hero in the romantic mold favored in the century's literature. Irving's Columbus was "a man of great and inventive genius" and his
(30) "ambition was lofty and noble, inspiring him with high thoughts, and an anxiety to distinguish himself by great achievements." Perhaps. But an effusive Irving got carried away. He said that Columbus's "conduct was characterized by the grandeur of his views and the magnanimity of his spirit. . . . Instead of ravaging the
(35) newly found countries . . . he sought to colonize and cultivate them, to civilize the natives." Irving acknowledged that Columbus may have had some faults, such as his part in enslaving and killing people, but offered the palliating explanation that these were "errors of the times."
(40)   William H. Prescott, a leading American historian of the conquest period, said of Columbus that "the finger of the historian will find it difficult to point to a single blemish in his moral character." Writers and orators of the nineteenth century ascribed to Columbus all the human virtues that were most prized in that
(45) time of geographic and industrial expansion, heady optimism, and an unquestioning belief in progress as the dynamic of history.

Most people living in America four centuries after the voyages of discovery had created the Columbus they wanted to believe in and were quite satisfied with their creation. But scholars were already
(50) finding grounds for a major reassessment of Columbus's reputation in history.

Passage 2

Why should one suppose that a culture like Europe's, steeped as it was in the ardor of wealth, the habit of violence, and the pride of intolerance, dispirited and adrift after a century and more of
(55) disease and famine and death beyond experience, would be able to come upon new societies in a fertile world, innocent and defenseless, and not displace and subdue, if necessary destroy, them? Why should one suppose such a culture would pause there to observe, to learn, to borrow the wisdom and the ways of a foreign, heathen
(60) people, half naked and befeathered, ignorant of cities and kings and metal and laws, and unschooled in all that the Ancients held

virtuous? Was not Europe in its groping era of discovery in the
fifteenth century in fact in search of salvation, as its morbid sonnets
said, or of that regeneration which new lands and new peoples—
(65) and of course new riches—would be presumed to provide?

And there was salvation there, in the New World, though it was
not of a kind the Europeans then understood. They thought first
that exploitation was salvation, and they went at that with a
vengeance, and found new foods and medicines and treasures, but
(70) that proved not to be; that colonization and settlement was
salvation, and they peopled both continents with conquerors, and it
was not that either. The salvation there, had the Europeans known
where and how to look for it, was obviously in the integrative tribal
ways, the nurturant communitarian values, the rich interplay with
(75) nature that made up the Indian cultures—as it made up, for that
matter, the cultures of ancient peoples everywhere, not excluding
Europe. It was there especially in the Indian consciousness, in what
Calvin Martin has termed *"the biological outlook on life,"* in which
patterns and concepts and the large teleological constructs of
(80) culture are not human-centered but come from the sense of being
at one with nature, biocentric, ecocentric.

However one may cast it, an opportunity there certainly was
once, a chance for the people of Europe to find a new anchorage in
a new country, in what they dimly realized was the land of Paradise,
(85) and thus find finally the way to redeem the world. But all they ever
found was half a world of nature's treasures and nature's peoples
that could be taken, and they took them, never knowing, never
learning the true regenerative power there, and that opportunity
was lost. Theirs was indeed a conquest of Paradise, but as is
(90) inevitable with any war against the world of nature, those who win
will have lost—once again lost, and this time perhaps forever.

1. In lines 12–16 of the first paragraph, the reference to the play by Lope
   de Vega serves to

     I. give an example of Columbus's reputation in Spain
    II. demonstrate how widespread Columbus's reputation had become
   III. exemplify how Columbus was already a myth and symbol of the
        discoverer

   (A) I only
   (B) II only
   (C) I and III only
   (D) II and III only
   (E) I, II, and III

2. In Passage 1 (line 19), the word "disposed" means
   (A) arranged
   (B) employed
   (C) settled
   (D) inclined
   (E) given away

3. In Passage 1 (line 28), the phrase "romantic mold" most nearly means
   (A) pattern concerned with love
   (B) idealized manner
   (C) visionary model
   (D) fictitious shape
   (E) escapist style

4. Of the following words used in the third paragraph of Passage 1, which most clearly reveals a judgment of the modern author as opposed to that of Washington Irving?
   (A) "mined" (line 27)
   (B) "ambition" (line 30)
   (C) "Perhaps" (line 32)
   (D) "magnanimity" (line 34)
   (E) "palliating" (line 38)

5. The major purpose of the Passage 1 is to
   (A) praise the daring and accomplishments of Columbus
   (B) survey the reputation of Columbus from the sixteenth through the nineteenth century
   (C) contrast the real Columbus of history with the mythic Columbus of the nineteenth century
   (D) describe the benefits and the damage of Columbus's voyages
   (E) reveal the unforeseen and harmful consequences of Columbus's voyages

6. With which of the following generalizations would the author of Passage 1 be most likely to agree?

    I. The values of a historical period are usually reflected by the heroes people of that time choose to idolize.
    II. What people believe about historical figures is usually what they wish to believe.
    III. Written history is usually a record of the truth as it is known at the time of writing.

    (A) I only
    (B) I and II only
    (C) I and III only
    (D) II and III only
    (E) I, II, and III

7. The questions of the first paragraph of Passage 2 (lines 52–65) serve chiefly to
    (A) raise doubts about issues that cannot be explained
    (B) defend and justify the actions of Europeans in the age of discovery
    (C) suggest areas which future historians might profitably explore
    (D) show how much easier it is to understand issues of the distant past with the objectivity given by time
    (E) reveal the author's ideas about the nature of Europeans at the time of Columbus's voyages

8. In Passage 2 (lines 61–62), the phrase "unschooled in all that the Ancients held virtuous" is used to

    I. reflect the European view of the American natives
    II. reveal a significant foundation of European culture in the period
    III. give a reason for the European contempt for the native Americans

    (A) III only
    (B) I and II only
    (C) I and III only
    (D) II and III only
    (E) I, II, and III

9. Which of the following does Passage 2 present as discovered and understood by the Europeans in America?
   (A) Human-centered cultures
   (B) New foods and medicines
   (C) Communitarian values
   (D) An Indian consciousness
   (E) An ecocentric culture

10. According to Passage 2, a *"biological outlook on life"* would be best defined as one in which
   (A) the interdependence of all life forms is understood
   (B) humans are the measure of all things
   (C) the needs of rich and poor are equally considered
   (D) the economic well-being of all races is emphasized
   (E) the primary motivation is survival of the species

11. The major purpose of Passage 2 is to
   (A) describe the benefits and damage of Columbus's discovery
   (B) present Columbus's discovery as a tragically missed opportunity to regenerate Europe
   (C) attack the greed and cruelty that inspired the European colonization of America
   (D) defend the European colonization of America as historically determined and unavoidable
   (E) evaluate as objectively as possible the meaning of the European incursion into the Americas

12. Of the five paragraphs in Passage 1, which one best prepares the reader for the contents of Passage 2?
   (A) The first (lines 1–16)
   (B) The second (lines 17–26)
   (C) The third (lines 27–39)
   (D) The fourth (lines 40–46)
   (E) The fifth (lines 47–51)

13. Compared to Passage 1, Passage 2 may be described by all of the following EXCEPT
   (A) more personal
   (B) more philosophical
   (C) more judgmental
   (D) more historical
   (E) more emotional

14. Compared to that of Passage 1, the prose of Passage 2 makes greater use of all of the following EXCEPT
    (A) words in series
    (B) rhetorical questions
    (C) understatements
    (D) repetitions
    (E) parallel phrases

15. Which of the following aptly describes a relationship between Passage 1 and Passage 2?

    I. Passage 1 predicts a reevaluation of Columbus's accomplishments, and Passage 2 makes that reevaluation.
    II. Passage 1 calls attention to the way the image of Columbus in each period reflects the values of that period, and Passage 2 presents an image that reflects late twentieth-century ideas.
    III. Passage 1 focuses upon the reputation of Columbus, while Passage 2 emphasizes his unique character.

    (A) III only
    (B) I and II only
    (C) I and III only
    (D) II and III only
    (E) I, II, and III

STOP. IF YOU FINISH BEFORE TIME IS CALLED, CHECK YOUR WORK ON THIS SECTION ONLY. DO NOT WORK ON ANY OTHER SECTION IN THE TEST.

SECTION 6: MATHEMATICAL REASONING

Time: 15 Minutes
10 Questions

DIRECTIONS

Solve each problem in this section by using the information given and your own mathematical calculations, insights, and problem-solving skills. Then select the one correct answer of the five choices given and mark the corresponding circle on your answer sheet. Use the available space on the page for your scratchwork.

Notes

(1) All numbers used are real numbers.
(2) Calculators may be used.
(3) Some problems may be accompanied by figures or diagrams. These figures are drawn as accurately as possible EXCEPT when it is stated in a specific problem that a figure is not drawn to scale. The figures and diagrams are meant to provide information useful in solving the problem or problems. Unless otherwise stated, all figures and diagrams lie in a plane.

Data That May Be Used for Reference

Area

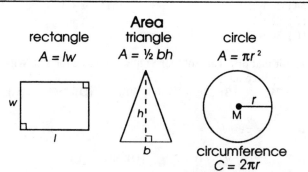

rectangle   triangle   circle

$A = lw$ $A = \frac{1}{2}bh$ $A = \pi r^2$

circumference
$C = 2\pi r$

Volume

rectangular solid   right circular cylinder

$V = lwh$ $V = \pi r^2 h$

Pythagorean Relationship

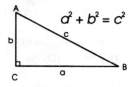

$$a^2 + b^2 = c^2$$

Special Triangles

30° – 60° – 90°   •   45° – 45° – 90°

A circle is composed of 360°
A straight angle measures 180°
The sum of the angles of a triangle is 180°

1. If $2x + 13$ represents an odd number, what must the next consecutive odd number be?
   (A) $2x + 15$ (D) $3x + 15$
   (B) $2x + 14$ (E) $4x + 1$
   (C) $3x + 13$

2. A suit that originally sold for \$120 was on sale for \$90. What was the rate of discount?
   (A) 75% (B) 33⅓%   (C) 30% (D) 25% (E) 20%

3. If $\sqrt{\dfrac{81}{x}} = \dfrac{9}{5}$, then $x =$

   (A) 5 (B) 9 (C) 25 (D) 50 (E) 53

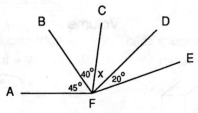

Note: Figure not drawn to scale.

4. If, in the figure above, $\angle CFD = \angle AFB$, then what is the degree measure of $\angle AFE$?
   (A) 40° (B) 45° (C) 150° (D) 160° (E) 180°

5. What is the value of x if the average of 93, 82, 79, and x is 87?
   (A) 87 (B) 90 (C) 93 (D) 94 (E) 348

SCHOOL-WIDE
EYE COLOR SURVEY

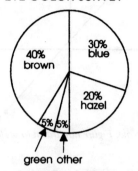

green other

6. Annette does a school-wide survey and publishes her results in the circle graph above. If 62 people at Annette's school have hazel eyes, how many have brown eyes?

    (A) 20   (B) 40   (C) 62   (D) 124   (E) 248

7. How many degrees has the minute hand moved on a clock from 4:00 P.M. to 4:12 P.M.?

    (A) 12   (B) 36   (C) 72   (D) 90   (E) 102

8. If $\dfrac{x^2 - 5x + 7}{x^2 - 4x + 10} = 1$, then $x =$

    (A) -3 (B) $\frac{1}{3}$ (C) $\frac{7}{10}$ (D) $\frac{17}{9}$ (E) 3

9. One angle of a triangle is 68°. The other two angles are in the ratio of 3:4. Which of the following is the number of degrees in the smallest angle of the triangle?

    (A) 16   (B) 34   (C) 48   (D) 64   (E) 68

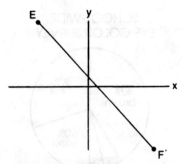

Note: Figure not drawn to scale.

10. If, in the graph above, point E has coordinates $(-3, 5)$ and point F has coordinates $(6, -7)$, then length of EF =
    (A) 21   (B) 15   (C) 7   (D) 5   (E) 3

STOP: IF YOU FINISH BEFORE TIME IS CALLED, CHECK YOUR WORK ON THIS SECTION ONLY. DO NOT WORK ON ANY OTHER SECTION IN THE TEST.

SECTION 7: MATHEMATICAL REASONING

Time: 30 Minutes
25 Questions

DIRECTIONS

Solve each problem in this section by using the information given and your own mathematical calculations, insights, and problem-solving skills. Then select the one correct answer of the five choices given and mark the corresponding circle on your answer sheet. Use the available space on the page for your scratchwork.

Notes

(1) All numbers used are real numbers.
(2) Calculators may be used.
(3) Some problems may be accompanied by figures or diagrams. These figures are drawn as accurately as possible EXCEPT when it is stated in a specific problem that a figure is not drawn to scale. The figures and diagrams are meant to provide information useful in solving the problem or problems. Unless otherwise stated, all figures and diagrams lie in a plane.

Data That May Be Used for Reference

Area

rectangle

$A = lw$

triangle

$A = \frac{1}{2} bh$

circle

$A = \pi r^2$

circumference

$C = 2\pi r$

Volume

rectangular solid

$V = lwh$

right circular cylinder

$V = \pi r^2 h$

Pythagorean Relationship

$$a^2 + b^2 = c^2$$

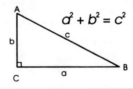

Special Triangles

30° – 60° – 90°

45° – 45° – 90°

A circle is composed of 360°
A straight angle measures 180°
The sum of the angles of a triangle is 180°

1. If $2x - 5 = 9$, then $3x + 2 =$
   (A) 44   (B) 23   (C) 16   (D) 14   (E) 7

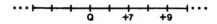

2. On the number line above, what is the point 15 units to the left of point Q?
   (A) 10   (B) 5   (C) 0   (D) −9   (E) −10

3. If $x = 3, y = 4$, and $z = -1$, what is the value of $2x + 3y^2 - z$?
   (A) 151   (B) 149   (C) 55   (D) 53   (E) 19

4. If cassette tapes cost $2.98 for a package of two tapes, how much change will Roy receive from a twenty-dollar bill if he purchases twelve tapes?
   (A) $2.02
   (B) $2.12
   (C) $2.18
   (D) $2.22
   (E) $3.02

5. $\dfrac{6^4 + 6^5}{6^4} =$

   (A) 36   (B) 31   (C) 30   (D) 7   (E) 6

6. Gasoline varies in cost from $0.96 to $1.12 per gallon. If a car's mileage varies from 16 to 24 miles per gallon, what is the difference between the most and least that the gasoline for a 480-mile trip will cost?
   (A) $ 5.12   (D) $14.40
   (B) $ 7.04   (E) $52.80
   (C) $11.52

7. Ernie cut a yardstick into two pieces, the larger piece being six inches more than the smaller. How could Ernie compute the size of the smaller piece, x?
   (A) $x + 6 = 36$ (D) $2x - 6 = 36$
   (B) $2x = 36$ (E) $2x + 6 = 30$
   (C) $x + x + 6 = 36$

$$\begin{array}{r} \square\square 4 \\ \times\ 8 \\ \hline 539\square \end{array}$$

8. The sum of the digits in the three boxes equals
   (A) 5   (B) 7   (C) 9   (D) 13   (E) 15

9. If the length and width of a rectangle are increased by x units, its perimeter is increased by how many units?
   (A) $4x$ (B) $2x$ (C) x^2 (D) x (E) $x + 4$

10. Which of the following ordered pairs (a, b) is NOT a member of the solution set of $2a - 3b = 6$?
    (A) $(6, 2)$ (D) $(4, \frac{2}{3})$
    (B) $(-3, -4)$ (E) $(0, 2)$
    (C) $(3, 0)$

11. Harriet planned to complete a certain task on Wednesday, January 1, but because of illness, the completion date was postponed 48 days. On which day of the week in February was the task completed?
    (A) Monday   (D) Thursday
    (B) Tuesday   (E) Friday
    (C) Wednesday

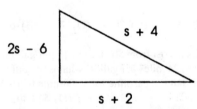

$2s - 6$

$s + 4$

$s + 2$

12. Which of the following expresses the perimeter of the above triangle?
    (A) $(2s - 6)(s + 4)$ (D) $4s + 12$
    (B) $\frac{1}{2}(2s - 6)(s + 4)$ (E) $4s - 12$
    (C) $4s$

13. What percent of $\frac{2}{3}$ is $\frac{1}{2}$?
    (A) 300%   (D) 50%
    (B) $133\frac{1}{3}$%   (E) $33\frac{1}{3}$%
    (C) 75%

14. How many inches are there in m yards and n feet?
    (A) $m + n$ (D) $3m + n$
    (B) $36m + 12n$ (E) $12(m + n)$
    (C) $36(m + n)$

15. A house is on the market for a selling price of $64,000. The buyer made a $1500 deposit, but fifteen percent of the selling price is needed for the down payment. How much more money does the buyer need for the down payment?
    (A) $3200   (D) $9600
    (B) $6400   (E) $11,100
    (C) $8100

16. The average of 9 numbers is 7, and the average of 7 other numbers is 9. What is the average of all 16 numbers?
    (A) 8   (B) 7⅞   (C) 7½   (D) 7¼   (E) 7⅛

17. If the volume and the total surface area of a cube are equal, how long must the edge of the cube be?
    (A) 2 units   (D) 5 units
    (B) 3 units   (E) 6 units
    (C) 4 units

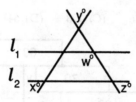

18. If $l_1 \parallel l_2, x = 60°$, and $w = 2z$, then $y + w =$
    (A) 60°   (B) 90°   (C) 120°   (D) 150°   (E) 180°

19. If # is a binary operation such that $a \, \# \, b$ is defined as

$$\frac{a^2 + b^2}{a^2 - b^2}$$

and $(a^2 - b^2 \neq 0)$, then what is the value of $a \, \# \, b$ if $2a = b$ and $a \neq 0$?

    (A) 1⅓   (B) ⅗   (C) −½   (D) −⅗   (E) −1⅔

20. If a pipe can drain a tank in t hours, what part of the tank does it drain in 3 hours?

    (A) $3t$ (B) $t/3$ (C) $t + 3$ (D) $3/t$ (E) $t - 3$

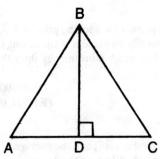

Note: Figure not drawn to scale.

21. In the figure above, BD $\perp$ AC, AB = 34, BD = 30, and BC = 34. What is the length of AC?

    (A) 8   (B) 18   (C) 30   (D) 32   (E) 34

22. What is the area of a square inscribed in a circle whose circumference is 16π?

    (A) 512   (B) 256   (C) 128   (D) 64   (E) 32

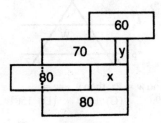

23. The horizontal length of each rectangle above is marked within. What is the total horizontal length of $x + y$?

    (A) 40   (D) 90

    (B) 50   (E) cannot be determined

    (C) 80

24. 750 times 45 equals P. Therefore, 750 times 44 equals

    (A) $P - 45$ (D) $44P$

    (B) $P - 750$ (E) $750P$

    (C) $P - 1$

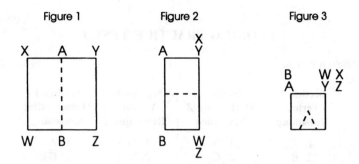

Figure 1   Figure 2   Figure 3

25. In figure 1 above, a square piece of paper is folded along dotted line AB so that X is on top of Y and W is on top of Z (figure 2). The paper is then folded again so that B is on top of A and WZ is on top of XY (figure 3). A small triangle is cut out of the folded paper as shown in figure 3. If the paper is unfolded, which of the following could be the result?

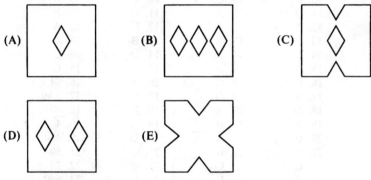

(A)

(B)

(C)

(D)

(E)

STOP. IF YOU FINISH BEFORE TIME IS CALLED, CHECK YOUR WORK ON THIS SECTION ONLY. DO NOT WORK ON ANY OTHER SECTION IN THE TEST.

SCORING PRACTICE TEST 1

Section 1 Verbal Reasoning	Section 2 Mathematical Reasoning	Section 3 Verbal Reasoning	Section 4 Mathematical Reasoning
1. A	1. B	1. B	1. A
2. B	2. C	2. C	2. C
3. A	3. C	3. D	3. C
4. C	4. C	4. E	4. A
5. D	5. D	5. B	5. D
6. C	6. D	6. A	6. A
7. B	7. E	7. B	7. C
8. D	8. B	8. D	8. A
9. C	9. B	9. B	9. A
10. C	10. C	10. C	10. B
11. B	11. A	11. C	11. B
12. A	12. A	12. E	12. A
13. E	13. A	13. B	13. A
14. C	14. E	14. D	14. C
15. A	15. B	15. A	15. C
16. E	16. C	16. A	16. 94
17. B	17. D	17. E	17. 9.49
18. D	18. A	18. E	18. 70
19. A	19. B	19. A	19. 4
20. C	20. A	20. D	20. 480
21. A	21. B	21. C	21. 50
22. C	22. C	22. B	22. 20
23. B	23. C	23. B	23. 640
24. C	24. D	24. B	24. 4/9
25. D	25. A	25. D	25. 48
26. A		26. B	
27. A		27. D	
28. D		28. D	
29. B		29. C	
30. E		30. A	
		31. A	
		32. E	
		33. C	
		34. D	
		35. C	

ANSWER KEY

Section 5 Verbal Reasoning	Section 6 Mathematical Reasoning	Section 7 Mathematical Reasoning
1. E	1. A	1. B
2. D	2. D	2. E
3. B	3. C	3. C
4. C	4. C	4. B
5. B	5. D	5. D
6. B	6. D	6. D
7. E	7. C	7. C
8. E	8. A	8. E
9. B	9. C	9. A
10. A	10. B	10. E
11. B		11. B
12. E		12. C
13. D		13. C
14. C		14. B
15. B		15. C
		16. B
		17. E
		18. E
		19. E
		20. D
		21. D
		22. C
		23. E
		24. B
		25. D

ANALYZING YOUR TEST RESULTS

The charts on the following pages should be used to carefully analyze your results and spot your strengths and weaknesses. The complete process of analyzing each subject area and each individual problem should be completed for each practice test. These results should then be reexamined for trends in types of errors (repeated errors) or poor results in specific subject areas. **This reexamination and analysis is of tremendous importance to you in assuring maximum test preparation benefit.**

Verbal Reasoning Analysis Sheet

Section 1	possible	completed	right	wrong
sentence completion	9	9	9	0
analogies	6	6	3	3
critical reading	15	15	11	4
Subtotal	30	30	23	7

Section 3	possible	completed	right	wrong
sentence completion	10	10	8	2
analogies	13	13	6	7
critical reading	12	12	5	7
Subtotal	35	35	19	16

Section 5	possible	completed	right	wrong
critical reading	15			
Subtotal	15			
Overall Verbal Totals	80			

Mathematical Reasoning Analysis Sheet

Section 2	possible	completed	right	wrong
multiple choice	25	25	19	6
Subtotal	25	25	19	6

Section 4	possible	completed	right	wrong
quantitative comparison	15	15	12	3
grid-ins	10	10	8	2
Subtotal	25	25	20	5

Section 6	possible	completed	right	wrong
multiple choice	10			
Subtotal	10			

Section 7	possible	completed	right	wrong
multiple choice	25			
Subtotal	25			
Overall Math Totals	85			

You can now use the Score Range Approximator on page 439 to convert your raw scores to an **approximate** scaled score.

WHY?????????????????????????????????

Analysis/Tally Sheet for Problems Missed

One of the most important parts of test preparation is analyzing **why** you missed a problem so that you can reduce the number of mistakes. Now that you have taken the practice test and checked your answers, carefully tally your mistakes by marking them in the proper column.

Reason for Mistakes

	Total Missed	Simple Mistake	Misread Problem	Lack of Knowledge	Lack of Time
Section 1: Verbal					
Section 3: Verbal					
Section 5: Verbal					
Subtotal					
Section 2: Math					
Section 4: Math					
Section 6: Math					
Section 7: Math					
Subtotal					
Total Math and Verbal					

Reviewing the above data should help you determine **why** you are missing certain problems. Now that you've pinpointed the type of error, compare it to other practice tests to spot other common mistakes.

COMPLETE ANSWERS AND EXPLANATIONS
FOR PRACTICE TEST 1

SECTION 1: VERBAL REASONING

Sentence Completion

1. (A) The adjective here should pick up the implications of *loved and hated,* not just one or the other. The word *controversial* (A) accounts for both. The other choices are not specifically related in any way to the rest of the sentence.

2. (B) You need a verb here describing the action of organisms with a meaning like developed or discovered. The best choice is (B), *evolved,* developed gradually, which also fits well with the detail of *thousands of years.* The wrong answers describe too conscious an action.

3. (A) Here you need words that are contradictory to the two givens: *affectionate* and *alert. Aloof* (A), *cruel* (B), or *selfish* (D) are possible first words, but *shrewd* (B), *lively* (C), and *nimble* (D) are not contradictions of *alert,* so the only possible right answer is (A).

4. (C) The first adjective offers a choice among five, any one of which would fit the first phrase. But since this fame is for an unfavorably regarded trait, the best choice is *notorious.* A hero is *famous, renowned, illustrious,* or *eminent,* but a man who talks too much is *notorious.* Since the action described confirms the reputation for long-windedness, *verified* is the only possible choice of the verbs.

5. (D) You know that Montana already is a senator who may run for reelection. Therefore, she is the *incumbent,* the holder of an office. The details of the sentence support this choice. Alhough the other nouns are not wholly unsuitable, none of them has any real connection with the details in the rest of the sentence.

6. (C) The first noun must be a term that refers to what is pledged to obtain a loan, a word like *pledge,* or *surety,* or *collateral,* or *deposit.* Only *profit* (D) can be eliminated. The verb must mean liquidate or get rid of, since he emerges *free of debt.* Only *discharge* (C) is left when you eliminate (A), (B), and (E). This confirms the sense of *collateral* being the best of the four available nouns.

7. (B) The missing word describes *absurdist* fiction and is parallel to the word *shocking.* Clearly, *banal* (A), *plausible* (C), *cozy* (D), and *familiar* (E) will not do. The adjective *radical* means favoring fundamental change or very leftist.

187

8. (D) The sense of the sentence calls for an adjective expressing strong feelings, since the writer is surprised by this response to an *insignificant issue.* Only choice (D) is logical.

9. (C) The sentence describes a division in the band, avant-garde instrumentalists and a popular-ballad crooner, so the first adjective should account for this split. The word *progressive* (A) fits only the band, while *old-fashioned* (B) and *predictable* (E) fit the singer. The word *inconsistent* is the best of the choices. The second adjective should describe *popular ballads,* and all except (B) (*unique*) will do.

Analogies

10. (C) The first noun here is an animal, the second a means of controlling it, as a *horse* is controlled by a *bridle.* The parallel is a *dog* controlled by a *leash.*

11. (B) The second of the two nouns is what the first uses to entice its prey: a *hunter* uses a *decoy* to attract ducks. The parallel is an *angler* (one who fishes) who uses a *lure* to attract fish. It is the human, not the mouse, who sets the mousetrap.

12. (A) The second of the two nouns is an example or type of the more general first word. One kind of *herb* is *oregano.* One kind of *poem* is a *ballad.*

13. (E) The two nouns denote an artist and the work he or she creates. A *choreographer* (the roots of the word are "dance" and "write" or "draw") designs the movements or contents of a *dance,* as the *playwright* is responsible for the contents of a *play.* A better parallel for (A) would have *composer* in place of *conductor.*

14. (C) These words are synonyms, both meaning to grow embittered or to become painful or infected. Though totally unlike *fester* and *rankle* in meaning, the relationship of *worship* and *adore* is similar. Both mean to love or honor greatly.

15. (A) The two words here are an adjective that could describe a person and a noun which would *not* be a quality of such a person. *Disinterested* (not *uninterested*) means fair or impartial. A *disinterested* person would avoid or not be characterized by *prejudice.* Similarly, a person who is *naive* (simple, artless) would not be characterized by *sophistication.*

Critical Reading

16. (E) Although *correspondence* can mean correlation, agreement, or similarity, here it means communication by letters. Gauguin's *correspondence* refers to the letters he wrote to France from the South Pacific.

17. (B) Gauguin's letter refers to the quotation from Poe which finds *singularity* (oddness, uniqueness, strangeness) in perfect beauty, and he is reminded of these lines by the beauty of his first Tahitian model.

18. (D) The passage points out that most of the artists before Gauguin had not painted Tahitians realistically, but *as idealized types,* altered to fit European tastes, just the opposite of choice (B). The passage goes on to point out that the Tahitian could *scarcely be distinguished from his African or Asian counterpart.*

19. (A) The reader can infer that Charles Giraud painted Tahitians before Gauguin did, but since the paintings have not survived, the author cannot know if Giraud followed other artists and painted to suit European ideas of beauty or if, like Gauguin, he painted the Tahitians as they really were. It is for this reason the author would like to see Giraud's work.

20. (C) The passage opposes the terms *Naturalism* and *Symbolism.* The naturalistic or realistic in Gauguin is alluded to in lines 23–25 (*straightforward*) and lines 35–38 (*naturalistically*), while lines 40–44 refer to the nonrealistic *Symbolist aspirations.*

21. (A) The two impulses in Gauguin that appear to be at odds are his wish to render the Tahitians as they really are and at the same time to reveal a *poetic image* of the *island's mysterious past.* The problem is discussed in the last 25 lines of the passage.

22. (C) The first paragraph is introductory and presents the opposing positions on global warming and greenhouse gases represented by the climatologist Jim Hansen and the politician John Sununu.

23. (B) Although *pit* (the verb) can mean to scar or remove the core of, the meaning here is sets in opposition or sets in competition.

24. (C) Since neither oxygen nor nitrogen absorb heat, neither (A) nor (B) is likely. The amount of carbon dioxide in the atmosphere can be increased by burning of fossil fuels (D). In choice (E), the opposite is

more likely to be true, since heat escapes as infrared radiation. Since carbon dioxide absorbs heat, a planet with more in its atmosphere would be warmer.

25. (D) Since oxygen and nitrogen, which are not greenhouse gases, form 99% of the atmosphere according to the second paragraph, the passage does not imply that greenhouse gases make up a large part of the atmosphere. The second paragraph also tells us that carbon dioxide absorbs large amounts of heat and that the release of carbon dioxide can lead to warming. The third paragraph adds that clearing and burning forests create carbon dioxide.

26. (A) If greenhouse gases absorb heat and nitrogen does not absorb heat (paragraph two), then nitrogen is not a greenhouse gas. The other four are mentioned in the second and third paragraphs of the passage.

27. (A) The first statement makes a point which logically questions the Marshall report theory that *without greenhouse gases to warm things up, the world would become cool in the next century.* If so, why was it not cool before there were greenhouse gases? The passage does not give us any information about economic predictions in the Marshall report, and in any case, since the report advocates the encouragement of greenhouse gases, this idea would not undermine its conclusions. Similarly, the third statement would not affect the arguments of the report, since oxygen is not a greenhouse gas.

28. (D) The word *skeptic* now usually means a person who habitually questions or doubts even matters generally accepted.

29. (B) The image of Mr. Sununu as a character in a Dracula film was probably intended to amuse the audience and to make the opponent seem a bit ridiculous. It would also suggest that the claims are melodramatic. A believer in the danger of too much greenhouse gas in the atmosphere would *not* be likely to suggest that the danger is imaginary, so the third statement is very unlikely.

30. (E) The final paragraph leaves the debate unresolved. Although a reader of the whole passage may feel a slight bias in favor of the climatologists, the final paragraph asserts that neither side can prove its case beyond a reasonable doubt.

SECTION 2: MATHEMATICAL REASONING

1. **(B)** Setting up an equation gives $\frac{1}{5}x = 2$. Multiplying both sides by 5,

$$(5)\tfrac{1}{5}x = 2(5)$$

Then
$$x = 10$$

And $\frac{1}{2}$ of 10 is 5.

2. **(C)** In the series 8, 9, 12, 17, 24 . . . ,

$$9 - 8 = 1$$
$$12 - 9 = 3$$
$$17 - 12 = 5$$
$$24 - 17 = 7$$

Hence, the difference between the next term and 24 must be 9, or

$$x - 24 = 9$$
$$x = 33$$

Hence, the next term in the series must be 33.

3. **(C)** The selling price for 1 dozen at 3 for $0.85 is

$$3 \times 4 = 12 = 1 \text{ dozen} = \$0.85 \times 4 = \$3.40$$

Hence, 6 dozen will yield $3.40 \times 6 = \$20.40$.

The store's cost for 6 dozen at \$1.80 per dozen is $\$1.80 \times 6 = \$10.80$.

Hence, the profit on 6 dozen of these items will be $\$20.40 - \$10.80$, or \$9.60.

4. **(C)** If $x = -1$,

$$x^4 + x^3 + x^2 + x - 3$$
$$= (-1)^4 + (-1)^3 + (-1)^2 + (-1) - 3$$
$$= 1 + (-1) + 1 + (-1) - 3$$
$$= 0 + 1 + (-1) - 3$$
$$= 1 + (-1) - 3$$
$$= 0 - 3$$
$$= -3$$

5. **(D)** Since $15 = 3 \cdot 5$, a number divisible by 15 must be divisible by both 3 and 5. A number is divisible by 3 if the sum of its digits is divisible by 3. A number is divisible by 5 if its last digit is 0 or 5. Since 46,335 is divisible by 3 and by 5, it is also divisible by 15.

6. **(D)** You should have a working knowledge of these expressions:

   sum—the result of addition
   difference—the result of subtraction
   product—the result of multiplication
   quotient—the result of division

   Therefore, the *product of two numbers* may be represented as $(x)(y)$. The *difference of the two numbers* may be either $x - y$ or $y - x$. The term *twice* indicates that the expression is to be multiplied by 1. Thus, the entire expression breaks down as follows:

   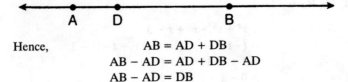

   The product of two numbers is equal to twice the difference of the two numbers
   $(x)(y)$ = 2 $(x - y)$

   Therefore, $(x)(y) = 2(x - y)$.

7. **(E)** $(5x + 2)(3x - 4) - (2x - 3)(x + 2)$
   $= (15x^2 + 6x - 20x - 8) - (2x^2 - 3x + 4x - 6)$
   $= (15x^2 - 14x - 8) - (2x^2 + x - 6)$
   $= 15x^2 - 14x - 8 - 2x^2 - x + 6$
   $= 13x^2 - 15x - 2$

8. **(B)** Since D is between A and B on $\overleftrightarrow{AB}$, we know that the sum of the lengths of the smaller segments AD and DB is equal to the length of the larger segment AB.

   A   D   B

   Hence, $AB = AD + DB$
   $AB - AD = AD + DB - AD$
   $AB - AD = DB$

9. **(B)** Since $a \otimes b = a^3 + b^2$,

   $$(-2) \otimes (-3) = (-2)^3 + (-3)^2$$
   $$= (-8) + 9$$
   $$= 1$$

10. (C) Since BD = CD, $\angle CBD = \angle C = 19°$.

Hence, $\angle BDC = 180° - (\angle CBD - \angle C)$
$= 180° - (19° + 19°)$
$= 180° - 38°$
$= 142°$

Then $\angle BDA = 180° - \angle BDC$
$= 180° - 142°$
$= 38°$

Since AB = AD, $\angle ABD = \angle BDA = 38°$.

Hence, $\angle A = 180° - (\angle BDA + \angle ABD)$
$= 180° - (38° + 38°)$
$= 180° - 76°$
$= 104°$

11. (A) The number of nickels that Angela has is x. Thus, the total value of those nickels (in cents) is $5x$. Angela also has twice as many dimes as nickels, or $2x$. The total value in cents of those dimes is $2x(10)$, or $20x$. Adding together the value of the nickels and dimes gives $5x + 20x$, or $25x$.

12. (A) If $x - 4 = y$, then $y - x = -4$. Hence, $(y - x)^3 = (-4)^3 = -64$.

13. (A) The perimeter of a rectangle with length l and width w is $2l + 2w$, Since the perimeter of the rectangle is $10x + 8$ and its length is $3x$,

$$\text{perimeter} = 2l + 2w$$
$$10x + 8 = 2(3x) + 2w$$
$$10x + 8 = 6x + 2w$$
$$10x + 8 - 6x = 6x + 2w - 6x$$
$$4x + 8 = 2w$$
$$\frac{4x + 8}{2} = \frac{2w}{2}$$
$$2x + 4 = w$$

Hence, the width of the rectangle is $2x + 4$.

14. **(E)** If $\dfrac{3}{7} = \dfrac{10}{x-4}$, then cross multiplying yields

$$3(x - 4) = (7)(10)$$
$$3x - 12 = 70$$
$$3x - 12 + 12 = 70 + 12$$
$$3x = 82$$

$$\dfrac{3x}{3} = \dfrac{82}{3}$$

$$x = {}^{82}\!/_3,\text{ or } 27\tfrac{1}{3}$$

15. **(B)** The car travels a total distance of 280 miles 7½ hours for the round trip. Its average speed in miles per hour is

$$280 \div 7\tfrac{1}{2} = \dfrac{280}{1} \div \dfrac{15}{2}$$

$$= \dfrac{280}{1} \cdot \dfrac{2}{15} = \dfrac{560}{15} = \dfrac{112}{3}$$

$$= 37\tfrac{1}{3}$$

You could have used your calculator here and simply divided 280 by 7.5, getting 37.333, or 37⅓.

16. **(C)** Since a and b must both be positive or both be negative, choice (C) III is the only answer that *must* be true.

17. **(D)** the slope (m) of a line passing through the points (x_1, y_1) and (x_2, y_2) is

$$m = \dfrac{y_2 - y_1}{x_2 - x_1}$$

Since $c = 1$ (see diagram), the line passes through $(-3, 5)$ and $(2, 9)$, and

$$m = \dfrac{9 - 5}{2 - (-3)} = \dfrac{4}{5}$$

Note that you could eliminate choices (A), (B), and (C) because they are all negative slopes, and the diagram shows a positive slope.

18. (A) If today Lucy is 14, then last year she was 13. Likewise, if Charlie's age now is C, then last year he was $C - 1$. Now, put these into an equation:

Lucy's age last year is three years older than twice Charlie's age last year.

$$13 = 2(C - 1) + 3$$

Transposing, $13 - 3 = 2(C - 1)$.

19. (B) $\angle XYZ$ is inscribed in a semicircle and is therefore a right angle. Hence, $\triangle XYZ$ is a right triangle and the Pythagorean theorem states

$$(XY)^2 = (XZ)^2 + (YZ)^2$$
$$(17)^2 = (XZ)^2 + (15)^2 \text{ (XY is a diameter)}$$
$$289 = (XZ)^2 + 225$$
$$289 - 225 = (XZ)^2$$
$$(XZ)^2 = 64$$
$$XZ = \sqrt{64}$$
$$XZ = 8$$

$$\text{area of } \triangle XYZ = \tfrac{1}{2}bh$$
$$= \tfrac{1}{2}(XZ)(YZ)$$
$$= \tfrac{1}{2}(8)(15)$$
$$= (4)(15)$$
$$= 60$$

20. (A) If 15 gumballs were picked from the bag, it is possible that 8 of them are red and 7 are green. On the next pick, however (the 16th), one is assured of having one gumball of each color.

21. (B) Since each letter repeats after every five vowels, divide 327 by 5, and the remainder will determine the vowel in that place of the pattern. Since $327 \div 5 = 65$ with a remainder of 2, the remainder of 2 indicates that the second vowel (e) will be the 327th letter.

22. (C) Let x = length of equal sides in feet and $x + 8$ = length of base in feet.

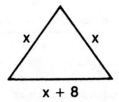

Since the perimeter is 89 feet,

$$x + x + x + 8 = 89$$
$$3x + 8 = 89$$
$$3x + 8 - 8 = 89 - 8$$
$$3x = 81$$

$$\frac{3x}{3} = \frac{81}{3}$$

$$x = 27$$

Hence, the length of the base is $x + 8$, or 35 feet.

23. (C) III only. The random sample indicates that 1500 out of 2500 New York moviegoers prefer comedies, or 60% of those polled prefer comedies. Of those polled, 500 out of 2500, or 20%, prefer dramas. Therefore, out of 8,000,000 total New York moviegoers, 60% should be found to prefer comedies (4,800,000), and 20% (1,600,000) should be found to prefer dramas. Only III reflects either of these estimates.

24. (D) Let x = the missing number. Since the average of x and z is y,

$$\tfrac{1}{2}(x + z) = y$$
$$2 \cdot \tfrac{1}{2}(x + z) = 2y$$
$$x + z = 2y$$
$$x + z - z = 2y - z$$
$$x = 2y - z$$

25. (A) Since the perimeter of the rhombus is 40, each side has length 10. Since the diagonals of a rhombus are perpendicular and bisect each other,

$$x^2 + 5^2 = 10^2$$
$$x^2 + 25 = 100$$
$$x^2 = 75$$
$$x = \sqrt{75}$$
$$x = 5\sqrt{3}$$

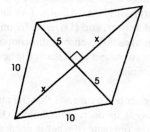

The area of a quadrilateral with perpendicular diagonals d_1 and d_2 is

$$\text{area} = \tfrac{1}{2} d_1 \cdot d_2$$
$$= \tfrac{1}{2}(10)(10\sqrt{3})$$
$$= 50\sqrt{3}$$

SECTION 3: VERBAL REASONING

Sentence Completion

1. (B) The *also* in the second half of the sentence signals that the verb is parallel to *prevent* in the first half. You can eliminate (C) and (D). The first adjective must mean something like reasonable or sensible, so (B) *logical* is a better choice than (A) *fanciful* or (E) *idle*, which mean just the opposite.

2. (C) The first noun must mean something like substitute but a word that will fit with the preposition *to*. Choice (A) *answer* is possible, (C) *alternative* is a good answer, and (D) *rejoinder* might work. The phrase *responsible for* (A) makes little sense in this context, and *involved in* (D) is awkward. The phrase *subject to* is clearly the best of the three and (C) the best of the five choices.

3. (D) The logic of the sentence suggests that the missing verb must mean something like prevent or decrease. Choices (B) *augment* (increase) and (C) *foster* are the opposite of what is needed. Neither *explain* (A) nor *exculpate* (E) (excuse) makes much sense, but *deter* (discourage, keep from doing) fits well.

4. (E) The sentence opposes the unpleasant *smoke, _____, and city* with the *_____ air and peace of the mountains,* so the first blank must be a noun similar in effect to *smoke,* while the second blank requires an adjective with pleasant denotation. In (A) and (B) the nouns are possible, but the adjectives are not. In (C) and (D), the noun choices cannot fit. Choice (E) correctly has the bad *hustle-bustle* and the good *exhilarating.*

5. (B) A situation requiring the choice between two unpleasant alternatives is the definition of the word *dilemma* and what this sentence describes. Some of the other choices are plausible, but since *dilemma* so exactly fits the situation, it is clearly the best.

6. (A) The word *combining* should alert you to look for a noun here that denotes a coming together of East and West. Choices (B), (C), and (D) are clearly wrong. Choice (A) *fusion,* the union of different things, fits well.

7. **(B)** The noun referring to what *allowed voters to decide* on an issue could be *statute* (A), *referendum* (B) (the most precise word), or *bill* (D). The missing adverb that describes the nine-to-one win must denote a very resounding margin of victory. Neither *meager* (A) nor *narrow* (D) will do. Again, the best answer uses the most specific noun as well as the most suitable adverb.

8. **(D)** The first blank requires a noun describing something a novel is based upon. Choices (A), (C), and (D) are possible. (B) and (E) are eliminated by the use of *upon which.* The second word must praise the book, since it is parallel with *intelligence* and the novel has been called *fine.* Choices (A) and (C) must be eliminated, and only (D) remains.

9. **(B)** The adjective *anachronistic* means representing something as existing at other than its proper time, such as a washing machine in the Middle Ages or a knight in armor at a football game. Choice (A) is a possibility, but (B) is more exact.

10. **(C)** Since she hoped to be undetected, she had to hide the card *furtively,* that is, stealthily, surreptitiously. The words *brazenly* (A) and *overtly* (B) contradict the opening phrase.

Analogies

11. **(C)** In this pair, the second noun is a carrier in which the first is carried. *Clothes* are carried in *luggage.* The best answer is (C), as *documents* are carried in a *briefcase.*

12. **(E)** There are two nouns here, and the second denotes the material of which the first is made. A *cymbal* is made of *brass.* The parallel pair is (E); a *violin* is made of *wood.* Note that words have several meanings, and *brass* here does *not* refer to the section of the orchestra that contains such instruments as the trumpet. A *cymbal* is part of the percussion section. The test will usually call for knowledge of the more obvious meanings of a word when there are several.

13. **(B)** The pair are related in length. A *decade* is ten years long; a *century* is one hundred years, or ten times longer. The related pair is *dime* and *dollar;* the first is one-tenth of the second, like *decade* to *century.*

14. **(D)** A *jury* must examine *evidence* in order to reach its verdict. Similarly, a *doctor* must examine *symptoms* to come to a diagnosis.

15. (A) The two verbs here denote to receive as the result of service or merit (*earn*) and to obtain by stealth, to steal, to pilfer, or to *filch*. The contrast is between verbs denoting a legitimate effort and a dishonest one. The best parallel is *create* as opposed to *plagiarize,* which is to take ideas or words from someone else and pass them off as one's own.

16. (A) Each of these verbs means to feel aversion to, but to *loathe* is a more intensive verb and means to *dislike* violently. The same relationship exists with to *praise* and to *extol,* which means to praise very highly.

17. (E) Though all of these words are related to astronomy, the relation of the two nouns in the question is of whole to part. A *constellation* is made up of more than one *star.* The best parallel is (E), the *solar system,* which contains more than one *planet.*

18. (E) The second of the two verbs here is like the first but with a suggestion of the sinister, not an exact synonym. Choices (A),(B), (C), and (D) are pairs of very similar meaning, but (E) adds the suggestion of underhandedness; to *snoop* is to *inquire* in a sneaky or prying manner.

19. (A) *Agar* (or agar-agar) is the medium in which a *bacterium* is grown. Choice (B) is a tempting answer, as a parasite does grow upon or within a host, but the terms are in the wrong order. The closest parallel is *potting soil,* a substance specifically used to grow a *plant* in.

20. (D) Both nouns describe falsehoods. *Slander* is a spoken false statement, while *libel* is written. The spoken-to-written difference is also used in a *speech* as opposed to an *essay.*

21. (C) The first adjective describes a person who would *not* be likely to demonstrate the quality denoted by the noun. A *credulous* (that is, gullible or very trusting) person would not be likely to harbor *doubt.* A *complacent* (that is, smug or self-satisfied) person is also unlikely to have *modesty.*

22. (B) These adjectives are opposites. *Supine* means lying face up, while *prone* means lying face down. The other pair of opposites is *light* and *dark.*

23. (B) A *surfeit* is an excess or oversupply; a *dearth* is a lack or scarcity, so the two words are opposites. The best parallel is the contrast of *flood* (too much water) and *drought* (a severe water shortage).

Critical Reading

24. (B) The passage explicitly refers to Celia and Dorothea as sisters. Although the passage does not mention their father's death, you know the jewels belonged to their mother, and since an uncle, not her father, gave them to Dorothea, it may be that the father is dead and they are in the uncle's care.

25. (D) That Dorothea has started an *infant school* in the village and is busy with plans for some buildings tells you at once that she is active and generous. There are no details in the passage to suggest that she is prying, idle, ambitious, or ineffectual, although she may be rich or philanthropic.

26. (B) The preceding sentence tells you that Dorothea's eyes are *full of laughter,* and her tone when she speaks again is *full* and *cordial.* She is teasing Celia good-naturedly, making fun of her sister's remark that it is *exactly six months to-day.* In this dialogue, it is Celia who has planned what she will say, while Dorothea speaks spontaneously. Dorothea has probably forgotten all about the jewels, while Celia has probably been thinking about them for some time.

27. (D) The phrase means disrespectful or lacking in respect. The reader must recognize that the verb *want* here means to lack, not the more common to wish for. Choice (C) confuses *wanting* and wanton.

28. (D) Celia does not wish to have all of the jewels, but she does want a share, and she expects to wear them. Unlike Dorothea, she is not at all Puritanical. She correctly anticipates that Dorothea might object to wearing jewelry, so she has prepared this defense on the moral grounds that she thinks will best convince Dorothea.

29. (C) Dorothea, who does not care about the jewels herself, has simply not realized that Celia really wants to wear them. In lines 32–33, the reader is told that this *discovery* is astonishing to her, and the moment she realizes Celia's true feeling, she rushes to open the cabinet. Celia's arguments would have been more effective if she had simply told Dorothea of her real wishes because Dorothea loves her sister and is eager to make her happy. Notice that Dorothea has said that the jewels would not be worn only before she realizes what Celia really wishes.

30. (A) *Deprecation* is disapproval, protest, as is suggested in this sentence by Dorothea's saying *no*. A lessening is a depreciation, while a removal is a deprivation.

31. (A) The adjective in this context comes from the verb meaning to annoy, to irk, as in to try one's patience. In some contexts, *trying* might mean attempting or determining, but here, irksome is the best definition.

32. (E) The *Puritanic toleration* is Dorothea's. She has given up all of the jewels to Celia and even encouraged her to wear them. Although this is in one way pleasing to Celia, it does put Dorothea in a position of moral superiority, which Celia finds annoying.

33. (C) Dorothea is the Puritan, and Celia is the *unenthusiastic sister,* that is, one who has not adopted the religious extremes of self-denial such as not wearing jewels.

34. (D) Although some of the answers here describe Dorothea accurately, only (D) points to an inconsistency. Dorothea regards wearing jewelry as somehow immoral, and yet, because she sees that Celia really wants to wear the jewels, she encourages her to do so. What is right for her sister would not be right for her.

35. (C) The passage is centrally concerned with delineating the two sisters. Although there is some mild comedy at the expense of both, the passage is not satiric, and it reveals as much love as friction between the sisters. They are not alike, and though Celia may take pleasure in jewels, the passage is not about the dangers of materialism. The author, the reader senses, is amused by and fond of both of these young women.

SECTION 4: MATHEMATICAL REASONING

Quantitative Comparison

1. (A) By inspection, both sides are exactly the same except that in column A you are adding $4 \cdot 10^2$ and in column B you are subtracting $4 \cdot 10^2$. Therefore, column A is greater. Solving for values would give

$3^2 + 4 \cdot 10^2 - 4^2$		$3^2 - 4 \cdot 10^2 - 4^2$
$9 + 4 \cdot 100 - 16$		$9 - 4 \cdot 100 - 16$
$9 + 400 - 6$		$9 - 400 - 16$
$409 - 16$		$-391 - 16$
393	$>$	-407

2. (C) Angles x and y are vertical angles formed by two intersecting lines. Therefore, they are equal. Vertical angles are always equal.

3. (C) Solving the top equation of $5y = 10$ gives $y = 2$. Substituting $y = 2$ into the second equation leaves

$$3x + 2(2) = 10$$
$$3x + 4 = 10$$
$$3x = 6$$

Therefore, $x = 2$, and columns A and B are equal.

4. (A) Since both sides have the factors $\frac{2}{5}$ and $\frac{5}{8}$, you may eliminate them from each column. Now compare $\frac{3}{7}$ and $\frac{4}{11}$ by cross multiplying upward.

$$33 \qquad\qquad 28$$
$$\frac{3}{7} \quad \diagdown\!\!\!\!\diagup \quad \frac{4}{11}$$

Since 33 is greater than 28, $\frac{3}{7}$ is greater than $\frac{4}{11}$.

5. (D) Trying some small values is required here, keeping in mind that x must be greater than 0. Let $x = 1$. Then

$$
\begin{array}{ccc}
3(1)^2 & & 2(1)^3 \\
3(1) & & 2(1) \\
3 & > & 2
\end{array}
$$

In this case, column A is greater. Now, try another value for x. Let $x = 2$. Then

$$
\begin{array}{ccc}
3(2)^2 & & 2(2)^3 \\
3(4) & & 2(8) \\
12 & < & 16
\end{array}
$$

In this case, column B is greater. Since there are different answers depending on the values chosen, the correct answer is (D), cannot be determined.

6. (A) In column A, a number greater than 1 is multiplied by itself 10 times. The answer will be greater than 1. But in column B, a number less than 1 (.23) is multiplied by itself 100 times. The answer in column B will be smaller than 1.

7. (C) To solve $a/6 = b/4$, cross multiply, giving $4a = 6b$. Then divide by 2, leaving $2a = 3b$.

8. (A) If the top angle were 90°, then x would be $3\sqrt{2}$. This could be calculated using the Pythagorean theorem.

$$
\begin{aligned}
a^2 + b^2 &= c^2 \\
3^2 + 3^2 &= x^2 \\
9 + 9 &= x^2 \\
18 &= x^2
\end{aligned}
$$

Therefore, $\sqrt{18} = x$

Simplified, this is $3\sqrt{2}$. But since the angle is larger than 90°, then the side across from 92° must be larger than $3\sqrt{2}$. The correct answer is (A).

9. (A) Since there are 180° in a triangle and 92° in one angle, that leaves 88° to be split equally between two angles. Thus, angle y is 44°. (The degrees must be split equally because angles across from equal sides are equal, and the triangle has two equal sides—isosceles.) The correct answer is (A).

10. (B) First multiply out column B.

$$4y^2 - 4y + 1 \qquad\qquad (2y + 1)^2$$
$$4y^2 - 4y + 1 \qquad\qquad 4y^2 + 4y + 1$$

Now, subtract out from both sides, getting

$$-4y \qquad\qquad +4y$$

Divide both sides by 4, getting

$$-y \qquad\qquad +y$$

Since y is a positive number between 0 and 1, column B is greater than column A.

11. (B) Since d is above the x axis, it must be positive, and c, being to the left of the y axis, must be negative. Therefore, $c < d$ because all negatives are less than all positives.

12. (A) Since point P is above the line containing points $(-2, 2)$, then d (actual distance) is greater than $|c|$. Therefore, $c + d$ is a positive number. Point Q is on the line. Therefore, e and f are additive inverses of each other, totaling 0. Since all positive numbers are greater than 0, then $c + d > e + f$.

13. (A) To find the number of degrees in the interior angles of a pentagon use the formula $180 \times (n - 2)$, where n is the number of sides. Therefore,

$$180 \times (5 - 2) = 180 \times 3 = 540$$
$$540° \qquad > \qquad 500°$$

Another method would be to draw the pentagon and break it into triangles connecting vertices (lines cannot cross) as shown below.

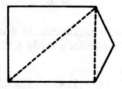

Multiplying the number of triangles (3) by 180 (degrees in a triangle) gives the same result, 540°.

14. (C) Simplifying the complex fraction in column A,

$$\cfrac{1}{1+\cfrac{1}{1+1/n}} = \cfrac{1}{1+\cfrac{1}{n/n+1/n}} = \cfrac{1}{1+\cfrac{1}{(n+1)/n}} = \cfrac{1}{1+\cfrac{n}{n+1}}$$

$$= \cfrac{1}{\cfrac{n+1}{n+1}+\cfrac{n}{n+1}} = \cfrac{1}{\cfrac{n+1+n}{n+1}} = \cfrac{1}{\cfrac{2n+1}{n+1}} = \cfrac{n+1}{2n+1}$$

15. (C) Extend line CO as shown.

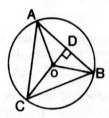

You now have triangle OBD, which is a $30° - 60° - 90°$ triangle. Since all $30° - 60° - 90°$ triangles are in proportion 1, $\sqrt{3}$, 2, and since side DB = half of $8\sqrt{3}$, or $4\sqrt{3}$, then side OB = 8. Therefore, OA + OB + OC = 8 + 8 + 8 = 24.

Grid-in Questions

16. Answer: 94—Since $x = -4$,

$$5x^2 - 3x + 2 = 5(-4)^2 - 3(-4) + 2$$
$$= 5(16) + 12 + 2$$
$$= 80 + 12 + 2$$
$$= 94$$

17. Answer: 9.49—For a 25-minute call, the first 3 minutes will cost $2.45, and the additional 22 minutes will cost $.32 per minute. The cost (C) for the call will be

$$C = \$2.45 + (22)(\$.32)$$
$$= \$2.45 + \$7.04$$
$$= \$9.49$$

18. Answer: 70—Let n = the original price of the jacket. 80% of n is $56.

$$(0.80) \cdot n = \$56$$
$$n = \$56 \div 0.8$$
$$n = \$70$$

19. Answer: 4—The volume of a cube with side of length x is x^3. Hence,

$$x^3 = 64$$
$$x = \sqrt[3]{64}$$
$$x = 4$$

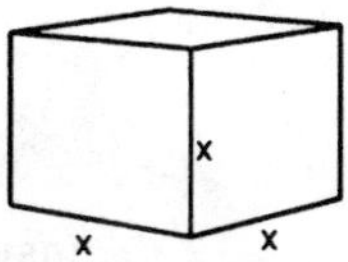

20. Answer: 480—You can quickly solve this problem by using your calculator. Total the four listed items: $840 + $460 + $320 + $120 = $1740. Subtract $1740 from the given total: $2220 − $1740 = $480. The lab workbooks cost $480.

21. Answer: 50—Begin by choosing a simple fraction, say $^{100}/_{100}$. If the numerator is tripled and the denominator is doubled, the resulting fraction will be $^{300}/_{200}$, or 1½. So the new fraction represents a 50% increase over the original fraction.

22. Answer: 20—Since $\ell_1 \| \ell_2$, the alternate interior angles have the same measure and

$$5x - 20 = 2x + 40$$
$$3x - 20 = 40$$
$$3x = 60$$
$$x = 20$$

23. Answer: 640—The phrase "how much more" indicates subtraction. Clothing was 13% of the total. Insurance was 5% of the total. So 13% − 5%, or 8%, more of the total of $8000 was spent on clothing than on insurance.

$$.08 \times \$8000 = \$640$$

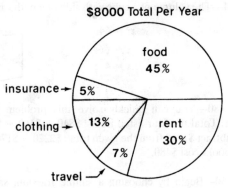

$8000 Total Per Year

24. Answer: 40—In △MXN, ∠MNX = 50°, ∠MXN = 90°, and ∠NMQ = 30°

$$\angle NMQ + \angle QMX = \angle NMX$$

So

$$50° + 90° + 30° + \angle QMX = 180°$$
$$170° + \angle QMX = 180°$$
$$\angle QMX = 10°$$

In △MPQ,   ∠QMP + ∠MPQ + ∠MQP = 180°
$$10° + 130° + \angle MQP = 180°$$
$$140° + \angle MQP = 180°$$
$$\angle MQP = 40°$$

Angle PXN is 90°. So the ratio of ∠MQP to angle PXN is 40/90, or 4/9.

25. Answer 48—Set up the equations as follows: Let t be the length of time it will take the plane to overtake the bus. Then $t + 4$ is the time that the bus has traveled before the plane starts. The distance that the bus has traveled by 1:00 P.M. is $50(t + 4)$, since distance equals rate times time ($d = rt$). The distance the plane will travel is $300t$. Now, equating these two (they will have to travel the same distance for one to overtake the other) gives $50(t + 4) = 300t$.

Solve the equation as follows:

$$50(t + 4) = 300t$$
$$50t + 200 = 300t$$
$$200 = 250t$$

Therefore $\quad\quad\quad\quad\quad\quad\quad\quad\quad \frac{4}{5} = t$

$\frac{4}{5}$ of an hour ($\frac{4}{5} \times 60$) is 48 minutes. Hence, it will take 48 minutes for the plane to overtake the bus.

SECTION 5: VERBAL REASONING

Critical Reading

1. (E) The sentence on Lope de Vega's play does all three. It gives an example of a play by a Spanish playwright using Columbus as a hero; it shows that Columbus's reputation had reached to the popular theater; and it gives an example of Columbus in his symbolic role as the *embodiment of that spirit driving humans to explore and discover.*

2. (D) The best of the five definitions here is inclined. Although the verb dispose can mean to arrange or to give away, the context here makes clear that the meaning is something like not inclined to struggle against the myth of Columbus, and the next sentence, as well as the rest of the paragraph, confirms this meaning.

3. (B) The nouns used for *mold* here—pattern, manner, model, shape, or style—are all adequate; *romantic* here is best defined by idealized. The word is explained further by the phrase *favored in the century's literature,* and the quotations from Irving that follow depict an idealized rather than a visionary, fictitious, or escapist hero.

4. (C) Since *ambition* and *magnanimity* are direct quotations from Irving, neither is possible. The word *mined* expresses no judgment, while *palliating* refers neutrally to Irving's inadequate explanation. The use of *Perhaps,* the only word in its sentence, expresses the author's reluctance to accept Irving's assessment of Columbus.

5. (B) The first paragraph surveys Columbus's reputation in the sixteenth and seventeenth centuries; the second, third, and fourth deal with the nineteenth century. Although the last paragraph predicts a reevaluation in the twentieth century, the passage does not deal with the hostile criticism of the explorer.

6. (B) The fourth paragraph explains how the nineteenth-century Columbus reflected what that period most valued, and the last paragraph refers to people creating *the Columbus they want to believe in.* The account of nineteenth-century historians' indifference to the Columbus documents discovered in 1825 contradicts the notion that history is truth as it known at the time of writing.

7. (E) Each of the questions reveals more of the author's ideas about the Europeans at the time of Columbus's voyages. The passage goes on to show how these limitations led to the exploitation of the New World. The paragraph does not defend or justify their actions.

8. (E) All three are accurate descriptions of the effects of the phrase. The phrase *a foreign, heathen people, half naked and befeathered, ignorant of cities and kings and metal and laws, and unschooled in all that the Ancients held virtuous* is the European view of the native Americans— superior, contemptuous of their ignorance of Greece and Rome, which had become important to Europe in the age of discovery. The point of view of this phrase is that of the fifteenth-century European, not that of the twentieth-century author.

9. (B) The second paragraph refers to *new foods and medicines* found in the New World.

10. (A) The passage presents the *biological outlook* as one in which humans have a *sense of being at one with nature,* where humans' relation to earth and all its life forms is more important than their relation to other humans. Choices (B) and (E) are just what the *biological outlook* is *not.* Choices (C) and (D) are concerned with economic rather than ecological well-being.

11. (B) The passage argues that, properly understood, the discovery might have brought regeneration to Europe, but the Europeans, tragically, could only exploit and destroy the new-found lands. The passage does criticize this European failure, but this criticism is not its real point. The passage does not describe the benefits of the discovery (A), and it is by no means objective (E).

12. (E) The last paragraph of Passage 1 refers to *a major reassessment of Columbus's reputation,* and Passage 2 presents a view of the consequences of Columbus's voyages totally unlike the heroic adulation of the first four paragraphs of the first passage.

13. (D) Passage 2 presents a highly personal, highly emotional, judgmental, philosophical view of Columbus's discovery. But it is not more historical than Passage 1. In fact, it presents only the view of its twentieth-century author, while Passage 1 samples opinions from several periods.

14. (C) The style of Passage 2 is characterized by its use of words in series, repetition, parallel phrases, and rhetorical questions. It does not use understatement. Some readers, no doubt, would argue that it depends on overstatement.

15. (B) The first two statements are just, but while Passage 1 focuses upon Columbus's reputation, Passage 2 does not even mention Columbus by name. The second passage does reevaluate the discovery of America. The second passage also presents an interpretation of the voyages of discovery that reflects the late twentieth-century concern for the wisdom of ancient cultures, for ecology, and for the dangers of warring against nature.

SECTION 6: MATHEMATICAL REASONING

1. (A) Since the difference between any two consecutive odd numbers is 2, the next odd number after $2x + 13$ would be

$$2x + 13 + 2 = 2x + 15$$

2. (D) The amount of discount was $120 - 90 = 30$. The rate of discount is a percent, so

$$\frac{\text{percent}}{100} = \frac{\text{is number}}{\text{of number}}$$

$$\frac{x}{100} = \frac{30}{120}$$

Cross multipliying $\qquad 120x = 3000$

$$\frac{120x}{120} = \frac{3000}{120}$$

$$x = 25$$

Hence, the rate of discount was 25%.

3. (C) $\sqrt{\dfrac{81}{x}} = \dfrac{9}{5}$

Squaring both sides,

$$\frac{81}{x} = \frac{81}{25}$$

Hence, $x = 25$.

4. (C) Since $\angle CFD = \angle AFB$, then $\angle CFD = 45°$ and $\angle AFE = 45° + 40° + 45° + 20° = 150°$.

5. (D) Average =

$$\frac{93 + 82 + 79 + x}{4} = 87$$

$$93 + 82 + 79 + x = 87 \cdot 4$$
$$254 + x = 348$$
$$x = 94$$

6. (D) According to the graph, 20% have hazel eyes, while 40% have brown eyes. This means that there are twice as many brown-eyed people as there are hazel-eyed people.

$$62 = \text{people with hazel eyes}$$
$$2 \times 62 = 124 \text{ people with brown eyes}$$

7. (C) On a clock, 60 minutes $= 360°$

Hence,
$$\frac{12 \text{ minutes}}{60 \text{ minutes}} = \frac{x°}{360°}$$

$$\frac{1}{5} = \frac{x}{360}$$

$$5x = 360$$

$$\frac{5x}{5} = \frac{360}{5}$$

$$x = 72$$

Hence, the minute hand has moved $72°$.

8. (A) Since $\dfrac{x^2 - 5x + 7}{x^2 - 4x + 10} = 1 = \frac{1}{1}$, cross multiply to get

$$x^2 - 5x + 7 = x^2 - 4x + 10$$
$$x^2 - 5x + 7 - x^2 = x^2 - 4x + 10 - x^2$$
$$-5x + 7 = -4x + 10$$
$$-5x + 7 + 4x = -4x + 10 + 4x$$
$$-x + 7 = 10$$
$$-x + 7 - 7 = 10 - 7$$
$$-x = 3$$
$$x = -3$$

9. (C) Let $3x =$ one angle and $4x =$ other angle.

$$3x + 4x + 68 = 180$$
$$7x + 68 = 180$$
$$7x = 112$$

$$x = 16$$
$$3x = 48$$
$$4x = 64$$

Hence, the smallest angle of the triangle is $48°$.

10. (B) If two points have coordinates (x_1, y_1) and (x_2, y_2), the distance, d, between these points is defined to be

$$d = \sqrt{(x_1 - x_2)^2 + (y_1 - y_2)^2}$$

Since E has coordinates $(-3, 5)$ and F has coordinates $(6, -7)$, the distance between E and F is

$$\begin{aligned}
EF &= \sqrt{(-3 - 6)2 + [5 - (-7)]^2} \\
&= \sqrt{(-9)^2 + (12)^2} \\
&= \sqrt{81 + 144} \\
&= \sqrt{225} \\
&= 15
\end{aligned}$$

SECTION 7: MATHEMATICAL REASONING

1. Solve for x.

$$2x - 5 = 9$$
$$2x = 14$$

Then
$$x = 7$$

Now substitute 7 for x.

$$3x + 2 = 3(7) + 2$$
$$= 21 + 2$$
$$= 23$$

2. (E) Note that since there is a mark between $+7$ and $+9$, that mark must equal $+8$. Thus, each mark equals 1. Counting back, point Q is at $+5$. Therefore, fifteen units to the left of $+5$ would be $+5 - 15 = -10$.

3. (C) $2x + 3y^2 - z = (2)(3) + 3(4)^2 - (-1)$
$$= 6 + 3(16) + 1$$
$$= 6 + 48 + 1$$
$$= 55$$

4. (B) To purchase twelve tapes, Roy must buy six packages. At \$2.98 per package, he spends \$17.88. His change from a twenty-dollar bill will be \$20.00 − \$17.88 = \$2.12.

5. (D) $\dfrac{6^4 + 6^5}{6^4} = \dfrac{6^4}{6^4} + \dfrac{6^5}{6^4}$

$$= 1 + 6$$
$$= 7$$

6. (D) The most the trip would cost is when gas costs \$1.12 and the milage is 16 mpg. Thus, \$1.12 × (480/16) = \$33.60. The least would be \$0.96 × (480/24) = \$19.20. The difference is thus \$14.40.

7. (C) If we call the smaller piece x, then the larger piece (6 inches bigger) must be $x + 6$. Since the two pieces together equal a yardstick,

$$x + (x + 6) = 36$$
$$x + x + 6 = 36$$

216

8. (E) For the multiplication problem to work correctly, the figures must be

$$\begin{array}{r} \boxed{6}\ \boxed{7}\ 4 \\ \times\ 8 \\ \hline 5\ \ 3\ \ 9\ \boxed{2} \end{array}$$

Thus, the sum of the boxed digits is 15.

9. (A) Perimeter of rectangle equals $2l + 2w$, where l is the length and w is the width. If the length and width are increased by x, the perimeter will be

$$2(l + x) + 2(w + x)$$
$$= 2l + 2x + 2w + 2x$$
$$= 2l + 2w + 4x$$

which is an increase of $4x$ units.

10. (E) In the ordered pair $(0, 2)$, $a = 0$ and $b = 2$. For $2a - 3b$,

$$2(0) - 3(2) = 0 - 6 = -6 \neq 6$$

Hence, the ordered pair $(0, 2)$ is not a member of the solution sets of $2a - 3b = 6$.

11. (B) Forty-eight days late is one day shy of exactly 7 weeks (7 weeks = $7 \times 7 = 49$ days). If the job were finished in 49 days, then it would have been completed on the same day, Wednesday. But since 48 is one day less than 7 weeks, the job was completed one day earlier than Wednesday: Tuesday.

12. (C) Perimeter is the sum of all sides. Thus,

$$(2s - 6) + (s + 4) + (s + 2) = \text{perimeter}$$

$$\begin{array}{r} 2s - 6 \\ s + 4 \\ s + 2 \\ \hline 4s + 0 = 4s \end{array}$$

13. (C) $\dfrac{\text{is number}}{\text{of number}} = \dfrac{\text{percent}}{100}$

$$\frac{1/2}{2/3} = \frac{x}{100}$$

Cross multiplying,

$$\frac{2}{3}x = 50$$

$$x = \frac{150}{2} = 75\%$$

14. (B) Since m yards = $36m$ inches and n feet = $12n$ inches, m yards and n feet = $(36m + 12n)$ inches.

15. (C) Fifteen percent of the selling price is needed for a down payment. Since the selling price of the house is \$64,000, 15% of the selling price equals

$$(.15)(\$64,000) = \$9600$$

The buyer has already paid \$1500 toward the deposit, so to figure how much *more* money is needed for the down payment, subtract \$1500 from \$9600.

$$\$9600 - \$1500 = \$8100$$

16. (B) If the average of 9 numbers is 7, then the sum of these numbers must be 9×7, or 63. If the average of 7 numbers is 9, then the sum of these numbers must be 7×9, or 63. The sum of all 16 numbers must be $63 + 63$, or 126. Hence, the average of all 16 numbers must be

$$126 \div 16 = \frac{126}{16} = 7^{14}\!/_{16} = 7\frac{7}{8}$$

17. (E) Let x equal the length of a side of the cube. The volume $V = x^3$, and the surface area $S = 6x^2$. Hence, $x = 6$.

18. **(E)** Since $\ell_1 \| \ell_2$, the corresponding angles formed on lines ℓ_1 and ℓ_2 are equal.

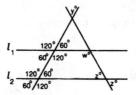

In any quadrilateral, the sum of interior degrees equals 360°. Therefore, $\angle w + \angle z = 180°$. If $w = 2z$, $\angle w = 120°$, and $\angle z = 60°$. Therefore,

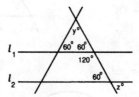

$\angle y = 60°$ (since there are 180° in a triangle). So the sum of $y + w = 60° + 120° = 180°$.

19. **(E)** The value of $a \# b =$

$$\frac{a^2 + b^2}{a^2 - b^2}$$

If $2a = b$, plug in $2a$ for b.

$$\frac{a^2 + (2a)^2}{a^2 - (2a)^2} = \frac{a^2 + 4a^2}{a^2 - 4a^2} = -\frac{5a^2}{3a^2} = -\frac{5}{3} = -1\tfrac{2}{3}$$

20. **(D)** Since it takes the pipe t hours to drain the tank completely, it will drain $1/t$ part of the tank each hour. Hence, in three hours, it will drain $3(1/t)$, or $3/t$, part of the tank.

21. **(D)** Since AB = BE = 34, △ABC is an isosceles triangle and altitude BD will bisect AC. Since △BDC is a right triangle, use the Pythagorean theorem, which says

$$(BC)^2 = (BD)^2 + (CD)^2$$
$$(34)^2 = (30)^2 + x^2$$
$$1156 = 900 + x^2$$
$$x^2 = 1156 - 900$$
$$x^2 = 256$$
$$x = \sqrt{256} = 16$$

Hence, CD = 16 = AD
$$AC = AD + DC$$
$$= 16 + 16$$
$$= 32$$

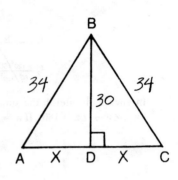

22. **(C)** Circumference = πd.

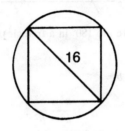

$$16\pi = \pi d$$
$$d = 16$$

diameter of circle = diagonal of square

area of square = ½(product of diagonals)

$$= \tfrac{1}{2} d_1 \times d_2$$
$$= \tfrac{1}{2}(16)(16) = 128$$

Hence, the area of the square is 128.

Alternate method: Using the Pythagorean theorem for isosceles right triangles gives $x^2 + x^2 = 16^2$, $2x^2 = 256$, and $x^2 = 128$, which is the area of the square.

23. **(E)** The horizontal length of x cannot be determined because there is no indication of the overlapping length of the rectangle to the left of x. If x cannot be determined, then $x + y$ cannot be determined.

24. (B) Drawing a picture may be helpful. 750 times 45 equals *P*.

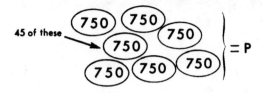

Note that 750 times 44 is the same as above but with one less circle. Therefore, it equals *P* − 750. If this is still difficult to understand, think in terms of dollars. You are paid $750 each week for 45 weeks. Therefore, your total pay (*P*) is $750 times 45. But suppose that you work only 44 weeks. Then your total pay will be *P* − one week's pay, or *P* − $750.

25. (D) Try it yourself with a scissors and square piece of paper.

PRACTICE TEST 2

PRACTICE TEST 2

ANSWER SHEET FOR PRACTICE TEST 2
(Remove This Sheet and Use It to Mark Your Answers)

SECTION 1

1 Ⓐ Ⓑ Ⓒ Ⓓ Ⓔ
2 Ⓐ Ⓑ Ⓒ Ⓓ Ⓔ
3 Ⓐ Ⓑ Ⓒ Ⓓ Ⓔ
4 Ⓐ Ⓑ Ⓒ Ⓓ Ⓔ
5 Ⓐ Ⓑ Ⓒ Ⓓ Ⓔ
6 Ⓐ Ⓑ Ⓒ Ⓓ Ⓔ
7 Ⓐ Ⓑ Ⓒ Ⓓ Ⓔ
8 Ⓐ Ⓑ Ⓒ Ⓓ Ⓔ
9 Ⓐ Ⓑ Ⓒ Ⓓ Ⓔ
10 Ⓐ Ⓑ Ⓒ Ⓓ Ⓔ
11 Ⓐ Ⓑ Ⓒ Ⓓ Ⓔ
12 Ⓐ Ⓑ Ⓒ Ⓓ Ⓔ
13 Ⓐ Ⓑ Ⓒ Ⓓ Ⓔ
14 Ⓐ Ⓑ Ⓒ Ⓓ Ⓔ
15 Ⓐ Ⓑ Ⓒ Ⓓ Ⓔ
16 Ⓐ Ⓑ Ⓒ Ⓓ Ⓔ
17 Ⓐ Ⓑ Ⓒ Ⓓ Ⓔ
18 Ⓐ Ⓑ Ⓒ Ⓓ Ⓔ
19 Ⓐ Ⓑ Ⓒ Ⓓ Ⓔ
20 Ⓐ Ⓑ Ⓒ Ⓓ Ⓔ
21 Ⓐ Ⓑ Ⓒ Ⓓ Ⓔ
22 Ⓐ Ⓑ Ⓒ Ⓓ Ⓔ
23 Ⓐ Ⓑ Ⓒ Ⓓ Ⓔ
24 Ⓐ Ⓑ Ⓒ Ⓓ Ⓔ
25 Ⓐ Ⓑ Ⓒ Ⓓ Ⓔ
26 Ⓐ Ⓑ Ⓒ Ⓓ Ⓔ
27 Ⓐ Ⓑ Ⓒ Ⓓ Ⓔ
28 Ⓐ Ⓑ Ⓒ Ⓓ Ⓔ
29 Ⓐ Ⓑ Ⓒ Ⓓ Ⓔ
30 Ⓐ Ⓑ Ⓒ Ⓓ Ⓔ

SECTION 2

1 Ⓐ Ⓑ Ⓒ Ⓓ Ⓔ
2 Ⓐ Ⓑ Ⓒ Ⓓ Ⓔ
3 Ⓐ Ⓑ Ⓒ Ⓓ Ⓔ
4 Ⓐ Ⓑ Ⓒ Ⓓ Ⓔ
5 Ⓐ Ⓑ Ⓒ Ⓓ Ⓔ
6 Ⓐ Ⓑ Ⓒ Ⓓ Ⓔ
7 Ⓐ Ⓑ Ⓒ Ⓓ Ⓔ
8 Ⓐ Ⓑ Ⓒ Ⓓ Ⓔ
9 Ⓐ Ⓑ Ⓒ Ⓓ Ⓔ
10 Ⓐ Ⓑ Ⓒ Ⓓ Ⓔ
11 Ⓐ Ⓑ Ⓒ Ⓓ Ⓔ
12 Ⓐ Ⓑ Ⓒ Ⓓ Ⓔ
13 Ⓐ Ⓑ Ⓒ Ⓓ Ⓔ
14 Ⓐ Ⓑ Ⓒ Ⓓ Ⓔ
15 Ⓐ Ⓑ Ⓒ Ⓓ Ⓔ
16 Ⓐ Ⓑ Ⓒ Ⓓ Ⓔ
17 Ⓐ Ⓑ Ⓒ Ⓓ Ⓔ
18 Ⓐ Ⓑ Ⓒ Ⓓ Ⓔ
19 Ⓐ Ⓑ Ⓒ Ⓓ Ⓔ
20 Ⓐ Ⓑ Ⓒ Ⓓ Ⓔ
21 Ⓐ Ⓑ Ⓒ Ⓓ Ⓔ
22 Ⓐ Ⓑ Ⓒ Ⓓ Ⓔ
23 Ⓐ Ⓑ Ⓒ Ⓓ Ⓔ
24 Ⓐ Ⓑ Ⓒ Ⓓ Ⓔ
25 Ⓐ Ⓑ Ⓒ Ⓓ Ⓔ

SECTION 3

1 Ⓐ Ⓑ Ⓒ Ⓓ Ⓔ	31 Ⓐ Ⓑ Ⓒ Ⓓ Ⓔ
2 Ⓐ Ⓑ Ⓒ Ⓓ Ⓔ	32 Ⓐ Ⓑ Ⓒ Ⓓ Ⓔ
3 Ⓐ Ⓑ Ⓒ Ⓓ Ⓔ	33 Ⓐ Ⓑ Ⓒ Ⓓ Ⓔ
4 Ⓐ Ⓑ Ⓒ Ⓓ Ⓔ	34 Ⓐ Ⓑ Ⓒ Ⓓ Ⓔ
5 Ⓐ Ⓑ Ⓒ Ⓓ Ⓔ	35 Ⓐ Ⓑ Ⓒ Ⓓ Ⓔ
6 Ⓐ Ⓑ Ⓒ Ⓓ Ⓔ	
7 Ⓐ Ⓑ Ⓒ Ⓓ Ⓔ	
8 Ⓐ Ⓑ Ⓒ Ⓓ Ⓔ	
9 Ⓐ Ⓑ Ⓒ Ⓓ Ⓔ	
10 Ⓐ Ⓑ Ⓒ Ⓓ Ⓔ	
11 Ⓐ Ⓑ Ⓒ Ⓓ Ⓔ	
12 Ⓐ Ⓑ Ⓒ Ⓓ Ⓔ	
13 Ⓐ Ⓑ Ⓒ Ⓓ Ⓔ	
14 Ⓐ Ⓑ Ⓒ Ⓓ Ⓔ	
15 Ⓐ Ⓑ Ⓒ Ⓓ Ⓔ	
16 Ⓐ Ⓑ Ⓒ Ⓓ Ⓔ	
17 Ⓐ Ⓑ Ⓒ Ⓓ Ⓔ	
18 Ⓐ Ⓑ Ⓒ Ⓓ Ⓔ	
19 Ⓐ Ⓑ Ⓒ Ⓓ Ⓔ	
20 Ⓐ Ⓑ Ⓒ Ⓓ Ⓔ	
21 Ⓐ Ⓑ Ⓒ Ⓓ Ⓔ	
22 Ⓐ Ⓑ Ⓒ Ⓓ Ⓔ	
23 Ⓐ Ⓑ Ⓒ Ⓓ Ⓔ	
24 Ⓐ Ⓑ Ⓒ Ⓓ Ⓔ	
25 Ⓐ Ⓑ Ⓒ Ⓓ Ⓔ	
26 Ⓐ Ⓑ Ⓒ Ⓓ Ⓔ	
27 Ⓐ Ⓑ Ⓒ Ⓓ Ⓔ	
28 Ⓐ Ⓑ Ⓒ Ⓓ Ⓔ	
29 Ⓐ Ⓑ Ⓒ Ⓓ Ⓔ	
30 Ⓐ Ⓑ Ⓒ Ⓓ Ⓔ	

CUT HERE

SECTION 4

1 Ⓐ Ⓑ Ⓒ Ⓓ Ⓔ	6 Ⓐ Ⓑ Ⓒ Ⓓ Ⓔ	11 Ⓐ Ⓑ Ⓒ Ⓓ Ⓔ
2 Ⓐ Ⓑ Ⓒ Ⓓ Ⓔ	7 Ⓐ Ⓑ Ⓒ Ⓓ Ⓔ	12 Ⓐ Ⓑ Ⓒ Ⓓ Ⓔ
3 Ⓐ Ⓑ Ⓒ Ⓓ Ⓔ	8 Ⓐ Ⓑ Ⓒ Ⓓ Ⓔ	13 Ⓐ Ⓑ Ⓒ Ⓓ Ⓔ
4 Ⓐ Ⓑ Ⓒ Ⓓ Ⓔ	9 Ⓐ Ⓑ Ⓒ Ⓓ Ⓔ	14 Ⓐ Ⓑ Ⓒ Ⓓ Ⓔ
5 Ⓐ Ⓑ Ⓒ Ⓓ Ⓔ	10 Ⓐ Ⓑ Ⓒ Ⓓ Ⓔ	15 Ⓐ Ⓑ Ⓒ Ⓓ Ⓔ

16 17 18

19 20 21

ANSWER SHEET FOR PRACTICE TEST 2
(Remove This Sheet and Use It to Mark Your Answers)

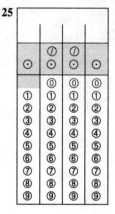

CUT HERE

ANSWER SHEET FOR PRACTICE TEST 2
(Remove This Sheet and Use It to Mark Your Answers)

SECTION 5

1 Ⓐ Ⓑ Ⓒ Ⓓ Ⓔ
2 Ⓐ Ⓑ Ⓒ Ⓓ Ⓔ
3 Ⓐ Ⓑ Ⓒ Ⓓ Ⓔ
4 Ⓐ Ⓑ Ⓒ Ⓓ Ⓔ
5 Ⓐ Ⓑ Ⓒ Ⓓ Ⓔ

6 Ⓐ Ⓑ Ⓒ Ⓓ Ⓔ
7 Ⓐ Ⓑ Ⓒ Ⓓ Ⓔ
8 Ⓐ Ⓑ Ⓒ Ⓓ Ⓔ
9 Ⓐ Ⓑ Ⓒ Ⓓ Ⓔ
10 Ⓐ Ⓑ Ⓒ Ⓓ Ⓔ

11 Ⓐ Ⓑ Ⓒ Ⓓ Ⓔ
12 Ⓐ Ⓑ Ⓒ Ⓓ Ⓔ
13 Ⓐ Ⓑ Ⓒ Ⓓ Ⓔ
14 Ⓐ Ⓑ Ⓒ Ⓓ Ⓔ

SECTION 6

1 Ⓐ Ⓑ Ⓒ Ⓓ Ⓔ
2 Ⓐ Ⓑ Ⓒ Ⓓ Ⓔ
3 Ⓐ Ⓑ Ⓒ Ⓓ Ⓔ
4 Ⓐ Ⓑ Ⓒ Ⓓ Ⓔ
5 Ⓐ Ⓑ Ⓒ Ⓓ Ⓔ

6 Ⓐ Ⓑ Ⓒ Ⓓ Ⓔ
7 Ⓐ Ⓑ Ⓒ Ⓓ Ⓔ
8 Ⓐ Ⓑ Ⓒ Ⓓ Ⓔ
9 Ⓐ Ⓑ Ⓒ Ⓓ Ⓔ
10 Ⓐ Ⓑ Ⓒ Ⓓ Ⓔ

SECTION 7

1 Ⓐ Ⓑ Ⓒ Ⓓ Ⓔ
2 Ⓐ Ⓑ Ⓒ Ⓓ Ⓔ
3 Ⓐ Ⓑ Ⓒ Ⓓ Ⓔ
4 Ⓐ Ⓑ Ⓒ Ⓓ Ⓔ
5 Ⓐ Ⓑ Ⓒ Ⓓ Ⓔ

6 Ⓐ Ⓑ Ⓒ Ⓓ Ⓔ
7 Ⓐ Ⓑ Ⓒ Ⓓ Ⓔ
8 Ⓐ Ⓑ Ⓒ Ⓓ Ⓔ
9 Ⓐ Ⓑ Ⓒ Ⓓ Ⓔ
10 Ⓐ Ⓑ Ⓒ Ⓓ Ⓔ

11 Ⓐ Ⓑ Ⓒ Ⓓ Ⓔ
12 Ⓐ Ⓑ Ⓒ Ⓓ Ⓔ
13 Ⓐ Ⓑ Ⓒ Ⓓ Ⓔ
14 Ⓐ Ⓑ Ⓒ Ⓓ Ⓔ
15 Ⓐ Ⓑ Ⓒ Ⓓ Ⓔ

16 Ⓐ Ⓑ Ⓒ Ⓓ Ⓔ
17 Ⓐ Ⓑ Ⓒ Ⓓ Ⓔ
18 Ⓐ Ⓑ Ⓒ Ⓓ Ⓔ
19 Ⓐ Ⓑ Ⓒ Ⓓ Ⓔ
20 Ⓐ Ⓑ Ⓒ Ⓓ Ⓔ

21 Ⓐ Ⓑ Ⓒ Ⓓ Ⓔ
22 Ⓐ Ⓑ Ⓒ Ⓓ Ⓔ
23 Ⓐ Ⓑ Ⓒ Ⓓ Ⓔ
24 Ⓐ Ⓑ Ⓒ Ⓓ Ⓔ
25 Ⓐ Ⓑ Ⓒ Ⓓ Ⓔ

26 Ⓐ Ⓑ Ⓒ Ⓓ Ⓔ
27 Ⓐ Ⓑ Ⓒ Ⓓ Ⓔ
28 Ⓐ Ⓑ Ⓒ Ⓓ Ⓔ
29 Ⓐ Ⓑ Ⓒ Ⓓ Ⓔ
30 Ⓐ Ⓑ Ⓒ Ⓓ Ⓔ

31 Ⓐ Ⓑ Ⓒ Ⓓ Ⓔ
32 Ⓐ Ⓑ Ⓒ Ⓓ Ⓔ
33 Ⓐ Ⓑ Ⓒ Ⓓ Ⓔ
34 Ⓐ Ⓑ Ⓒ Ⓓ Ⓔ
35 Ⓐ Ⓑ Ⓒ Ⓓ Ⓔ

SECTION 1: VERBAL REASONING

Time: 30 Minutes
30 Questions

In this section, choose the best answer for each question and blacken the corresponding space on the answer sheet.

Sentence Completion

DIRECTIONS

Each blank in the following sentences indicates that something has been omitted. Consider the lettered words beneath the sentence and choose the word or set of words that best fits the whole sentence.

1. Understanding the _____ that separate us from each other can also enable us to _____ the complex fabric of our society.
   (A) differences ... appreciate
   (B) truths ... combat
   (C) traditions ... resolve
   (D) similarities ... enrich
   (E) fears ... complete

2. What is most needed in a discussion of immigration are solid facts, not wishful thinking, realities, not _____.
   (A) explanations
   (B) reasons
   (C) ideas
   (D) fears
   (E) myths

3. South Korea's industrial production fell six percent last year, the largest annual _____ since 1980, fueling fears that the _____ economy is slipping deeper into recession.
   (A) figure ... flourishing
   (B) decrease ... steady
   (C) decline ... sagging
   (D) change ... lethargic
   (E) drop ... booming

4. By gradually winning the support of both liberals and conservatives, both rich and poor, the governor has demonstrated that her remarkable _____ skills go side by side with her willingness to speak openly and _____ on controversial issues.
   (A) interpersonal . . . equivocally
   (B) diplomatic . . . frankly
   (C) organizational . . . covertly
   (D) personal . . . deceptively
   (E) intimidating . . . obscurely

5. Slander and libel laws stand as a protection of an individual's reputation against the _____ dissemination of falsehoods.
   (A) unintentional
   (B) inevitable
   (C) inferential
   (D) irresponsible
   (E) incontestable

6. Presenting love as foolish, compromised, or dangerous, his love songs are frankly _____.
   (A) lyrical
   (B) antiromantic
   (C) conventional
   (D) melodic
   (E) sentimental

7. By showing that the trainer's voice _____ gave commands to the horse, he was able to _____ the clever ruse that contended an animal could add and subtract.
   (A) ostensibly . . . confirm
   (B) never . . . debunk
   (C) covertly . . . unmask
   (D) unwittingly . . . prove
   (E) potentially . . . defend

8. For an actor so changeable and unpredictable, even the word _____ seems inadequate.
   (A) immutable
   (B) mercurial
   (C) stoical
   (D) placid
   (E) obstinate

9. A _____ is distrustful of human goodness and sincerity, while a
   _____ has a hatred of people in general.
   - (A) pessimist ... ingrate
   - (B) siren ... tyrant
   - (C) altruist ... anarchist
   - (D) cynic ... misanthrope
   - (E) philanthropist ... misogynist

Analogies

DIRECTIONS

In each question below, you are given a related pair of words or phrases.
Select the lettered pair that *best* expresses a relationship similar to that in
the original pair of words.

10. TUNE : PIANO ::
    - (A) erase : pencil
    - (B) focus : camera
    - (C) transmit : plague
    - (D) ripen : fruit
    - (E) examine : biologist

11. ISLAND : OCEAN ::
    - (A) tree : forest
    - (B) automobile : highway
    - (C) radio : sound
    - (D) star : zodiac
    - (E) oasis : desert

12. SQUARE : CUBE ::
    - (A) triangle : hexagon
    - (B) trapezoid : quadrangle
    - (C) circle : sphere
    - (D) pentagon : pentagram
    - (E) addition : subtraction

13. ZIRCON : DIAMOND ::
    - (A) gold : silver
    - (B) garnet : ruby
    - (C) oyster : pearl
    - (D) necklace : bracelet
    - (E) emerald : sapphire

14. COMPLAISANT : COURTESY ::
    (A) offensive : smile
    (B) wise : riches
    (C) eager : inaction
    (D) vain : correctness
    (E) greedy : gluttony

15. GAUCHE : GRACE ::
    (A) impecunious : wealth
    (B) ignorant : fool
    (C) prejudiced : bigotry
    (D) conservative : reserve
    (E) proud : vanity

Critical Reading

DIRECTIONS

Questions follow each of the passages below. Using only the stated or implied information in each passage and in its introduction, if any, answer the questions.

Questions 16–21 are based on the following passage.

The following passage is from The Autobiography of Benjamin Franklin.

In 1732 I first publish'd my *Almanack,* under the name of *Richard Saunders;* it was continu'd by me about twenty-five years, commonly call'd *Poor Richard's Almanack.* I endeavor'd to make it both entertaining and useful, and it accordingly came to be in such
(5) demand, that I reap'd considerable profit from it, vending annually near ten thousand. And observing that it was generally read, scarce any neighborhood in the province being without it, I consider'd it as a proper vehicle for conveying instruction among the common people, who bought scarcely any other books; I therefore filled all
(10) the little spaces that occurr'd between the remarkable days in the calendar with proverbial sentences, chiefly such as inculcated industry and frugality, as the means of procuring wealth, and thereby securing virtue; it being more difficult for a man in want, to act always honestly, as, to use here one of those proverbs, *it is hard*
(15) *for an empty sack to stand upright.*

These proverbs, which contained the wisdom of many ages and nations, I assembled and form'd into a connected discourse prefix'd to the Almanack of 1757, as the harangue of a wise old man

to the people attending an auction. The bringing all these scatter'd
(20) counsels thus into a focus enabled them to make greater impres-
sion. The piece, being universally approved, was bought by the
clergy and gentry, to distribute gratis among their poor parish-
ioners and tenants. In Pennsylvania, as it discouraged useless
expense in foreign superfluities, some thought it had its share of
(25) influence in producing that growing plenty of money which was
observable for several years after its publication.

I considered my newspaper, also, as another means of communi-
cating instruction, and in that view frequently reprinted in it
extracts from the *Spectator,* and other moral writers; and some-
(30) times publish'd little pieces of my own. Of these are a Socratic
dialogue, tending to prove that, whatever might be his parts and
abilities, a vicious man could not properly be called a man of sense;
and a discourse on self-denial, showing that virtue was not secure
till its practice became a habitude, and was free from the
(35) opposition of contrary inclinations.

In the conduct of my newspaper, I carefully excluded all libelling
and personal abuse. Whenever I was solicited to insert any thing of
that kind, and the writers pleaded, as they generally did, the liberty
of the press, and that a newspaper was like a stage-coach, in which
(40) any one who would pay had a right to a place, my answer was, that I
would print the piece separately if desired, but that I would not
take upon me to spread his detraction; and that, having contracted
with my subscribers to furnish them with what might be either
useful or entertaining, I could not fill their papers with private
(45) altercation, in which they had no concern, without doing them
manifest injustice.

16. In line 13, the word "want" means
   (A) custom
   (B) captivity
   (C) covetousness
   (D) desire
   (E) need

17. According to the passage, the best way to become virtuous is to first
    become
   (A) wealthy
   (B) educated
   (C) self-knowing
   (D) reasonable
   (E) self-serving

18. With which of the following ideas about the freedom of the press would Franklin be likely to disagree?

   I. A person who is willing to pay for printing in a newspaper should be allowed to publish whatever he or she chooses.

  II. The primary obligation of the free press is to its subscribers.

 III. Personal disputes do not belong in the public press.

(A) I only
(B) II only
(C) III only
(D) I and II only
(E) I and III only

19. Franklin's refusal to publish in his newspaper any personal abuse was based on his belief that
(A) the newspaper might be prosecuted for libel
(B) personal abuse should not be printed for any price
(C) false personal attacks are too difficult to distinguish from attacks that are based on fact
(D) a newspaper's responsibility is to furnish its subscribers with worthy reading matter
(E) anyone who has paid for an item has the right to have it printed

20. The passage suggests that Franklin's principal profession was as a
(A) politician
(B) inventor
(C) printer
(D) scientist
(E) novelist

21. According to the passage, in both his almanac and newspaper, Franklin hoped to combine
(A) profit and religion
(B) wisdom and appeal to a large public
(C) ideas of thrift and virtue
(D) instruction and entertainment
(E) comedy and tragedy

Questions 22–30 are based on the following passage.

Immediately after *Hubble*'s launch, operators at the National Aeronautics and Space Administration Goddard Space Flight Center and at the Space Telescope Science Institute began an extensive series of systems checks and calibrations. The first test
(5) images revealed an inherent focusing problem, technically known as spherical aberration. A close examination of the images revealed that the telescope's main mirror had been ground to the wrong shape: it is two microns flatter at the edges than stipulated by design (a micron is one millionth of a meter). Small though the
(10) error may seem, it is a gross mistake by the standards of modern precision optics.

The shape of the mirror makes it impossible to focus all the light collected by *Hubble* to a single point. *Hubble*'s designers intended that the telescope should be able to concentrate 70 percent of the
(15) light of a point source—a distant star, for example—into a spot 0.1 arcsecond across (an arcsecond is a tiny angle, equal to 1/1,800 the apparent diameter of the moon). Actually, only 15 percent of the light falls into this central image; the other 85 percent spills over into an unwanted halo several arcseconds in diameter.
(20)   Various other difficulties have surfaced. Twice each orbit, when *Hubble* passes in and out of the earth's shadow, the sudden temperature change causes the telescope's large solar cell panels to flap up and down about 30 centimeters every 10 seconds. The resulting jitter can disrupt the telescope's pointing system and
(25) cause additional blurring of astronomical images. Two of *Hubble*'s six gyroscopes have failed, and a third works only intermittently; the telescope needs at least three gyroscopes to perform its normal science operations. Faulty electrical contacts threatened to shut down the High-Resolution Spectrograph.
(30)   NASA hopes to address some of these problems in 1994, when astronouts are scheduled to visit *Hubble*. They will attempt to replace the telescope's solar panels and two of the gyroscopes. The astronauts may also try to install a package of corrective optics and an upgraded Wide Field and Planetary Camera if the new devices
(35) are completed by then.

In the meantime, scientists have quickly learned how to wring as much performance from the space telescope as possible. Because *Hubble*'s mirror was ground to fine precision and because its error is well understood, computer enhancement can restore many
(40) images to their intended sharpness. The resulting astronomical views have eloquently refuted some early pessimism about the

telescope's scientific capabilities. Regrettably, attaining such resolution often involves discarding the smeared halos that appear
around celestial targets, literally throwing away most of the light
(45) captured by *Hubble*.

The greatest blow to *Hubble*'s scientific mission therefore has
been not a loss of resolution but a loss of sensitivity. *Hubble* was
designed to be able to detect objects a billion times fainter than
those visible to the human eye. At present, the telescope is limited
(50) to observing objects roughly 20 times brighter than intended.
Hubble cannot detect some particularly elusive targets, such as
extremely distant galaxies and quasars or possible planets around
nearby stars. Astronomers have had to postpone many of their
potentially most significant observations until the telescope is fixed.
(55)   Although designed to home in on some of the most remote
cosmic objects, *Hubble* has proved well suited to studying objects
within the solar system. For example, it has captured stunning
views of the giant planets, Jupiter and Saturn. NASA's two *Voyager*
space probes closely scrutinized Jupiter in 1979 and Saturn in 1980
(60) and 1981. The space telescope can routinely produce images of
Jupiter and Saturn comparable in detail to those obtained by the
Voyagers only a few days before their closest approaches to the two
planets.

22. In line 5, the word "inherent" means
    (A) correctable, insignificant
    (B) theoretical, hypothetical
    (C) serious, grave
    (D) innate, basic
    (E) suppressing, holding back

23. How much greater a percentage of the light of a point source would
    have been concentrated into an arcsecond spot if the mirror of the
    Hubble telescope had been ground correctly?
    (A) 15 percent
    (B) 30 percent
    (C) 55 percent
    (D) 70 percent
    (E) 80 percent

24. It can be inferred from the third paragraph that the telescope is subjected to sharp temperature changes because the temperature is
    (A) affected by its proximity to the moon
    (B) affected by the presence of the earth's shadow
    (C) affected by the proximity of other planets to the earth
    (D) affected by the earth's atmosphere
    (E) much higher as the telescope moves away from the sun

25. According to the passage, all of the following have been troubled or defective EXCEPT
    (A) solar cell panels
    (B) gyroscopes
    (C) main mirror
    (D) High-Resolution Spectrograph
    (E) lens

26. The word "address" as used in line 30 means
    (A) write to
    (B) use a proper form
    (C) apply itself
    (D) take a stand
    (E) repair

27. Which of the following best describes the difference between a telescope's sensitivity and its resolution?
    (A) Sensitivity is response to light or sound waves; resolution is its ability to separate an image into parts.
    (B) Sensitivity is the condition of receiving accurately outside stimuli; resolution is the capability of making darker shades lighter.
    (C) Sensitivity is its ability to perceive light; resolution is its ability to make the parts of an image visible.
    (D) Sensitivity is the distance at which a telescope can pick up foreign objects; resolution is the image of these objects.
    (E) Sensitivity is what is always lost in an image when resolution is gained.

28. The last paragraph of the passage provides
    (A) a summary of the arguments of the whole passage
    (B) an irrelevant comparison of the *Hubble Telescope* and the *Voyager* probes
    (C) a personal anecdote of the author
    (D) a contradiction of the assertions of the third paragraph (lines 20–29) of the passage
    (E) a rebuttal of media claims that the *Hubble Telescope* is a failure

29. In line 55, the phrase "home in on" is best paraphrased by
    (A) fall upon rapidly
    (B) expose clearly
    (C) fix upon
    (D) be comfortable with
    (E) photograph

30. The purpose of the passage as a whole is to
    (A) assess the accomplishments and shortcomings of the *Hubble Telescope*
    (B) compare the successes of the *Hubble Telescope* with those of other space telescopes
    (C) explain why the media disappointment with the *Hubble Space Telescope* is unjustified
    (D) remind readers of what the *Hubble Telescope* may accomplish after repairs are made
    (E) explain why the loss of sensitivity in the *Hubble Telescope* is compensated by a gain in resolution

STOP. IF YOU FINISH BEFORE TIME IS CALLED, CHECK YOUR WORK ON THIS SECTION ONLY. DO NOT WORK ON ANY OTHER SECTION IN THE TEST.

SECTION 2: MATHEMATICAL REASONING

Time: 30 Minutes
25 Questions

DIRECTIONS

Solve each problem in this section by using the information given and your own mathematical calculations, insights, and problem-solving skills. Then select the one correct answer of the five choices given and mark the corresponding circle on your answer sheet. Use the available space on the page for your scratchwork.

Notes

(1) All numbers used are real numbers.
(2) Calculators may be used.
(3) Some problems may be accompanied by figures or diagrams. These figures are drawn as accurately as possible EXCEPT when it is stated in a specific problem that a figure is not drawn to scale. The figures and diagrams are meant to provide information useful in solving the problem or problems. Unless otherwise stated, all figures and diagrams lie in a plane.

Data That May Be Used for Reference

Area

rectangle
$A = lw$

triangle
$A = \frac{1}{2} bh$

circle
$A = \pi r^2$

circumference
$C = 2\pi r$

Volume

rectangular solid
$V = lwh$

right circular cylinder
$V = \pi r^2 h$

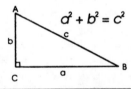

Pythagorean Relationship

$a^2 + b^2 = c^2$

Special Triangles

30° – 60° – 90°

45° – 45° – 90°

A circle is composed of 360°
A straight angle measures 180°
The sum of the angles of a triangle is 180°

1. A man purchased 4 pounds of steak priced at $3.89 per pound. How much change did he receive from a twenty-dollar bill?
   (A) $44.66   (D) $4.44
   (B) $15.56   (E) $4.34
   (C) $ 4.46

2. If a number is divisible by 7 but is not divisible by 21, then the number cannot be divisible by
   (A) 2   (B) 3   (C) 5   (D) 8   (E) 10

3. If $.0039y = 39$, then $y =$
   (A) 10   (B) 100   (C) 1000   (D) 10,000   (E) 100,000

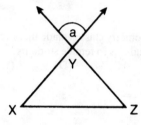

4. In $\triangle XYZ$, XY = 10, YZ = 10, and $\angle a = 84°$. What is the degree measure of $\angle Z$?
   (A) 96°   (B) 84°   (C) 48°   (D) 42°   (E) 24°

5. If $a = \sqrt{b}$ and $b = 81$, what is the value of $\sqrt{a}$?
   (A) ⅓   (B) 3   (C) 9   (D) 81   (E) 100

6. A plumber charges $45 for the first hour of work and $20 per hour for each additional hour of work after the first. What would be the total bill for labor if the plumber works for 6 consecutive hours?
   (A) $ 65   (D) $165
   (B) $120   (E) $180
   (C) $145

| 6″ | 2″ | 10″ | 2″ | 5″ |

7. Above are the measures of rainfall for five consecutive days during the winter. For the measure of those five days, which of the following is true?

    I. The median equals the mode.
    II. The median equals the arithmetic mean.
    III. The range equals the median.

  (A) I only
  (B) II only
  (C) III only
  (D) I and II only
  (E) I and III only

8. Three-fifths of a geometry class is made up of female students. What is the ratio of male students to female students?
  (A) ⅖   (B) ⅗   (C) ⅔   (D) 5⁄3   (E) ½

9. If $a = p + prt$, then $r =$

  (A) $\dfrac{a - 1}{t}$

  (B) $\dfrac{a - p}{pt}$

  (C) $a - p - pt$

  (D) $\dfrac{a}{t}$

  (E) $\dfrac{a + p}{pt}$

10. What is the slope of the line for the equation $6x + y = 3$?
  (A) 6   (B) 3   (C) −2   (D) −6   (E) −9

11. Maria plans to make sandwiches for a picnic. She has three types of bread from which to choose (rye, sourdough, and white), four types of meat from which to choose (salami, bologna, ham, and pastrami), and three types of cheese from which to choose (swiss, cheddar, and jack). If Maria will only use one type of bread, one type of meat, and one type of cheese on each sandwich, how many different kinds of sandwiches can Maria make?

(A) 3   (B) 4   (C) 10   (D) 17   (E) 36

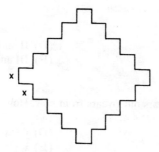

12. In the figure above, all line segments meet at right angles, and each segment has a length of x. What is the area of the figure in terms of x?

(A) $25x$ (B) $36x$ (C) $36x^2$ (D) $41x^2$ (E) $41x^3$

13. If $x - y = 15$ and $3x + y = 13$, then $y =$

(A) -8 (B) -7 (C) 7   (D) 8   (E) 15

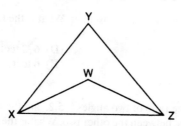

14. WX and WZ are angle bisectors of the base angles of isosceles triangle XYZ above. If $Y = 80°$, what is the degree measure of $\angle XWZ$?

(A) 65°   (B) 80°   (C) 100°   (D) 130°   (E) 160°

15. If $m^2 + n^2 = 12$ and $mn = 9$, then $(m + n)^2 =$

(A) 12   (B) 24   (C) 30   (D) 42   (E) 48

16. The perimeter of a rectangle is 42, and its length is 8 more than its width. What is the length of the rectangle?
    (A) 25   (B) 17   (C) 16½   (D) 14½   (E) 6½

17. If x, y, and z are consecutive positive integers greater than 1, not necessarily in that order, then which of the following is (are) true?

    I. $x > z$
    II. $x + y > z$
    III. $yz > xz$
    IV. $xy > y + z$

    (A) I only   (D) II and IV only
    (B) II only   (E) III and IV only
    (C) II and III only

18. Rajiv will be y years old x years from now. How old will he be z years from now?
    (A) $y - x + z$ (D) $y - x - z$
    (B) $y + x + z$ (E) $x + z - y$
    (C) $y + x - z$

19. The average of three numbers is 55. The second is 1 more than twice the first, and the third is 4 less than three times the first. What is the largest number?
    (A) 165   (B) 88   (C) 80   (D) 57   (E) 28

20. The area of a square is 72 square feet. What is the length of a diagonal of the square?
    (A) 36 feet   (D) $6\sqrt{2}$ feet
    (B) $18\sqrt{2}$ feet   (E) 6 feet
    (C) 12 feet

21. In a triangle, the ratio of two angles is 5:2, and the third angle is equal to the difference between the other two. What is the number of degrees in the smallest angle?
    (A) 36   (B) 25⅗   (C) 25⅖   (D) 18   (E) 9

22. If $(a, b) \oplus (c, d) = (ac - bd, ad)$, then $(-2, 3) \oplus (4, -1) =$
    (A) $(-5, 2)$ (D) $(-11, -2)$
    (B) $(-5, -2)$ (E) $(-5, -3)$
    (C) $(-11, 2)$

23. A collection of 25 coins consists of nickels, dimes, and quarters. There are three times as many dimes as nickels and three more dimes than quarters. What is the total value of the collection in dollars and cents?
   (A) $3.65
   (B) $3.25
   (C) $2.25
   (D) $1.65
   (E) $1.25

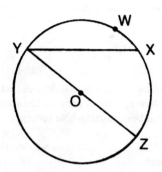

24. On the circle with center O above, arc YWX equals 100°. Which of the following is the degree measure of ∠XYZ?
   (A) 130°   (B) 100°   (C) 80°   (D) 50°   (E) 40°

25. If m and n are integers and $\sqrt{mn} = 10$, which of the following CANNOT be a value of $m + n$?
   (A) 25   (B) 29   (C) 50   (D) 52   (E) 101

STOP. IF YOU FINISH BEFORE TIME IS CALLED, CHECK YOUR WORK ON THIS SECTION ONLY. DO NOT WORK ON ANY OTHER SECTION IN THE TEST.

SECTION 3: VERBAL REASONING

Time: 30 Minutes
35 Questions

In this section, choose the best answer for each question and blacken the corresponding space on the answer sheet.

Sentence Completion

DIRECTIONS

Each blank in the following sentences indicates that something has been omitted. Consider the lettered words beneath the sentence and choose the word or set of words that best fits the whole sentence.

1. With the benefit of _____, it is easy to see the mistakes we made last week or last year.
   (A) hindsight
   (B) prophecy
   (C) insight
   (D) tactfulness
   (E) nostalgia

2. The pamphlet argues that imagination is not a gift _____ to poets, but something everyone possesses.
   (A) relevant
   (B) inimical
   (C) unique
   (D) unrestricted
   (E) conducive

3. That "less is more" is a(n) _____ upon which all of the governor's conservation program is based.
   (A) hope
   (B) question
   (C) enigma
   (D) image
   (E) paradox

4. Though McCarthy tried to provoke a _____, Eisenhower ignored all the senator's _____ as if he had not heard them.
   (A) fight . . . avocations
   (B) compromise . . . overtures
   (C) confrontation . . . accusations
   (D) condemnation . . . motives
   (E) consensus . . . implications

5. Again and again, out of indifference or sheer stupidity, we have _____ our resources, assuming that there was no end to the earth's _____ to recover from our mistakes.
   (A) invested . . . resolve
   (B) expanded . . . ability
   (C) wasted . . . failure
   (D) husbanded . . . inability
   (E) squandered . . . capacity

6. Despite _____ reports of freewheeling spending on political candidates by large corporations, most business contributions are _____ divided between the two major parties.
   (A) lurid . . . equitably
   (B) shocking . . . unfairly
   (C) unfair . . . secretly
   (D) favorable . . . evenly
   (E) encouraging . . . carefully

7. With characteristic understatement, Webster called his client's embezzlement of four million dollars a regretted _____.
   (A) peccadillo
   (B) crime
   (C) atrocity
   (D) theft
   (E) enormity

8. Keynes's theory that unemployment is caused by a(n) _____ disposition to save cannot explain the high unemployment in _____ countries that have no savings at all.
   (A) simple . . . wealthy
   (B) bizarre . . . prosperous
   (C) orderly . . . rich
   (D) individualistic . . . successful
   (E) excessive . . . indigent

9. His biographer believed that Pierce's _____ was caused by his _____ to travel and his refusal to read about any position different from his own.
   (A) parochialism ... reluctance
   (B) insularity ... readiness
   (C) bigotry ... zeal
   (D) narrow-mindedness ... eagerness
   (E) magnanimity ... failure

10. Though she was _____ by the medical establishment, Dr. Sandstrom bravely continued her work until other doctors could no longer deny the _____ of her theories.
    (A) ignored ... conviction
    (B) vilified ... probability
    (C) encouraged ... originality
    (D) supported ... credibility
    (E) attacked ... tenets

Analogies

DIRECTIONS

In each question below, you are given a related pair of words or phrases. Select the lettered pair that *best* expresses a relationship similar to that in the original pair of words.

11. COWHAND : HERD ::
    (A) wolf : fold
    (B) chef : cuisine
    (C) shepherd : flock
    (D) snowmobile : snow
    (E) newspaper : editor

12. MOTH : WOOL ::
    (A) earthworm : potato
    (B) termite : wood
    (C) ant : aphid
    (D) silkworm : silk
    (E) lizard : scale

13. DOCUMENT : PASSPORT ::
    (A) mirror : looking glass
    (B) league : team
    (C) pen : ball-point
    (D) army : captain
    (E) ice cream : dessert

14. PATTERN : DRESSMAKER ::
    (A) rule : carpenter
    (B) recipe : chef
    (C) composer : musician
    (D) canvas : sailmaker
    (E) novel : novelist

15. LIABILITY : IMMUNITY ::
    (A) pardon : amnesty
    (B) debit : credit
    (C) real estate : property
    (D) equinox : winter
    (E) fidelity : honesty

16. PLAN : INTRIGUE ::
    (A) move : slink
    (B) fear : doubt
    (C) run : hasten
    (D) eat : devour
    (E) boil : seethe

17. REQUEST : REQUIREMENT ::
    (A) solicitation : contribution
    (B) hope : faith
    (C) aspiration : inspiration
    (D) inquiry : interrogation
    (E) question : answer

18. SWEET : SACCHARINE ::
    (A) loud : deafening
    (B) quiet : still
    (C) bright : dark
    (D) initial : first
    (E) delicious : tasty

19. ABBOT : MONASTERY ::
   (A) nun : convent
   (B) conductor : orchestra
   (C) priest : bishop
   (D) author : book
   (E) runner : marathon

20. KNOT : BOWLINE ::
   (A) atoll : lagoon
   (B) state : senator
   (C) musician : pianist
   (D) volcano : lava
   (E) book : index

21. LEARNING : PEDANT ::
   (A) city : mayor
   (B) music : violinist
   (C) revenge : destroyer
   (D) politics : candidate
   (E) discipline : martinet

22. JINGO : CHAUVINIST ::
   (A) pain : analgesic
   (B) opera : oratorio
   (C) toady : sycophant
   (D) satirist : booster
   (E) doctor : lawyer

23. ACCRETE : DIMINISH ::
   (A) wax : wane
   (B) divide : subtract
   (C) decline : erode
   (D) augment : increase
   (E) tremble : waver

Critical Reading

DIRECTIONS

Questions follow the passage below. Using only the stated or implied information in the passage and in its introduction, if any, answer the questions.

Questions 24–35 are based on the following passage.

Playfully, we call them "shrinks," acknowledging each time we do so that the psychiatrist's precursor was the head-shrinking witchdoctor, the original healer of souls. Often we use the name sardonically, implying that a certain residue of mumbo-jumbo still
(5) clings to our supposedly enlightened science of the mind. But by the same token might there not be something of at least marginal value to be found in the supposedly superstitious practice of witchdoctoring? Have traditional cultures anything to teach our industrial society about the meaning of sanity? The anthropologist
(10) Marshall Sahlins, assembling a composite picture of life among the hunters and gatherers, once undertook to reconstruct a "stone-age economics" from which he believed we might learn something about the meaning of wealth and poverty. Is there a "stone-age psychiatry" that can be mined for similarly heuristic insights?
(15)   Until well into this century, even trained anthropological observers tended to regard tribal healers as charlatans whose practices were mere quackery. Some scholars classified all shamans as psychotics whose practices were "witchcraft" in the most pejorative meaning of the word. The terms used ranged from the politely
(20) technical ("neurotic-epileptoid type") to the bluntly dismissive ("veritable idiots"), but all came down to regarding tribal therapy as the mad treating the mad. Thanks largely to the work of Claude Levi-Strauss and subsequent studies in transcultural psychiatry, we have since come to see that tribal societies possess spiritual and
(25) psychotherapeutic traditions that may be more effective in the treatment of their own people than Western medicine, especially when it comes to mental and emotional disorders. The anthropologist I. M. Lewis, standing the question on its head, has gone so far as to suggest that our psychotherapy might be viewed as a scaled
(30) down subspecies of traditional healing. "The more meaningful equivalence," he observes, "is that psychiatry, and especially psychoanalysis, as Jung would perhaps have admitted much more freely than most Freudians would care to, represent limited and imperfect forms of shamanism." The remark is not entirely fair to
(35) Freud, who readily acknowledged that tribal healers can be as

adept as many psychiatrists at creating a "condition of expectant faith" that can have great therapeutic effect.

Perhaps the most marked difference between psychotherapy old and new is the complexity and breadth of traditional healing. In (40) tribal societies, the distinction between the physical and psychic is far less rigid than we understand it to be. One might almost say that traditional medicine regards all disease as psychosomatic, in the sense that the psyche is implicated in its etiology. Even a frozen foot may be treated by Eskimo shamans as a psychic disturbance. (45) Therefore, thoughts, dreams, memories, emotions must be mobilized in its cure. The province of stone-age psychiatry is a broad one.

E. Fuller Torrey, taking issue with the "psychiatric imperialism" of Western society, points out that healing has everything to do (50) with the cultural bond that unites therapist and client. A common worldview, a shared diagnostic vocabulary, mutually respected ideas and principles make for the trust and conviction without which healing may be impossible. But if we have learned that tribal techniques can be more effective than modern psychiatry in (55) treating native people, this knowledge may have little direct value for us—unless we can find some common ground with tribal peoples that allows us to borrow a portion of their culture. That common ground may be the ground of desperation. If our relations with nature are as deeply failed as the environmental crisis (60) suggests, we may have to look for help wherever we can find it, including insights long absent from our own society. Where else are these to be found but in the experience of our fellow humans living different lives in a different world?

Traditional therapy can be stubbornly parochial; it is embedded (65) in a place and a history, in the rhythms of climate, in the contours of a landscape where the birds and beasts have been close companions for centuries. In local lore, a river, a mountain, a grove may take on the personality of a tribal elder, a presence named and known over the generations. Artifacts assume a peculiarly evoca- (70) tive power. The *manangs* of Borneo come to their patients bearing a bundle filled with strange implements: the horns of the giant beetle, a quartz amulet that is "the stone of light," a wild boar's tusk that can retrieve lost souls. What can these things mean to us? They seem like the proverbial "eye of newt and toe of frog" that (75) make witchcraft appear so ludicrous. Yet the effectiveness of the shaman's method largely lies in its emotional specificity. What we as modern observers achieve by our efforts to universalize is, at last, something of our own, a new creation that may lack the color and force of the original.

24. In the first paragraph, the author uses the word "shrinks" (line 1) in order to

   I. jokingly refer to the forerunners of the contemporary psychiatrist
   II. suggest a distrust of contemporary psychiatry
   III. remind readers of the potential value in the traditional practices

   (A) I only
   (B) I and II only
   (C) I and III only
   (D) II and III only
   (E) I, II, and III

25. The first paragraph cites the work of anthropologist Marshall Sahlins in order to suggest that
   (A) if the stone age can teach us about economics, perhaps it can teach us about psychiatry
   (B) the problems of poverty in our era can be solved by consulting stone-age economics
   (C) the stone-age notions of rich and poor are irrelevant in today's complex civilization
   (D) modern anthropologists need not limit their studies to the life-styles of lost civilizations
   (E) modern psychiatry is dependent upon ancient ideas

26. The passage argues that tribal medical treatment may be
   (A) more universally effective than modern methods
   (B) more effective in treating people living in civilized countries than modern methods
   (C) about as effective as Western methods in treating members of tribal societies
   (D) more effective than Western methods in treating mental disorders of tribal members
   (E) more effective than Western methods in treating mental disorders of non-Western nations

27. The passage implies that one reason for the success within a tribe of tribal medicine is that
   (A) some tribal doctors may use curative herbs
   (B) the patient expects to be cured
   (C) some tribal doctors have Western training
   (D) the patients are not really sick
   (E) some tribal doctors refuse to use amulets

28. Which of the following would be likely to be treated by ancient psychotherapy but not by modern?
    (A) Depression
    (B) Broken arm
    (C) Fear of crowds
    (D) Schizophrenia
    (E) Mental illness

29. The word "marked" in line 38 means
    (A) signaled
    (B) indicated
    (C) scored
    (D) conspicuous
    (E) recorded

30. Which of the following best expresses the meaning of the phrase 'between the physical and psychic" in line 40?
    (A) Between body and mind
    (B) Between the sensual and sensuous
    (C) Between the real and supernatural
    (D) Between logic and the uncanny
    (E) Between sensory and extrasensory perception

31. In line 42, the word "psychosomatic" can be best defined as
    (A) curable by herbal medicine or spells
    (B) contagious
    (C) originating in the mind
    (D) imaginary
    (E) subject to treatment by witchcraft

32. Freud and E. Fuller Torrey agree upon the importance in healing of
    (A) mutual trust between doctor and patient
    (B) a conviction of the superiority of shamanism to psychiatry
    (C) the patient's desire to be cured
    (D) a conviction of the superiority of psychiatry to shamanism
    (E) a genuine belief in the efficacy of witchcraft

33. In line 48, the phrase "taking issue with" can be best defined as
    (A) departing from
    (B) resulting from
    (C) disagreeing with
    (D) proceeding with
    (E) siding with

34. Anticipating the skepticism that might arise from taking ancient medicine seriously, the author has deliberately used all of the following words and phrases to mock ancient medicine or its practitioners EXCEPT
    (A) "mumbo-jumbo" (line 4)
    (B) "charlatans" (line 16)
    (C) "psychotics" (line 18)
    (D) "eye of newt and toe of frog" (line 74)
    (E) "shaman's method" (line 76)

35. The purpose of the passage as a whole is to
    (A) question the usefulness of modern psychotherapy as opposed to tribal healing methods
    (B) assert the superiority of tribal methods to Western psychiatric procedures
    (C) urge the study of tribal medicine and tribal ways to abet Western psychiatry
    (D) criticize Western civilization's arrogant dismissal of tribal lore
    (E) reconstruct as far as it is possible some principles of stone-age mental therapy

STOP. IF YOU FINISH BEFORE TIME IS CALLED, CHECK YOUR WORK ON THIS SECTION ONLY. DO NOT WORK ON ANY OTHER SECTION IN THE TEST.

SECTION 4: MATHEMATICAL REASONING

Time: 30 Minutes
25 Questions

DIRECTIONS

This section is composed of two types of questions. Use the 30 minutes allotted to answer both question types. Your scratchwork should be done on any available space in the section.

Notes

(1) All numbers used are real numbers.
(2) Calculators may be used.
(3) Some problems may be accompanied by figures or diagrams. These figures are drawn as accurately as possible EXCEPT when it is stated in a specific problem that a figure is not drawn to scale. The figures and diagrams are meant to provide information useful in solving the problem or problems. Unless otherwise stated, all figures and diagrams lie in a plane.

Data That May Be Used for Reference

Area

rectangle	triangle	circle
$A = lw$	$A = \frac{1}{2} bh$	$A = \pi r^2$

circumference
$C = 2\pi r$

Volume

rectangular solid	right circular cylinder
$V = lwh$	$V = \pi r^2 h$

Pythagorean Relationship

$$a^2 + b^2 = c^2$$

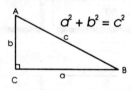

Special Triangles

30° – 60° – 90°

45° – 45° – 90°

A circle is composed of 360°
A straight angle measures 180°
The sum of the angles of a triangle is 180°

Quantitative Comparison

DIRECTIONS

In this section, you will be given two quantities, one in column A and one in column B. You are to determine a relationship between the two quantities and mark—

(A) if the quantity in column A is greater than the quantity in column B.
(B) if the quantity in column B is greater than the quantity in column A.
(C) if the quantities are equal.
(D) if the comparison cannot be determined from the information that is given.
AN (E) RESPONSE WILL NOT BE SCORED.

Notes

(1) Sometimes, information concerning one or both of the quantities to be compared is given. This information is not boxed and is centered above the two columns.
(2) All numbers used are real numbers. Letters such as a, b, m, and x represent real numbers.
(3) In a given question, if the same symbol is used in column A and column B, that symbol stands for the same value in each column.

	Column A	**Column B**
1.	35% of 50	50% of 35

$$x^2 = 36$$

2.	6	x

3.	$3\sqrt{2}$	$\sqrt{17}$

Questions 4–5 refer to the diagram.

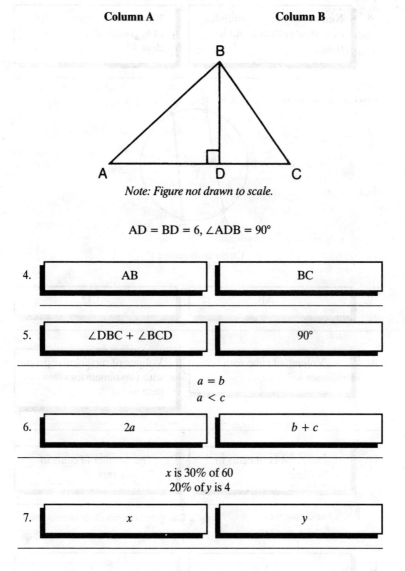

Column A   **Column B**

B

A   D   C

Note: Figure not drawn to scale.

AD = BD = 6, ∠ADB = 90°

| 4. | AB | BC |

| 5. | ∠DBC + ∠BCD | 90° |

$$a = b$$
$$a < c$$

| 6. | $2a$ | $b + c$ |

x is 30% of 60
20% of *y* is 4

| 7. | x | y |

	Column A	Column B

8. Number of integer multiples of 8, greater than 8, but less than 50 | Number of integer multiples of 6, greater than 6, but less than 40

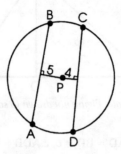

Circle with center P

9. AB | CD

10. Volume of cube with side 6 | Volume of rectangular prism with two dimensions less than 6

11. The number of cents in $8n$ dimes | The number of cents in $3n$ quarters

$$5x + y = 2$$
$$x + 3y = 6$$

12. x | y

Column A   **Column B**

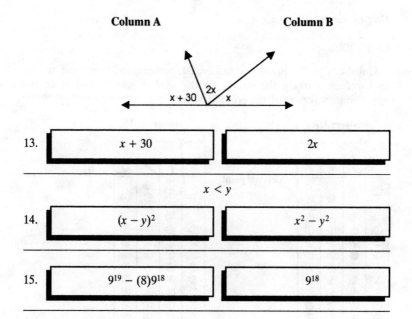

13.

| $x + 30$ | $2x$ |

$x < y$

14.

| $(x - y)^2$ | $x^2 - y^2$ |

15.

| $9^{19} - (8)9^{18}$ | 9^{18} |

Grid-in Questions

DIRECTIONS

Questions 16–25 require you to solve the problem and enter your answer by carefully marking the circles on the special grid. Examples of the appropriate way to mark the grid follows.

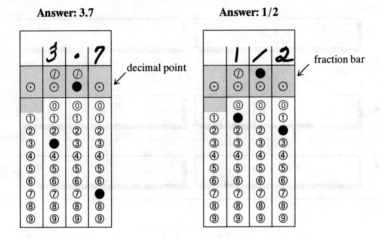

Answer: 3.7

decimal point

Answer: 1/2

fraction bar

Answer 1½

Do not grid in mixed numbers in the form of mixed numbers. **Always** change mixed numbers to improper fractions or decimals.

Change to 1.5   or   Change to 3/2

Answer: 123

Space permitting, answers may start in any column. Each grid-in answer below is correct.

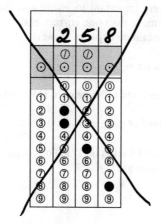

Note: Circles must be filled in correctly to receive credit. Mark only one circle in each column. No credit will be given if more than one circle in a column is marked. Example:

Answer: 258
No credit!!!!

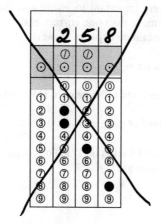

Answer: 8/9

Accuracy of decimals: Always enter the most accurate decimal value that the grid will accommodate. For example: An answer such as .8888 . . . can be gridded as .888 or .889. Gridding this value as .8, .88, or .89 is considered inaccurate and therefore **not acceptable.** The acceptable grid-ins of 8/9 are:

8/9   .888   .889

Be sure to write your answers in the boxes at the top of the circles before doing your gridding. Although writing out the answers above the columns is not required, it is very important to insure accuracy. Even though some problems may have more than one correct answer, grid only **one answer.** Grid-in questions contain no negative answers.

16. If $x + \frac{3}{5}x = 1$, then $x =$

17. In a class of 35 students, 60% are girls. How many boys are in the class?

18. What is the average of $\frac{1}{4}$, $\frac{1}{6}$, and $\frac{1}{12}$?

19. If a car averages 317.9 miles on 17 gallons of gas, how many miles will it travel on 5 gallons of gas?

Springfield High School's average SAT scores
over a five-year period were

	MATH	VERBAL
1989	520	540
1990	515	532
1991	518	528
1992	510	525
1993	507	510

20. What was the mean (average) of the verbal SAT scores for the five-year period 1989 through 1993?

21. The ratio of the measures of the angles of a quadrilateral is 3:5:7:9. What is the degree measure of the smallest angle?

22. If Jim takes 6 days to paint a house alone and Mike takes 8 days to paint the same house alone, what part of the job will be completed if both boys work for 2 days?

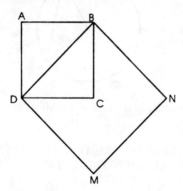

23. In square ABCD above, AB = 5. What is the area of square BDMN?

Car Sales

24. In the graph above, if each point aligns exactly with a grid mark or aligns halfway between two grid marks, what was the greatest percentage increase between two consecutive years? (Disregard the % sign when gridding your answer.)

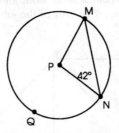

25. What is the measure in degrees of arc MQN in the circle above with center P?

STOP. IF YOU FINISH BEFORE TIME IS CALLED, CHECK YOUR WORK ON THIS SECTION ONLY. DO NOT WORK ON ANY OTHER SECTION IN THE TEST.

SECTION 5: VERBAL REASONING

Time: 15 Minutes
14 Questions

In this section, choose the best answer for each question and blacken the corresponding space on the answer sheet.

Critical Reading

DIRECTIONS

Questions follow the two passages below. Using only the stated or implied information in each passage and in its introduction, if any, answer the questions.

Questions 1–14 are based on the following passages.

The two passages that follow are about the conductor of the modern symphony orchestra. The first was written in the 1950s by a well-known composer-conductor. The second was written in the 1960s by a well-known composer.

Passage 1

There was an era of the so-called violin-conductor, whose main duty was to start and stop the orchestra and generally keep the flow of the music going. This was all well and good as long as orchestras were small enough. But around Beethoven's time, orchestras began
(5) getting larger and larger, and it soon became apparent that somebody had to be up there to keep the players together. So conducting as we know it is actually less than 150 years old.

The first real conductor in our sense of the word was Mendelssohn, who founded a tradition of conducting based on the
(10) concept of precision, as symbolized in the wooden stick we call the baton. Mendelssohn dedicated himself to an exact realization of the score he was conducting, through manipulation of that baton. There soon arrived, however, a great dissenter named Richard Wagner who declared that everything Mendelssohn was doing was
(15) wrong and that any conductor worth his salt should personalize the score he was conducting by coloring it with his own emotions and his own creative impulse. And so out of the clash of these two points of view the history of conducting was born; and there arose all those great names in conducting, as well as all the fights that go
(20) on about them right up to our own time. Mendelssohn fathered the

267

"elegant" school, whereas Wagner inspired the "passionate" school of conducting. Actually, both attitudes are necessary, the Apollonian and the Dionysian, and neither one is completely satisfactory without the other. Both of them can be badly abused,
(25) as we know from having heard performances that seemed clear but were dry as dust, and others in which passion became simple distortion.

The ideal modern conductor is a synthesis of the two attitudes, and this synthesis is rarely achieved. In fact, it's practically
(30) impossible. Almost any musician can be a conductor, even a pretty good one; but only a rare musician can be a great one. This is not only because it is so hard to achieve the Mendelssohn-Wagner combination, but also because the conductor's work encompasses such a tremendous range. Unlike an instrumentalist or a singer, he
(35) has to play on an orchestra. His instrument is one hundred human instruments, each one a thorough musician, each with a will of his own; and he must cause them to play like one instrument with a single will. Therefore, he must have enormous authority, to say nothing of psychological insight in dealing with this large group—
(40) and all this is just the beginning. He must be a master of the mechanics of conducting. He must have an inconceivable amount of knowledge. He must have a profound perception of the inner meanings of music, and he must have uncanny powers of communication. If he has all this, he is the ideal conductor

Passage 2

(45)   Conducting, like politics, rarely attracts original minds, and the field is more for the making of careers and the exploitation of personalities—another resemblance to politics—than a profession for the application of exact and standardized disciplines. A conductor may actually be less well equipped for his work than his
(50) players, but no one except the players need know it, and his career is not dependent on them in any case, but on the society women (including critics) to whom his musical qualities are of secondary importance. The successful conductor can be an incomplete musician, but he must be a compleat angler. His first skill *has* to be
(55) power politics.

In such people the incidence of ego disease is naturally high to begin with, and I hardly need add that the disease grows like a tropical weed under the sun of a pandering public. The results are that the conductor is encouraged to impose a purely egotistical,
(60) false, and arbitrary authority, and that he is accorded a position out

of all proportion to his real value in the musical, as opposed to the music-business, community. He soon becomes a "great" conductor, in fact, or as the press agent of one of them recently wrote me, a "titan of the podium," and as such is very nearly the worst
(65) obstacle to genuine music-making. "Great" conductors, like "great" actors, are unable to play anything but themselves; being unable to adapt themselves to the work, they adapt the work to themselves, to their "style," their mannerisms. The cult of the "great" conductor also tends to substitute looking for listening, so that to
(70) conductor and audience alike (and to reviewers who habitually fall into the trap of describing a conductor's appearance rather than the way he makes music sound, and of mistaking the conductor's gestures for the music's meanings), the important part of the performance becomes the gesture.

(75)   If you are incapable of listening, the conductor will show you what to feel. Thus, the film-actor type of conductor will act out a life of Napoleon in "his" *Eroica*[1], wear an expression of noble suffering on the retreat from Moscow (TV having circumvented the comparatively merciful limitation to the dorsal view) and one of
(80) ultimate triumph in the last movement, during which he even dances the Victory Ball. If you are unable to listen to the music, you watch the corybantics[2], and if you *are* able, you had better not go to the concert.

[1] *Eroica* = a symphony by Beethoven originally dedicated to Napoleon
[2] corybantics = dancing

1. From Passage 1, the reader can infer that in the seventeenth century

    I. orchestras did not employ a conductor
   II. orchestras were smaller than they are today
  III. orchestral players were better trained and more skillful

(A) I only
(B) II only
(C) I and II only
(D) I and III only
(E) I, II, and III

2. From its use in Passage 1 (lines 20–24) it can be inferred that the word "Apollonian" means
   (A) sunny and optimistic
   (B) Wagnerian
   (C) emotionally intense
   (D) Bacchic
   (E) clear and elegant

3. According to Passage 1, instrumentalists and singers have an advantage over a conductor because they
   (A) have only to do what the conductor directs
   (B) need not master the mechanics of conducting
   (C) must cope with only one instrument, not a hundred
   (D) must be able to read music
   (E) need not understand the meaning of a score

4. Of which of the following kinds of conductor described in Passage 1 would the author of that passage be most likely to approve?
   (A) One "dedicated . . . to an exact realization of the score" (lines 11–12)
   (B) One "coloring [the score] with his own emotions and his own creative impulse" (lines 16–17)
   (C) One whose performances "seemed clear but were dry as dust" (lines 25–26)
   (D) One in whose performances "passion became simple distortion" (lines 26–27)
   (E) One who is both "elegant" and "passionate" and can "personalize the score" (lines 21, 15–16)

5. By adding the parenthetical phrase "including critics" (line 52) the author of Passage 2 suggests all of the following EXCEPT:
   (A) Music critics and society women are alike.
   (B) Music critics are more interested in orchestras than in orchestra conductors.
   (C) Music critics are more important to a conductor's success than are the conductor's musical abilities.
   (D) Music critics are less interested in musical ability than are orchestra players.
   (E) Music critics are less able to judge musical qualities than are musicians.

6. The author of Passage 2 believes that politicians are
   (A) original thinkers
   (B) career-minded
   (C) highly disciplined professionals
   (D) modest and self-effacing
   (E) indifferent to power

7. By the phrase "the incidence of ego disease is naturally high" (line 56), the author of the Passage 2 means
   (A) there is a great deal of illness among musicians
   (B) conductors are rarely sick
   (C) conducting is a dangerous and demanding profession
   (D) conductors are very self-centered
   (E) orchestras are likely to thrive in tropical countries

8. In Passage 2, the distinction implied in lines 58–62 between the "music-business community" and the "musical community" is that
   (A) in the music-business community, conductors are undervalued
   (B) in the music-business community, composers are overvalued
   (C) in the musical community, music is more important than personality
   (D) only the music-business community is concerned with money
   (E) the music-business community is concerned with popular music, and the musical community with classical music

9. The phrase "TV having circumvented the comparatively merciful limitation to the dorsal view" (lines 78–79) in Passage 2 can be best understood to mean
   (A) television has brought conductors to a much larger audience than ever before
   (B) television allows the viewer to see and hear details of a performance that are not clear in the concert hall
   (C) television distorts both the sound and the appearance of a symphony concert
   (D) television unfortunately allows the viewers to see the front of the conductor
   (E) television programs have the fortunate advantage of being easily turned off

10. In the last paragraph of Passage 2, the phrase "if you *are* able" refers to

    I. visualize the "Victory Ball"
   II. "listen to the music"
  III. "watch the corybantics"

    (A) II only
    (B) III only
    (C) I and III only
    (D) II and III only
    (E) I, II, and III

11. The author of Passage 2 either directly or obliquely makes fun of all of the following EXCEPT
    (A) conductors
    (B) politicians
    (C) the musical public
    (D) music critics
    (E) orchestral players

12. Of the following kinds of conductor described in Passage 1, which would the author of Passage 2 be most likely to approve?
    (A) One "dedicated . . . to an exact realization of the score" (lines 11–12)
    (B) One "coloring [the score] with his own emotions and his own creative impulse" (lines 16–17)
    (C) One whose performances "seemed clear but were dry as dust." (lines 25–26)
    (D) One in whose performances "passion become simple distortion" (lines 26–27)
    (E) One who is both "elegant" and "passionate" and can "personalize the score" (lines 21, 15–16)

13. Which of the following words is used in both passages but with totally different connotations?
    (A) "conductor"
    (B) "exact"
    (C) "music"
    (D) "great"
    (E) "orchestra"

14. That both passages were written at midcentury rather than very recently is suggested by their

   I. assumption that an orchestra will be led by a conductor rather than by a concert-master
   II. assumption that a conductor is a male
   III. assumption that a performance may be reviewed by a music critic

   (A) I only
   (B) II only
   (C) III only
   (D) I and II only
   (E) I, II, and III

STOP. IF YOU FINISH BEFORE TIME IS CALLED, CHECK YOUR WORK ON THIS SECTION ONLY. DO NOT WORK ON ANY OTHER SECTION IN THE TEST.

SECTION 6: MATHEMATICAL REASONING

Time: 15 Minutes
10 Questions

DIRECTIONS

Solve each problem in this section by using the information given and your own mathematical calculations, insights, and problem-solving skills. Then select the one correct answer of the five choices given and mark the corresponding circle on your answer sheet. Use the available space on the page for your scratchwork.

Notes

(1) All numbers used are real numbers.
(2) Calculators may be used.
(3) Some problems may be accompanied by figures or diagrams. These figures are drawn as accurately as possible EXCEPT when it is stated in a specific problem that a figure is not drawn to scale. The figures and diagrams are meant to provide information useful in solving the problem or problems. Unless otherwise stated, all figures and diagrams lie in a plane.

Data That May Be Used for Reference

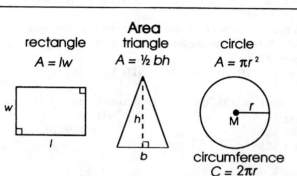

Area

rectangle

$A = lw$

triangle

$A = \frac{1}{2}bh$

circle

$A = \pi r^2$

circumference

$C = 2\pi r$

Volume

rectangular solid

$V = lwh$

right circular cylinder

$V = \pi r^2 h$

Pythagorean Relationship

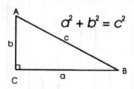

$a^2 + b^2 = c^2$

Special Triangles

$30° - 60° - 90°$

$45° - 45° - 90°$

A circle is composed of 360°
A straight angle measures 180°
The sum of the angles of a triangle is 180°

1. What is .25% of 12?
   (A) ³⁄₁₀₀   (B) ³⁄₁₀   (C) ⅓   (D) 3   (E) 300

2. A square 4 inches on a side is cut up into smaller squares 1 inch on a side. What is the maximum number of such squares that can be formed?
   (A) 4   (B) 8   (C) 16   (D) 36   (E) 64

3. If a book costs $5.70 after a 40% discount, what was its original price?
   (A) $2.28   (D) $9.12
   (B) $6.10   (E) $9.50
   (C) $7.98

4. $\dfrac{\frac{2}{3} - \frac{1}{2}}{\frac{1}{6} + \frac{1}{4} + \frac{2}{3}} =$

   (A) ²⁄₁₃   (B) ²⁄₉   (C) ¹³⁄₂₀   (D) 1¹⁄₁₃   (E) 3¼

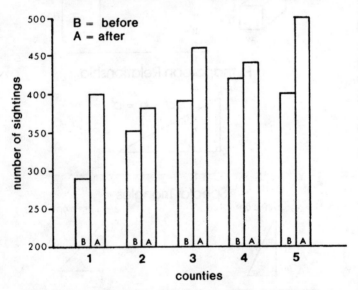

Number of Wild Bear Sightings Before and After Conservation Measures in Five Different Counties

5. According to the graph above, which county had the most bear sightings before the conservation measures?
   (A) 1   (B) 2   (C) 3   (D) 4   (E) 5

6. If $(x + 1)$ times $(2x + 1)$ is an odd integer, then x must be
   (A) an odd integer   (D) a composite number
   (B) an even integer   (E) a negative number
   (C) a prime number

7. There are 36 students in a certain geometry class. If two-thirds of the students are boys and three-fourths of the boys are under six feet tall, how many boys in the class are under six feet tall?
   (A) 6   (B) 12   (C) 18   (D) 24   (E) 27

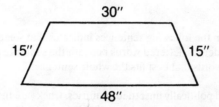

8. What is the area of the trapezoid above in square inches?
   (A) 108   (B) 234   (C) 368   (D) 468   (E) 585

9. Three factories of Conglomerate Corporation are capable of manufacturing hubcaps. Two of the factories can each produce 100,000 hubcaps in 15 days. The third factory can produce hubcaps 30% faster. Approximately how many days would it take to produce a million hubcaps with all three factories working simultaneously?
   (A) 38   (B) 42   (C) 44   (D) 46   (E) 50

10. What is the area in square yards of an equilateral triangle if the length of one of its sides is 12 yards?
   (A) $18\sqrt{3}$ (B) $36\sqrt{3}$ (C) 72   (D) $72\sqrt{3}$ (E) 216

STOP. IF YOU FINISH BEFORE TIME IS CALLED, CHECK YOUR WORK ON THIS SECTION ONLY. DO NOT WORK ON ANY OTHER SECTION IN THE TEST.

SECTION 7: VERBAL REASONING

Time: 30 Minutes
35 Questions

In this section, choose the best answer for each question and blacken the corresponding space on the answer sheet.

Sentence Completion

DIRECTIONS

Each blank in the following sentences indicates that something has been omitted. Consider the lettered words beneath the sentence and choose the word or set of words that best fits the whole sentence.

1. In poor and politically unsettled countries, trucks are the only means of getting in or out, public transportation being virtually _____.
   (A) indecipherable
   (B) ubiquitous
   (C) indifferent
   (D) inadequate
   (E) nonexistent

2. Parker is known for the _____ of her stories, many of them less than three pages long.
   (A) wit
   (B) sincerity
   (C) cynicism
   (D) economy
   (E) development

3. Because most parents who watched *Sesame Street* as children are likely to regard the show as _____ viewing for their children, an advertiser can _____ a very large young audience.
   (A) educational . . . alienate
   (B) obligatory . . . rely on
   (C) compulsory . . . avoid
   (D) required . . . apprehend
   (E) habitual . . . expect

4. A fiscal _____, Lloyd would sell shares when all the best economic advisors were recommending against doing so.
   (A) conservative
   (B) maverick
   (C) investor
   (D) Tory
   (E) moderate

5. The clothes she designs for men are conservative, but her fashions for women are more _____.
   (A) liberal
   (B) flamboyant
   (C) tasteful
   (D) expensive
   (E) conventional

6. His _____ protests against elephant poaching, an illegal but enormously _____ pursuit, put the warden at risk.
   (A) vigorous . . . unpopular
   (B) realistic . . . costly
   (C) unregarded . . . profitable
   (D) outspoken . . . lucrative
   (E) tactful . . . popular

7. Although it is _____ that scientists will discover even smaller particles, we have theoretical reasons to believe that we _____ or are very close to a knowledge of nature's ultimate building blocks.
   (A) unlikely . . . have misapprehended
   (B) uncertain . . . have approached
   (C) possible . . . have reached
   (D) probable . . . have avoided
   (E) moot . . . have acquired

8. Contrary to several sports writers' opinion, Valdez is neither _____ nor _____, but an affable and articulate young man.
   (A) sullen . . . winsome
   (B) genial . . . quiet
   (C) morose . . . reticent
   (D) gracious . . . impolite
   (E) aggressive . . . well spoken

9. In 1900, Spanish operatic composers faced a problem of language, for if works were not written in Italian, singers of international stature _____ to sing them.
   (A) refused
   (B) hoped
   (C) vocalized
   (D) desired
   (E) preferred

10. The reason for reduced spending on arms throughout the world is not _____, but _____, not a change in thinking, but a shortage of money.
    (A) ideological ... economic
    (B) personal ... political
    (C) pacifist ... practical
    (D) local ... universal
    (E) liberal ... conservative

Analogies

DIRECTIONS

In each question below, you are given a related pair or words or phrases. Select the lettered pair that *best* expresses a relationship similar to that in the original pair of words.

11. CLIPPER SHIP : SAIL ::
    (A) automobile : windshield
    (B) train : baggage
    (C) dirigible : helium
    (D) submarine : propeller
    (E) seaplane : pontoon

12. NURSERY : PLANTS ::
    (A) classroom : teacher
    (B) department store : charge account
    (C) radio : news
    (D) bakery : bread
    (E) cobbler : shoes

13. WITCH : SORCERER ::
    (A) surgeon : anesthetist
    (B) playwright : dramatist
    (C) contralto : baritone
    (D) cook : waitress
    (E) director : editor

14. JANITOR : BUILDING ::
    (A) rider : horse
    (B) fisherman : fire
    (C) violinist : orchestra
    (D) ranger : forest
    (E) police officer : judge

15. BREAKFAST : DINNER ::
    (A) lark : nightingale
    (B) stone : wood
    (C) tent : tepee
    (D) radar : sonar
    (E) realism : rationalism

16. RING : BRACELET ::
    (A) log : pencil
    (B) tennis ball : basketball
    (C) trash barrel : wastebasket
    (D) mile : yard
    (E) square : cube

17. WALNUT : WOOD ::
    (A) parsnip : vegetable
    (B) bulb : tulip
    (C) apple : seed
    (D) chair : living room
    (E) spice : recipe

18. CALORIE : HEAT ::
    (A) weight : menu
    (B) exercise : muscle
    (C) personality : psychiatrist
    (D) omen : bird
    (E) acre : area

19. POPE : CARDINALS ::
    (A) supreme court : senate
    (B) abbess : abbots
    (C) bishop : dioceses
    (D) lama : temple
    (E) president : electoral college

20. TRIAL : SUMMATION ::
    (A) composition : coda
    (B) newspaper : editorial
    (C) drama : exposition
    (D) serial : episode
    (E) ballot : election

21. CAPRICIOUS : WHIM ::
    (A) indecisive : idea
    (B) optimistic : hope
    (C) parsimonious : poverty
    (D) garrulous : talk
    (E) philanthropic : cynicism

22. URBANITY : BUMPKIN ::
    (A) wit : comedian
    (B) egotism : show-off
    (C) tolerance : bigot
    (D) timidity : grammarian
    (E) literacy : librarian

Critical Reading

DIRECTIONS

Questions follow the passage below. Using only the stated or implied information in the passage and in its introduction, if any, answer the questions.

Questions 23–35 are based on the following passage.

Acid rain, in the past half decade, has been added to the technological world's litany of fears. Like carbon dioxide, it is an unintended by-product of the Industrial Revolution. Evidence strongly suggests that pollutants in the atmosphere are acidifying
(5) rains, lakes, and streams.

The problem is not well understood. It is not even well named. The words would sound less sinister if it were commonly known that all rains and snows are naturally acidic. A substance's acidity is measured on the pH scale, in which 7 is perfectly neutral, neither
(10) acidic nor alkaline. Speaking very roughly, the average pH of rain in nature—though it varies from place to place on the globe— is thought to be 5.6, which is slightly acidic.

In many parts of the industrial world, however, and in forested country far downwind of factory country, the pH of rains and snows
(15) is much lower. Rainfall in the eastern United States is currently estimated by the Environmental Protection Agency to be about pH 4.5. The pH scale is logarithmic, which means that as one counts down the scale, each integer is 10 times more acidic than normal. And they often come worse. "One long rainfall in the autumn of
(20) 1978 holds a dubious national record," environmentalist and writer John Luoma reports in his book *Troubled Skies, Troubled Waters.* "Instruments registered values less than pH 2, a level six to eight times more acidic than vinegar and some five thousand times more acidic than normal rain."

(25)   The pollutants responsible for this increase are chiefly sulfur dioxide and the oxides of nitrogen. Swirled and cooked together with other gases and chemicals in the atmosphere, they can combine to form, among other things, sulfuric acid, which then falls on our country's soil and gathers in our lakes.

(30)   Those lakes most at risk are in territory that was scraped clean of topsoil during the last advances and retreats of the ice age. In the great chain of wilderness lakes that extends from northern Minnesota into Canada; in the Appalachians; and in much of Scandinavia, the ice scoured right down to the bedrock, and the new soil that
(35) has collected there is still quite thin. These regions are poor in the kind of natural alkaline rock, like limestone, that elsewhere helps to neutralize acid rain. Many of their lakes have been greatly acidified, altering their chemistry in complex ways that are only beginning to be understood. Fish in these lakes have died off. The
(40) water is eerily clear and clean, because in it so little life survives.

Ironically, part of the problem is an engineering feat that was once seen as the problem's solution. Coal-burning plants such as Kyger Creek, and the General James M. Gavin plant, both in Cheshire, Ohio, have built huge smokestacks (Gavin's is over 1,000
(45) feet high) to loft their emissions of sulfur dioxide and nitrogen oxides high into the atmosphere and keep these wastes from sickening their neighbors in Cheshire. The gases are borne

extraordinary distances in the upper atmosphere, where they have
plenty of time and space to recombine into sulfuric acid, which
(50) then falls thousands of miles from Kyger Creek and Gavin. Tall
stacks help convert acid rain from a local to an environmental
problem.

Environmentalists and industrialists agree that acid rain is
poorly understood and must be studied further. But they disagree
(55) about what to do in the meanwhile. Some argue for several kinds of
preventive action now. For instance, expensive "scrubbers" could
be installed immediately by plants such as Kyger Creek and Gavin
to clean sulfur dioxides from the stacks' emissions. But many other
people—including most of those who would have to pay to install
(60) the scrubbers—think the expense premature. The issue has as
many sides as any in climatology. Some of the chemical emissions
in question even make good fertilizer. Notes climatologist Reid
Bryson of the University of Wisconsin, "It may be the old saying
about a silver lining to every cloud—but here in Wisconsin, when
(65) they cleaned up the sulfur emissions from one of our local power
plants, the farmers in the area had to start adding sulfur to their
fields."

Though the debate continues, Jon Luoma says, "the difficulties
in the way of reducing acid rain are not so much scientific as
(70) political."

23. The second paragraph describes acid rain as "not even well named"
because
  (A) rain is naturally acid
  (B) no liquids are perfectly neutral
  (C) some rains are alkaline
  (D) the public cannot understand the meaning of the phrase
  (E) the phrase makes acid rain appear to be a serious problem

24. The first sentence of the third paragraph refers to "forested country far
downwind of factory country" as having rains and snows of low pH
because
  (A) industrial pollution travels upwind
  (B) the pH scale is logarithmic
  (C) rainfall is heavier in forested country
  (D) all rainfall is acidic
  (E) pollution from factories is blown here by winds

25. From the information in the third paragraph, it can be inferred that the pH of vinegar is probably
    (A) 2
    (B) 4
    (C) 6
    (D) 7
    (E) 8

26. In the third paragraph, the phrase "a dubious national record" is best taken to mean a
    (A) record not scientifically confirmed
    (B) record not generally accepted as a record
    (C) record not expected to endure
    (D) local rather than an international record
    (E) record not worth achieving

27. Of the following, which would be the most alkaline?
    (A) A liquid with a pH of 3
    (B) A liquid with a pH of 5
    (C) A liquid with a pH of 7
    (D) A liquid with a pH of 9
    (E) A liquid with a pH of 11

28. The passage suggests that an area with limestone may be harmed less by acid rain because
    (A) no rain will run off into lakes and streams
    (B) streams will be more abundant and faster flowing
    (C) the limestone may neutralize the acid
    (D) the limestone will absorb less water than other rocks
    (E) limestone is a natural by-product of coal burning

29. As it is used in line 40, the word "eerily" means
    (A) scrupulously
    (B) immaculately
    (C) strangely
    (D) partially
    (E) ostensibly

30. In line 41, the adverb "ironically" is used because
    - (A) the smokestacks failed to protect Cheshire
    - (B) the result is the opposite of what was expected
    - (C) the builders of the smokestacks failed to consider the problems of acid rain
    - (D) smokestacks cannot solve the problems of acid rain
    - (E) engineers, rather than scientists, were responsible for the construction

31. In line 41, the word "feat" means
    - (A) failure
    - (B) foundation
    - (C) attempt
    - (D) achievement
    - (E) sleight of hand

32. In the seventh paragraph, the reference to "the old saying about a silver lining to every cloud" is used because
    - (A) some effects of acid rain are beneficial
    - (B) there is hope that someday acid rain problems will be eliminated
    - (C) acid rain falls far from the source of pollution
    - (D) the solution to the problem of acid rain is political, not scientific
    - (E) lakes in some regions are now clear and clean because of acid rain

33. The chief antagonists in the debate about how to deal with causes of acid rain are most likely to be
    - (A) industrial polluters and farmers
    - (B) industrialists and environmentalists
    - (C) the federal government and private landowners
    - (D) farmers whose soils benefit from acid rain and farmers whose soils do not
    - (E) foresters and fishermen

34. The passage implies that acid rain could be reduced by all of the following EXCEPT
    - (A) emission controls on smokestacks
    - (B) reduction of coal burning in industry
    - (C) reduction of sulfur dioxide in the atmosphere
    - (D) reduction of the use of sulfur as fertilizer
    - (E) reduction of oxides of nitrogen in the atmosphere

35. That "the difficulties in the way of reducing acid rain are not so much scientific as political" is due chiefly to the fact that
    (A) scientists do not yet fully understand acid rain
    (B) the side effects of acid rain can be beneficial as well as harmful
    (C) many scientists believe preventive measures should be undertaken immediately
    (D) acid rain falls on areas at great distances from the source of pollution
    (E) the cost of cleaning sulfur dioxides from smokestacks may be paid by the federal government

STOP. IF YOU FINISH BEFORE TIME IS CALLED, CHECK YOUR WORK ON THIS SECTION ONLY. DO NOT WORK ON ANY OTHER SECTION IN THE TEST.

SCORING PRACTICE TEST 2

ANSWER KEY

Section 1 Verbal Reasoning	Section 2 Mathematical Reasoning	Section 3 Verbal Reasoning	Section 4 Mathematical Reasoning
1. A	1. D	1. A	1. C
2. E	2. B	2. C	2. D
3. C	3. D	3. E	3. A
4. B	4. C	4. C	4. D
5. D	5. B	5. E	5. C
6. B	6. C	6. A	6. B
7. C	7. B	7. A	7. B
8. B	8. C	8. E	8. C
9. D	9. B	9. A	9. B
10. B	10. D	10. B	10. D
11. E	11. E	11. C	11. A
12. C	12. D	12. B	12. B
13. B	13. A	13. C	13. B
14. E	14. D	14. B	14. D
15. A	15. C	15. B	15. C
16. E	16. D	16. A	16. 5/8
17. A	17. B	17. D	17. 14
18. A	18. A	18. A	18. 1/6
19. D	19. C	19. B	19. 93.5
20. C	20. C	20. C	20. 527
21. D	21. A	21. E	21. 45
22. D	22. A	22. C	22. 7/12
23. C	23. A	23. A	23. 50
24. B	24. E	24. E	24. 100
25. E	25. C	25. A	25. 264
26. C		26. D	
27. C		27. B	
28. E		28. B	
29. C		29. D	
30. A		30. A	
		31. C	
		32. A	
		33. C	
		34. E	
		35. C	

288

ANSWER KEY

Section 5 Verbal Reasoning	Section 6 Mathematical Reasoning	Section 7 Verbal Reasoning
1. C	1. A	1. E
2. E	2. C	2. D
3. C	3. E	3. B
4. E	4. A	4. B
5. B	5. D	5. B
6. B	6. B	6. D
7. D	7. C	7. C
8. C	8. D	8. C
9. D	9. D	9. A
10. A	10. B	10. A
11. E		11. D
12. A		12. D
13. D		13. C
14. B		14. D
		15. A
		16. B
		17. A
		18. E
		19. E
		20. A
		21. B
		22. C
		23. A
		24. E
		25. A
		26. E
		27. E
		28. C
		29. C
		30. B
		31. D
		32. A
		33. B
		34. D
		35. D

ANALYZING YOUR TEST RESULTS

The charts on the following pages should be used to carefully analyze your results and spot your strengths and weaknesses. The complete process of analyzing each subject area and each individual problem should be completed for each practice test. These results should then be reexamined for trends in types of errors (repeated errors) or poor results in specific subject areas. **This reexamination and analysis is of tremendous importance to you in assuring maximum test preparation benefit.**

Verbal Reasoning Analysis Sheet

Section 1	possible	completed	right	wrong
sentence completion	9			
analogies	6			
critical reading	15			
Subtotal	30			

Section 3	possible	completed	right	wrong
sentence completion	10			
analogies	13			
critical reading	12			
Subtotal	35			

Section 5	possible	completed	right	wrong
critical reading	14			
Subtotal	14			

Section 7	possible	completed	right	wrong
sentence completion	10			
analogies	12			
critical reading	13			
Subtotal	35			

Overall Verbal Totals	114			

Mathematical Reasoning Analysis Sheet

Section 2	possible	completed	right	wrong
multiple choice	25			
Subtotal	25			

Section 4	possible	completed	right	wrong
quantitative comparison	15			
grid-ins	10			
Subtotal	25			

Section 6	possible	completed	right	wrong
multiple choice	10			
Subtotal	10			
Overall Math Totals	60			

You can now use the Score Range Approximator on page 439 to convert your raw scores to an **approximate** scaled score.

WHY?????????????????????????????????

Analysis/Tally Sheet for Problems Missed

One of the most important parts of test preparation is analyzing **why** you missed a problem so that you can reduce the number of mistakes. Now that you have taken the practice test and checked your answers, carefully tally your mistakes by marking them in the proper column.

Reason for Mistakes

	Total Missed	Simple Mistake	Misread Problem	Lack of Knowledge	Lack of Time
Section 1: Verbal					
Section 3: Verbal					
Section 5: Verbal					
Section 7: Verbal					
Subtotal					
Section 2: Math					
Section 4: Math					
Section 6: Math					
Subtotal					
Total Math and Verbal					

Reviewing the above data should help you determine **why** you are missing certain problems. Now that you've pinpointed the type of error, compare it to other practice tests to spot other common mistakes.

COMPLETE ANSWERS AND EXPLANATIONS
FOR PRACTICE TEST 2

Sentence Completion

1. (A) The first noun could be any of the five except *similarities,* although at first glance, (A) *differences* looks like the best. The second blank needs a verb that follows from *understanding,* and (A) *appreciate* is the closest to the earlier word. Choices (B) and (C) make little sense with the *fabric* metaphor (how can one *resolve* or *combat* a *fabric?*).

2. (E)The phrase *facts, not wishful thinking* is parallel to *realities, not _____ ,* so you need a word that is opposite to *realities* and similar in effect to *wishful thinking.* Only *myths* describes something that contrasts with *realities.*

3. (C) The verb *fell* tells you that the first noun must mean *decline* or fall. Choices (B) *decrease,* (C) *decline,* and (E) *drop* are all possibilities. The adjective describing this economy must also denote falling, so you can eliminate *steady* (B) and *booming* (E), but (C) *sagging* is appropriate.

4. (B) The first adjective must be consistent with the information that the skills have won over both liberals and conservatives. Choices (A), (B), and (D) would fit, but *organizational* (C) or *intimidating* (E) would not. The second blank requires an adverb that parallels or accords with *openly.* Both *equivocally* (ambiguously) and *deceptively* are clearly the opposite of what is needed. The correct choice is *frankly* (B).

5. (D) The missing adjective here should describe the actions of a slanderer. The noun *dissemination* means spreading abroad; the action of spreading a *libel* or *slander* is not well described by any of these choices except by *irresponsible* (D)

6. (B) The final adjective must describe songs that satirize *love* as *foolish* or *compromised.* Much the best choice is *antiromantic.* The four other choices conflict with the assertion of the first half of the sentence.

7. (C) If signaling the horse by the voice is part of a *clever ruse,* the missing adverb must be something signifying secretly or without being observed. Only *covertly* (C) has this meaning. The verb that fills the second blank must mean something like expose, and *unmask* (C) fits the requirement.

8. **(B)** The needed word here is a strong way of saying *changeable* or *unpredictable*. Of the five choices, *mercurial* (volatile, *changeable*) is clearly the best.

9. **(D)** The sentence presents two related definitions and is a straightforward test of vocabulary. A *cynic* distrusts *human goodness;* a *misanthrope* hates *people in general.* A *pessimist* looks on the dark side of things and expects the worst; an *ingrate* is an ungrateful person. A *siren* is a temptress; a *tyrant* is an absolute ruler, usually a cruel or despotic one. An *altruist* is unselfishly concerned for the welfare of others; an *anarchist* opposes all forms of government. A *philanthropist* is a generous lover of humankind; a *misogynist* is person who hates women.

Analogies

10. **(B)** The words here are a verb (*tune*) and a noun (*piano*), with the verb describing an action that must be performed before the noun can function properly. As a *piano* must be *tune*d, so a *camera* must be *focus*ed. This is a better choice than **(D)** (*ripen* : *fruit*) because although *fruit* should *ripen* before it's eaten, both the *camera* and *piano* are mechanical objects, and the verbs require some manual action.

11. **(E)** An *island* is land surrounded by *water,* an *oasis* is a place of water surrounded by the dry sands of a *desert.*

12. **(C)** A *square* is a four-sided figure of two dimensions. With three dimensions, it becomes a *cube.* The parallel geometric figures are the two-dimensional *circle* that in three dimensions will be a *sphere.*

13. **(B)** A *zircon* is a mineral that can be cut to resemble a *diamond,* but it is far cheaper. Similarly, a *garnet* is a red, semiprecious stone that is used in jewelry to replace the much more valuable *ruby.*

14. **(E)** The pairing here combines an adjective and a noun, and the noun is a quality which would characterize a person whom the adjective describes. A *complaisant* person—that is someone who is polite or obliging—would be characterized by *courtesy.* Similarly, a *greedy* person would be likely to be guilty of *gluttony.* Choice **(B)** is possible but a less good choice since, although the *wise* may become *rich,* it is less certain than that the *greedy* are *glutton*ous.

15. (A) This is also a pair linking an adjective and a noun, but in this case, the noun denotes a characteristic a person described by the adjective would lack. The adjective *gauche* (the French for "left") means awkward or without *grace*. Similarly, an *impecunious* (having no money) person would be without *wealth*.

Critical Reading

16. (E) As it is used here, *want* means need or poverty rather than a wish or desire for something.

17. (A) Franklin's first paragraph makes the point that procuring wealth will secure virtue, for it is much harder for a person in need to resist a temptation to act dishonestly than for one who has no worry about the next meal. Although Franklin would, no doubt, encourage self-knowledge, education, and reason, the passage specifically cites wealth as security for virtue.

18. (A) Although Franklin was willing to print personal abuse for a fee, he insisted on doing so separately from his newspaper. He did so because he believed in his obligation to the subscribers of his newspaper, who had no concern with private altercations. He would *disagree* only with the first of these three statements.

19. (D) Franklin believed that his obligation to his subscribers required him to print material that was useful or entertaining, materials worth their subscription fees.

20. (C) Although Franklin is remembered as a statesman, scientist, and inventor, his chief means of support, as this passage implies, was as a printer.

21. (D) The first and last paragraphs refer to Franklin's wish to make his publications *entertaining and useful* (line 4) and *useful or entertaining* (line 44).

22. (D) The word *inherent* means innate, inborn, existing in something as a basic characteristic. The problem is *inherent* because the mirror had been ground to the wrong shape.

23. (C) If the mirror had been ground correctly, it would have concentrated 70 percent instead of 15 percent of the light—that is, 55 percent more than the present 15 percent.

24. **(B)** The passage refers to sudden temperature changes when the telescope passes in and out of the earth's shadow.

25. **(E)** The passage makes no mention of defects in the lens of the telescope.

26. **(C)** As it is used here, the verb means to apply (oneself) to, to deal with, to encounter.

27. **(C)** A telescope's sensitivity is its ability to respond to light (rather than to sound), and the resolution, which can be computer enhanced, is the ability to make the image that it detects visible and clear. Of the five choices, (C) offers the best definitions.

28. **(E)** The last paragraph deals chiefly with the telescope's success with objects within the solar system. This success is sufficient to rebut media claims of failure, for *Hubble* makes it possible for astronomers to see the planets well whenever they wish to do so.

29. **(C)** The phrase to *home in on* (also used for automatic weapons) means to fix upon, to track, to pick out and follow home. It refers here to the distant objects that *Hubble* is unable to *home in on*.

30. **(A)** The passage as a whole gives a balanced view of the *Hubble Space Telescope*. It admits the disappointments and specifies several tasks that the instrument is not yet able to handle. But it also points out the areas in which the telescope has been successful—not *revolutionary*, but useful to astronomers.

SECTION 2: MATHEMATICAL REASONING

1. (D) The 4 pounds of steak would cost

$$4 \times \$3.89 = \$15.56$$

The change from a twenty-dollar bill would be

$$\begin{array}{r} \$20.00 \\ -15.56 \\ \hline \$\ 4.44 \end{array}$$

2. (B) For a number to be divisible by 21, it must be divisible by 3 and by 7, since $21 = 3 \times 7$. Hence, if a number is divisible by 7 but not by 21, it cannot be divisible by 3.

3. (D) $.0039y = \dfrac{39}{10,000} y = 39$

$$y = \dfrac{(10,000)}{39} \times (39)$$

$$y = 10,000$$

Or, using your calculator, divide 39 by .0039.

4. (C) Since $XY = YZ = 10$, then $\triangle XYZ$ is an isoceles triangle and $\angle X = \angle Z$. $\angle Y = 84°$, since it forms a vertical angle with the given angle.

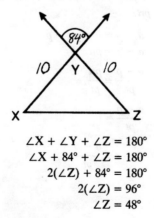

$$\angle X + \angle Y + \angle Z = 180°$$
$$\angle X + 84° + \angle Z = 180°$$
$$2(\angle Z) + 84° = 180°$$
$$2(\angle Z) = 96°$$
$$\angle Z = 48°$$

Hence, the measure of $\angle Z = 48°$.

299

5. (B) If $a = \sqrt{b}$ and $b = 81$, then $a = \sqrt{81}$, or $a = 9$. So the value of $\sqrt{a}$ is $\sqrt{9} = 3$.

6. (C) If the plumber works for 6 consecutive hours, the charge is $45 for the first hour plus $20 for each of the five additional hours:

$$\$45 + 5(\$20) = \$45 + \$100 = \$145$$

7. (B) II only. The arithmetic mean is the average (sum divided by number of items), or $6 + 2 + 10 + 2 + 5 = 25$ divided by $5 = 5$.

The median is the middle number after the numbers have been ordered: 2, 2, 5, 6, 10. The median is 5.

The mode is the most frequently appearing number: 2.

The range is the highest minus the lowest, or $10 - 2 = 8$.

Therefore, only II is true: the median (5) equals the mean (5).

8. (C) Since three-fifths of the class are females, then two-fifths of the class are males. Hence, the ratio of males to females is

$$\tfrac{2}{5} \text{ to } \tfrac{3}{5} = \frac{\tfrac{2}{5}}{\tfrac{3}{5}}$$

$$= \tfrac{2}{5} \div \tfrac{3}{5}$$

$$= \tfrac{2}{5} \cdot \tfrac{5}{3}$$

$$= \tfrac{2}{3}$$

9. (B) Since $a = p + prt$,

$$a - p = p + prt - p$$

$$a - p = prt$$

$$\frac{a - p}{pt} = \frac{prt}{pt}$$

$$\frac{a - p}{pt} = r$$

Hence,

$$r = \frac{a - p}{pt}$$

10. (D) First change the equation to slope-intercept form $y = mx + b$, where m is the slope and b is the y intercept.

$$6x + y = 3$$
$$\underline{-6x \qquad\qquad -6x}$$
$$y = 3 - 6x \quad \text{or} \quad -6x + 3$$

Next, you can see that in the equation $y = -6x + 3$, -6 is in the m position and is therefore the slope.

11. (E) Total number of different combinations ("how many different kinds") is found by multiplying the number of ways for each item. Therefore, three different breads times four different meats times three different cheeses = $3 \times 4 \times 3 = 36$.

12. (D) Breaking the figure into squares of side x by adding lines gives

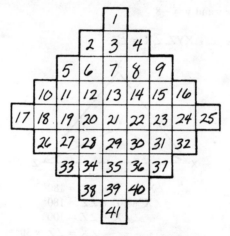

Remember, each square has area x^2. Then the total area is $41x^2$. Choices (A), (B), and (E) are not possible because area must be in square units.

13. (A) Adding the two equations,

$$x - y = 15$$
$$3x + y = 13$$
$$\overline{4x \qquad = 28}$$

$$\frac{4x}{4} = \frac{28}{4}$$

$$x = 7$$

Since $x = 7$	or	Since $x = 7$
and $x - y = 15$		and $3x + y = 13$
$7 - y = 15$		$3(7) + y = 13$
$7 - 7 - y = 15 - 7$		$21 + y = 13$
$-y = 8$		$21 - 21 + y = 13 - 21$
$y = -8$		$y = -8$

Hence, $x = y$ and $y = -8$.

14. (D) In isoceles $\triangle XYZ$, $\angle X = \angle Z$.

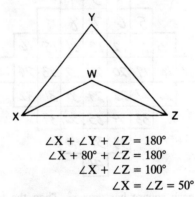

$$\angle X + \angle Y + \angle Z = 180°$$
$$\angle X + 80° + \angle Z = 180°$$
$$\angle X + \angle Z = 100°$$
$$\angle X = \angle Z = 50°$$

Since WX bisects $\angle YXZ$ and WZ bisects $\angle YZX$,

$$\angle YXW = \angle WXZ = \angle YZW = \angle WZX = 25°$$

Hence, on $\triangle XWZ$,

$$\angle XWZ + \angle WXZ + \angle WZX = 180°$$
$$\angle XWZ + 25° + 25° = 180°$$
$$\angle XWZ + 50° = 180°$$
$$\angle XWZ = 130°$$

15. (C) $(m + n)^2 = (m + n)(m + n)$
$$= m^2 + mn + mn + n^2$$
$$= m^2 + 2mn + n^2$$
$$= (m^2 + n^2) + (2mn)$$

Since $m^2 + n^2 = 12$ and $mn = 9$,

$$(m^2 + n^2) + (2mn) = 12 + 2(9)$$
$$= 12 + 18$$
$$= 30$$

16. (D) Let x = width and $x + 8$ = length.

Since the perimeter of the rectangle is 42,

$$2x + 2(x + 8) = 42$$
$$2x + 2x + 16 = 42$$
$$4x + 16 = 42$$
$$4x = 26$$
$$x = {}^{26}\!/_4 = 6\frac{1}{2}$$
$$x + 8 = 14\frac{1}{2}$$

Hence, the length of the rectangle is $14\frac{1}{2}$.

17. (B) Adding any two of three consecutive positive integers greater than 1 will always be greater than the other integer. Therefore, II is true. The others cannot be determined because they depend on values and/or the order of $x, y,$ and z.

18. (A) Since Rajiv will be y years old x years from now, he is $y - x$ years old now. Hence, z years from now he will be $y - x + z$ years old.

19. (C) Let x = first number, $2x + 1$ = second number, and $3x - 4$ = third number. Since the average of the three numbers is 55,

$$\frac{x + (2x + 1) + (3x - 4)}{3} = 55$$

Multiplying both sides of the equation by 3,

$$x + (2x + 1) + (3x - 4) = 165$$
$$6x - 3 = 165$$
$$6x - 3 + 3 = 165 + 3$$
$$6x = 168$$
$$\frac{6x}{6} = \frac{168}{6}$$
$$x = \frac{168}{6}$$
$$x = 28 = \text{first number}$$
$$2x + 1 = 57 = \text{second number}$$
$$3x - 4 = 80 = \text{third number}$$

Hence, the largest number is 80.

20. (C) Area of the square = ½ × product of diagonals

$$= \tfrac{1}{2}d_1 d_2$$
$$= \tfrac{1}{2}d^2 \text{ (since } d_1 = d_2 \text{ in a square)}$$

Hence, $\tfrac{1}{2}d^2 = 72$
$$d^2 = 144$$
$$d = 12 \text{ feet}$$

21. (A) Let $5x$ = first angle, $2x$ = second angle, and $5x - 2x = 3x$ = third angle. Since the sum of the angles in any triangle is $180°$,

$$5x + 2x + 3x = 180°.$$
$$10x = 180°$$
$$\frac{10x}{10} = \frac{180°}{10}$$
$$x = 18°$$

Hence,
$$5x = 90°$$
$$2x = 36°$$
$$3x = 54°$$

The smallest angle will have a measure of $36°$.

22. (A) $(-2, 3) \oplus (4, -1) = [(-2)(4) - (3)(-1), (-2)(-1)]$
$$= [(-8) - (-3), (2)]$$
$$= (-5, 2)$$

23. (A) Let n = number of nickels, $3n$ = number of dimes, and $3n - 3$ = number of quarters. Since there are 25 coins in the collection,

$$n + 3n + (3n - 3) = 25$$
$$7n - 3 = 25$$
$$7n = 28$$
$$n = 4 \text{ nickels} = \$0.20$$
$$3n = 12 \text{ dimes} = \$1.20$$
$$3n - 3 = 9 \text{ quarters} = \$2.25$$

Hence, the total value of the collection is

$$\$0.20 + \$1.20 + \$2.25 = \$3.65$$

24. (E) Since arc YXZ is a semicircle, its measure is 180°.

$$arc\ XZ = arc\ YXZ - arc\ YWX$$
$$= 180° - 100°$$
$$= 80°$$

Since an inscribed angle = ½(intercepted arc),

$$\angle XYZ = ½(arcXZ)$$
$$= ½(80°)$$
$$= 40°$$

Hence, ∠XYZ has a measure of 40°.

25. (C) Since $\sqrt{mn} = 10$, $mn = 100$, and the possible values for m and n would be

1 and 100
2 and 50
4 and 25
5 and 20
10 and 10

Since none of these combinations yields $m + n = 50$, choice (C) is correct.

SECTION 3: VERBAL REASONING

Sentence Completion

1. (A) The informative phrase here is *mistakes we made last week or last year*. These mistakes we understand by looking back, by *hindsight*. None of the other choices fits the rest of the sentence so well.

2. (C) The parallel phrases here are *something everyone possesses* and *imagination is not a gift _____ to poets*. The right word must be the opposite of universal, since the *not* precedes it. The best choice is *unique*, different from all others. With *not*, this is equivalent to *something everyone possesses*.

3. (E) The phrase *less is more* is not a *hope*, a *question* (that would be "is less more?"), an *enigma* (riddle), or an *image*. It is a *paradox*, an apparent self-contradiction, since less *should* be less, not more.

4. (C) Choices (A), (C) and (D) would seem to fit the first blank, but the second noun, which describes something the senator did that the president ignored, could be only (B) or (C), and (B) has already been eliminated. Both of the nouns in (C) make very good sense in this context.

5. (E) Since the action is described as stupid and indifferent, it cannot be something that has helped our resources, so we are left with two possible answers: *wasted* (C) or *squandered* (E). The second blank must be a word meaning ability; *capacity* (E) makes good sense, but *failure* (C) does not.

6. (A) Reports of *freewheeling* corporate spending are unlikely to be *favorable* or *encouraging,* but choices (A) and (B) fit well, and (C) is a possibility. The *despite* at the beginning of the sentence tells us that the reports are not true, and the missing adverb should be very different from *freewheeling*. Both (B) *unfairly* and (C) *secretly* contradict the *despite,* but (A) makes good sense. The reports must be *lurid,* that is, sensational or startling, and the adverb is *equitably,* that is, fairly or even-handedly.

7. (A) The first phrase tells us the crime will be described by an *understatement*. Choices (B), (C), (D), and (E) all call a crime a crime, but *peccadillo* suggests that stealing four million dollars is insignificant, a minor fault, a petty crime. This is *understatement*.

307

8. (E) The second adjective modifies *countries that have no savings at all,* so it cannot be any of the words meaning rich (A, B, C, and D). The correct choice is *indigent,* that is, poor. Although (A), (C), or (E) might have fit the first blank, choice (E) also makes the most sense.

9. (A) The sentence tells us that Pierce refused to read about positions different from his own. You need first a noun to describe a quality of a man like this, and all of the answers except (E) are possibilities. The second blank calls for a word to go with *to travel* that will also fit this parochial, or insular, or bigoted, or narrow-minded man. The right answer must mean something like *failure* or refusal. Either (A) or (E) will do, but only (A) has the first word right.

10. (B) If the doctor must be brave to continue her work, the missing verb must describe something to be resisted. The best choices are *vilified* (B) and *attacked* (E). The result of the brave work is acceptance by other doctors of the *probability* or the *tenets* of her theories. *Tenets* usually refers to doctrines or principles of a school of thought and is not quite right in this context. But both *vilified* (reviled, defamed) and *probability* fit well.

Analogies

11. (C) The two nouns here describe a caretaker and the group for which that person is responsible. Here the clear parallel is the *cowhand,* who oversees a *herd* of cattle, and the *shepherd,* who oversees a *flock* of sheep.

12. (B) A clothes *moth* is an insect which feeds upon *wool* or fur. The closest parallel is another insect, the *termite,* which feeds upon *wood.* The first term of the other choices does not actually feed upon the second term, although they may have some connection.

13. (C) A *passport* is a type of *document.* If the order of choice (E) were reversed, the parallel would be a good one, but the question puts the specific example (*passport*) as the second term. Choice (C) is the correct answer because a *ball-point* is a type of *pen.*

14. (B) A *dressmaker* uses a *pattern* to guide the making of an article of clothing just as a *chef* uses a *recipe* to make food. The first term is a plan or guide rather than a tool, material, or product.

15. (B) These nouns are opposites. An *immunity* is an exemption or release from an obligation such as taxes or prosecution, while *liability* is an obligation or responsibility for something. The only pair of antonyms among the answer choices is (B) where *debit,* an entry of money owed, is the opposite of *credit,* an entry of money received or to be received.

16. (A) Both words here are verbs, although in another context they might be nouns. To *intrigue* is to *plan* or scheme in a secret or underhanded way. The parallel is *move* and *slink* (to move in a sneaking manner).

17. (D) *Request* and *requirement* here are nouns; the difference between them is the element of force or compulsion in *requirement* as opposed to the voluntary *request.* A similar difference is approximated in the pairing of *inquiry* (a question or a questioning) and *interrogation* (a questioning in a formal examination, especially of a witness). The correspondence is not exact, but it is clearly the closest of the five choices.

18. (A) The second of these two adjectives is an intensive form of the first. *Saccharine* means very *sweet,* even too *sweet.* Choices (B), (C), (D), and (E) are either synonyms or antonyms (C), but *deafening* is intensely *loud.*

19. (B) An *abbot* is a monk who is the head, not merely a member, of a *monastery,* so the two nouns present a person in charge and what he or she is in charge of. The best choice here is the *conductor* of an *orchestra.*

20. (C) A *bowline* is a kind of *knot* as a *pianist* is a kind of *musician.* None of the other options is close.

21. (E) A *pedant* is a person who is narrow-minded, stressing details of *learning* which he or she professes rigorously. Similarly, a *martinet* is a strict disciplinarian, who enforces *discipline* with equal concern. The second term here is a person and the first that which the person is narrowly interested in.

22. (C) A *chauvinist* is not, as is often assumed, simply a male who blindly champions maleness. The word originally denoted any militant, unreasoning supporter of a country, that is, a *jingo.* The word is now also used to describe mindless supporters of a gender or a race. The terms here are synonyms, as are *toady* (a flatterer) and *sycophant* (also a flatterer).

23. (A) To *accrete* is to grow by being added to, while to *diminish* is to grow smaller, its antonym. The verbs *wax* and *wane* are also opposites and, in fact, are synonyms for *accrete* and *diminish.*

Critical Reading

24. (E) The first paragraph cites our using the word *shrinks playfully* and, in the second sentence, as a means of suggesting a criticism of modern psychotherapy. The third sentence asks (and suggests an affirmative answer) if *witchdoctoring* might have *at least marginal value.*

25. (A) The allusion to Sahlins's *stone-age economics* is intended to suggest the possibility of a stone-age psychiatry that may have some relevance to the modern world. The idea is advanced tentatively, in the form of a question that concludes the paragraph.

26. (D) The passage never makes outrageous claims for tribal therapy, but it does assert that it *may be more effective in the treatment of their own people,* with the added qualification *especially when it comes to mental and emotional disorders.*

27. (B) The second paragraph concludes with a reference to the *condition of expectant faith,* Freud's words of praise for tribal healers who create this feeling that can have a *great therapeutic effect.* That is, a patient who expects to be healed is more likely to recover.

28. (B) The third paragraph describes the much greater range of ills that traditional shamans would treat, including a frozen foot. Modern psychotherapists can be expected to deal with the mental afflictions of choices (A), (C), (D), or (E) but not with the broken arm.

29. (D) The word *marked* is an adjective here meaning conspicuous or obvious.

30. (A) The phrase is best paraphrased by between body and mind. Although *psychic* as a noun can mean a person sensitive to forces beyond the physical world, here it means that which is of the mind.

31. (C) As it is used in this context, *psychosomatic* means originating in the mind and carries no suggestion of imaginary or unreal.

32. (A) Freud, the second paragraph says, believed in the importance of the *condition of expectant faith* based on the patient's trust in the therapist's skill. Torrey, in the fourth paragraph, insists upon the importance of the *cultural bond* uniting the therapist and the client. The best answer here is choice (A).

33. (C) To take issue with is to argue, disagree, contest with. Torrey is disagreeing with assumed superiority of the Western scientist.

34. (E) The author deliberately uses the words *mumbo-jumbo, charlatans, psychotics,* and *eye of newt* not because he agrees with them but because he realizes that many of his readers approach this subject with these prejudices. The phrase *shaman's method* does not have the pejorative denotation or connotations of the four other choices.

35. (C) The passage is suggesting that we study tribal lore before we dismiss it because it may have uses even in modern Western society. The passage is not so unrealistic as to assert that tribal medicine is superior to Western, and its chief purpose is not to criticize the West.

SECTION 4: MATHEMATICAL REASONING

Quantitative Comparison

1. (C) This comparison should be made without any actual computation as follows:

35% of 50	50% of 35
$.35 \times 50$	$.50 \times 35$

   Since 35×50 is on each side and each column's answer has two decimal places, the quantities are equal. Or

$^{35}/_{100} \times 50$		$^{50}/_{100} \times 35$
$^{1}/_{100} \times 35 \times 50$	$=$	$^{1}/_{100} \times 50 \times 35$

2. (D) Solving $x^2 = 36$ gives $+6$ and -6. Therefore, x can be equal to 6 or -6, making no comparison possible.

3. (A) Changing the form of column A by squaring 3 and then multiplying it by 2 to get everything under the radical sign leaves the simple comparison $\sqrt{18} > \sqrt{17}$.

4. (D) The length of side AB is determinable by using the Pythagorean theorem, but since DC is not known, BC cannot be determined. Note that you cannot make a determination by measuring.

5. (C) Since there are 180° in a triangle and $\angle BDC$ is 90°, the remaining two angles, $\angle DBC$ and $\angle BCD$, must total 90°.

6. (B) If $a = b$ and $a < c$, then the following substitutes make the comparison simpler.

$2a$	$b + c$
$a + a$	$b + c$

   Since $a = b$, then

$a + b$	$b + c$

   Now, canceling b's from each column leaves

a	$<$	c

312

7. (B) Solve the first problem as follows:

$$x \text{ is } 30\% \text{ of } 60$$

Substituting "=" for "is" and "·" for "of" ($30\% = \frac{3}{10}$)

Then
$$x = (\frac{3}{10}) \cdot 60$$
$$x = 18$$

Solve the second problem as follows

$$20\% \text{ of } y \text{ is } 4 \ (20\% = \frac{1}{5})$$
$$(\frac{1}{5}) \cdot y = 4$$
$$(\frac{1}{5})y = 4$$

Multiplying by $\frac{5}{1}$ gives

Then
$$(\frac{5}{1}) \cdot (\frac{1}{5})y = 4 \cdot (\frac{5}{1})$$
$$y = 20$$

8. (C) The integer multiples of 8 greater than 8 but less than 50 are 16, 24, 32, 40, and 48. Column A is therefore 5. The integer multiples of 6 greater than 6 but less than 40 are 12, 18, 24, 30, and 36. Therefore, column B is also 5. The correct answer is (C).

9. (B) The chord that is closer to the center of the circle will be longer than the chord that is farther from the center. Hence, CD > AB.

10. (D) Volume of a cube with side 6 is $6 \times 6 \times 6 = 216$. Volume of a rectangular prism with two dimensions less than 6 is not determinable because the third dimension is needed. Therefore, no comparison can be made.

11. (A) Since there are 10 cents in each dime, the number of cents in $8n$ dimes is

$$10(8n) = 80n$$

Since there are 25 cents in each quarter, the number of cents in $3n$ quarters is

$$25(3n) = 75n$$

Hence, the number of cents in $8n$ dimes is greater than the number of cents in $3n$ quarters. Or you can disregard the n, since it is the same positive number on each side. Thus you are actually comparing 80¢ in column A and 75¢ in column B.

12. (B) Solving the systems of equations as follows by first multiplying the bottom equation by -5 gives

$$5x + y = 2$$
$$-5x + -15y = -30$$

Now, adding equations leaves

$$-14y = -28$$
Therefore, $$y = 2$$

Substituting $y = 2$ into the original second equation gives

$$x + 3(2) = 6$$
Then $$x + 6 = 6$$
and $$x = 0$$
Therefore $$x < y$$

13. (B) Since the three angles whose measures are given as x, $2x$, and $x + 30$ form a straight line,

$$x + 2x + (x + 30) = 180$$
$$4x + 30 = 180$$
$$4x = 150$$
$$x = 150 \div 4$$
$$x = 37.5$$
$$2x = 75$$
$$x + 30 = 67.5$$
Hence, $$2x > x + 30$$

14. **(D)** Substituting $x = 0$ and $y = 1$,

	$(x - y)^2$		$x^2 - y^2$
	$(0 - 1)^2$		$(0)^2 - (1)^2$
Then	1	$>$	-1

Now, substituting $x = -1$ and $y = 0$,

	$(-1 - 0)^2$		$(-1)^2 - (0)^2$
	$(-1)^2$		$(-1)^2$
Then	1	$=$	1

Since different values give different comparisons, no comparison can be made.

15. **(C)** It would be much too time consuming to multiply out 9^{19} or 9^{18}. Therefore, the quick way to solve this problem is to factor out column A as follows:

$$9^{19} - (8)9^{18}$$
$$(9^1)(9^{18}) - (8)9^{18}$$
$$(9^1 - 8)(9^{18})$$
$$(1)(9^{18})$$

Thus, they are equal.

Grid-in Questions

16. Answer: $\frac{5}{8}$—Multiplying both sides of the equation by the LCD of 5,

$$5(x + \tfrac{3}{5}x) = 5(1)$$
$$5x + 3x = 5$$
$$8x = 5$$
$$x = \tfrac{5}{8}$$

17. Answer: 14—Since 60% of the students are girls, 40% of the students are boys. Hence,

$$40\% \text{ of } 35 = (.40)(35)$$
$$= 14 \text{ boys}$$

18. Answer: 1/6—The average of any three numbers is equal to the sum of the numbers divided by 3.

$$\frac{1}{4} + \frac{1}{6} + \frac{1}{12} = \frac{3}{12} + \frac{2}{12} + \frac{1}{12}$$

The sum $$= \frac{6}{12}$$

$$= \frac{1}{2}$$

The average of the numbers is

$$\frac{1}{2} \div 3 = \frac{1}{2} \cdot \frac{1}{3} = 1/6$$

19. Answer: 93.5—

$$\frac{317.9 \text{ miles}}{17 \text{ gallons}} = \frac{x \text{ miles}}{5 \text{ gallons}}$$

$$17x = (317.9)(5)$$
$$17x = 1589.5$$
$$x = 1589.5 \div 17$$
$$x = 93.5 \text{ miles}$$

20. Answer: 527—The total of the five verbal SAT scores is 2.635. Dividing that total by 5 (the number of scores) gives 527 as the average.

21. Answer: 45—Since the sum of the measures of the angles of a quadrilateral is 360 and the ratio of the angle measures is 3:5:7:9,

$$3x + 5x + 7x + 9x = 360$$
$$24x = 360$$
$$x = 360 \div 24$$
$$x = 15$$

The smallest angle is $3x = (3)(15) = 45$.

22. Answer: 7/12—If Jim works for 2 days, he will complete 2/6, or 1/3, of the job. If Mike works for 2 days, he will complete 2/8, or 1/4, of the job. Together they will complete

$$1/3 + 1/4 = 4/12 + 3/12 = 7/12 \text{ of the job}$$

23. Answer: 50—Since BD is a diagonal of square ABCD,

$$BD = 5\sqrt{2}$$

$$\begin{aligned} \text{The area of square BDMN} &= (BD)^2 \\ &= (5\sqrt{2})^2 \\ &= 25 \times 2 \\ &= 50 \end{aligned}$$

24. Answer: 100—The greatest increase is indicated by the steepest rise in the graph lines, between 1991 and 1992. But you are looking for the greatest *percentage* increase, which means the increase as compared to the starting point. To find percentage increase:

$$\frac{\text{amount of increase}}{\text{starting point}} = \text{percentage increase}$$

Car Sales

1989–1990	20 to 25	$5/20 = 25\%$ increase
1990–1991	25 to 50	$25/25 = 100\%$ increase
1991–1992	50 to 90	$40/50 = 80\%$ increase
1992–1993	decrease	

25. Answer: 264—In $\triangle$MNP, PM = PN and $\angle$PMN = $\angle$PNM = 42°. Also, in $\triangle$MNP,

$$\angle PMN + \angle PNM + \angle MPN = 180°$$
$$42° + 42° + \angle MPN = 180°$$
$$84° + \angle MPN = 180°$$
$$\angle MPN = 96°$$

Since $\angle$MPN is a central angle,   arc MN = 96°

Also,   arc MN + arc MQN = 360°
$$96° + \text{arc MQN} = 360°$$
$$\text{arc MQN} = 264°$$

Critical Reading

1. (C) The passage makes no comment on the skills of the players in the earlier period as opposed to today. The first paragraph tells us that orchestra conducting is *less than 150 years old* and that it became necessary because orchestras began to increase in size in the late 1700s.

2. (E) The sentence structure suggests that *Apollonian* and *Dionysian* are parallel to *Mendelssohn* and *Wagner,* to *elegant* and *passionate,* and to *clear* and *emotional.* Although Apollo is the sun god, the best choice here is *clear* and *elegant.*

3. (C) The third paragraph discusses the difficulties of conducting, citing the conductor's having to *play* upon an instrument of one hundred musicians, while the singer or orchestral player must deal with only one.

4. (E) The author of Passage 1 presents the *ideal modern conductor* as a synthesis of the *elegant* and the *passionate* schools (lines 15–16, 20–22).

5. (B) The snide parenthesis manages to suggest that music critics are society ladies who are less interested in and less able to judge musical abilities than are musicians. Like the society women, the critics are more important to a conductor's success than are a conductor's real musical abilities. The sentence does not imply that critics are more interested in the players than in the conductor.

6. (B) The author compares conductors and politicians, suggesting that both are careerists. They are, like conductors, conspicuously *not* original, disciplined, modest, or indifferent to power.

7. (D) The phrase is in fact saying that conductors are self-centered, are egoists.

8. (C) The passage suggests that in the *musical community*—that is, the community of musicians and music lovers— music is paramount. In the *music-business community,* however, with its cult of personality, music is not the main concern. Although choices (D) and (E) may well be true, the passage does not deal with these issues.

9. (D) What the sentence in its roundabout way is really saying is that television, unfortunately, makes it possible for viewers to see the front of the conductor. In the concert hall, the conductor's back is to the audience, but television has made it possible for viewers to see every grimace of the conductor. To circumvent is to go around or to avoid, and *dorsal* means back.

10. (A) The phrase refers to *listen to the music.* The author implies that it will be so bad you had much better have stayed at home.

11. (E) At one time or another, the passage mocks or directly attacks conductors, politicians, the public, and the critics, but it spares the instrumentalists who play in the orchestras.

12. (A) Unlike the author of Passage 1, the author of Passage 2 wants no part of the conductor's personality or feelings to interfere with what the composer has written. The ideal performance would be *an exact realization of the score.* Since the second author is a composer, while the first is a conductor, these preferences are understandable.

13. (D) Both passages use the word *great,* but Passage 2 always puts quotation marks around the word. The author is quoting the word from people like the author of the first passage (and may, in fact, have the first passage specifically in mind), but *"great"* in the second passage is said with a sneer. It refers to so-called *"great"* conductors whose qualifications have too little to do with music.

14. (B) Both passages assume that a conductor will be male. Since that time, a small but increasing number of female conductors have appeared before the public. In addition, a gender-neutral style of writing has become more common.

SECTION 6: MATHEMATICAL REASONING

1. (A) $\dfrac{\text{percent}}{100} = \dfrac{\text{is number}}{\text{of number}}$

$$\dfrac{.25}{100} = \dfrac{x}{12}$$

Cross multiplying, $\quad 100x = 3.00$

$$\dfrac{100x}{100} = \dfrac{3.00}{100}$$

$$x = .03, \text{ or } \tfrac{3}{100}$$

2. (C) The maximum number of squares 1 inch by 1 inch will be 16.

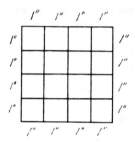

3. (E) Let x = original price. Then

$$x - .40x = 5.70$$
$$.60x = 5.70$$
$$x = 9.50$$

Hence, the book originally cost $9.50.

4. (A) Multiply the numerator and denominator by 12 (LCD).

$$\dfrac{12(\tfrac{2}{3} - \tfrac{1}{2})}{12(\tfrac{1}{6} + \tfrac{1}{4} + \tfrac{2}{3})} = \dfrac{8 - 6}{2 + 3 + 8} = \tfrac{2}{13}$$

5. (D) According to the graph, the tallest "B" (before) bar is county 4.

6. (B) Solve this problem by plugging in simple numbers. Start with 1, an odd integer.

$$(1 + 1) \text{ times } (2 \cdot 1 + 1)$$
$$= (2) \text{ times } (2 + 1)$$
$$= 2 \cdot 3$$
$$= 6 \text{ (not odd)}$$

Now, try 2, an even integer.

$$(2 + 1) \text{ times } (2 \cdot 2 + 1)$$
$$= (3) \text{ times } (4 + 1)$$
$$= 3 \cdot 5$$
$$= 15 \text{ (an odd integer)}$$

7. (C) Since two-thirds of the students are boys, $\frac{2}{3}(36) = 24$ boys in the class. Out of the 24 boys in the class, three-fourths of them are under six feet tall, or $\frac{3}{4}(24) = 18$ boys under six feet tall.

8. (D) Since the area of a trapezoid $= \frac{1}{2} \cdot h \cdot (b_1 + b_2)$, we need to find the altitude, h. Draw altitudes in the figure as follows:

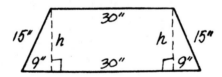

Since the triangles formed are right triangles, use the Pythagorean theorem, which says

$$c^2 = a^2 + b^2$$
$$15^2 = 9^2 + h^2$$
$$225 = 81 + h^2$$
$$h^2 = 225 - 81$$
$$h^2 = 144$$
$$h = \sqrt{144} = 12 \text{ inches}$$

Hence, the area of the trapezoid will be

$$\frac{1}{2} \cdot h \cdot (b_1 + b_2) = \frac{1}{2} \cdot 12 \cdot (30 + 48)$$
$$= (6)(78)$$
$$= 468 \text{ square inches}$$

9. **(D)** First, calculate the rates of production per day. Two of the factories each make $100,000/15 \cong 6667$ hubcaps per day. The third plant makes $1.3 \times 6667 \cong 8667$ hubcaps per day. The total production rate is $8667 + 2(6667) = 22,001$ hubcaps per day. At that rate, it would take 45.5 days to produce a million hubcaps.

10. **(B)** Area = ½ × base × altitude.

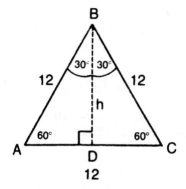

Since $\triangle BCD$ is a 30–60–90 triangle,

$$h = \frac{\sqrt{3}}{2}\,(BC)$$

$$= \frac{\sqrt{3}}{2}\,(12)$$

$$= 6\sqrt{3}$$

Hence,   area of $\triangle ABC = \frac{1}{2}(AC)(BD)$

$$= \frac{1}{2}(12)(6\sqrt{3})$$

$$= (6)(6\sqrt{3})$$

$$= 36\sqrt{3} \text{ square yards}$$

SECTION 7: VERBAL REASONING

Sentence Completion

1. (E) If trucks are the *only* means of transport, then there can be no public transportation, and a word that denotes this is needed. The best choice is *nonexistent,* that is, not in existence.

2. (D) The clue in the second part of the sentence describes the stories as often *less than three pages long.* Although any one of the answers could make sense, only *economy* is specifically related to the short length of the stories.

3. (B) For the first blank, each of the first four choices would be suitable, but the second blank requires a verb that follows from the parental sympathy with the program. Either (B) or (E) is appropriate, but *obligatory* is a better adjective choice than *habitual.*

4. (B) The missing word must describe someone who acts in opposition to the *best economic advisors.* Choices (A), (D), and (E) all denote a conservative, and choice (C) is neutral. A *maverick* is a person who acts independently, deriving from the term for an unbranded, lost calf that any rancher could claim.

5. (B) The *but* signals a word that is very different from *conservative* in meaning. Although *liberal* in some contexts is the opposite of *conservative,* that use refers to politics, not clothing, and the best choice here is (B) *flamboyant,* which means ornate or showy.

6. (D) If the protests put the warden at risk, they were probably *vigorous* or *outspoken* and not *tactful, realistic,* or *unregarded,* although *realistic* might work. *Poaching* is *illegal* but also very "something" that makes people risk breaking the law. The possibilities here are *profitable* or its synonym *lucrative.* The best choice, then, is (D), which has *outspoken protests* and *lucrative pursuit.*

7. (C) The *Although* signals the possibility of smaller particles being found, so (B) and (C) are the best first words. With the phrase *or are very close to* in the sentence, *have approached* is redundant, while *have reached* makes good sense.

8. (C) The blanks must be the opposites or contradictions of *affable* and *articulate,* given the *neither* and *nor.* Of the choices, not *morose* and not *reticent* would be the closest to *affable* and *articulate.* The adjectives *sullen, quiet,* or *aggressive* could work but not paired with the words given here.

9. (A) If there is a *problem* for Spanish composers, the missing word must be *refused.* With (B), (D), or (E), there would be no problem, and (C) makes no sense.

10. (A) The two missing adjectives modify *reason* and are defined by *not a change in thinking* and *but a shortage of money.* The choices that most clearly refer to belief and money are *ideological* and *economic.*

Analogies

11. (D) The motion of the *clipper ship* depends upon the *sail* as the motion of the *submarine* depends upon the *propeller.* Although helium may hold the dirigible up, it is not the force that moves the airship.

12. (D) A *nursery* is a place where *plants* are sold. A *bakery* is a place where *bread* is sold.

13. (C) *Witch* refers to a female with supernatural powers, a sorceress. The male is called a *sorcerer.* Similarly, a female singer in a lower register is a *contralto,* while a male is a *baritone.*

14. (D) The *janitor* is the person in charge of the maintenance of *building* property. The parallel here is a *ranger,* who is responsible for the *forest.*

15. (A) The nouns describe meals, one of the morning, one of the evening. The *lark* is conventionally presented as a dawn singer, while the *nightingale* is associated with evening or night. While it is true that *dinner* can also describe a midday meal, no answer choice provides a morning/midday option.

16. (B) A *ring* and a *bracelet* have the same shape, but the bracelet is larger. A *tennis ball* and a *basketball* are both spheres, with the larger second.

17. (A) *Walnut* is a kind of *wood* as a *parsnip* is a kind of *vegetable.*

18. (E) A *calorie* is a unit that measures *heat* as an *acre* is a unit of measurement for *area.*

19. (E) The *pope* is elected by the college of *cardinals* as a president is chosen by the *electoral college.*

20. (A) The *summation* is the final summing up of arguments in a *trial.* In a musical *composition,* the passage that brings it to an end is the *coda.*

21. (B) The adjective *capricious* describes a person who is governed by *whim* as *optimistic* describes a person who is governed by *hope.*

22. (C) A *bumpkin,* a loutish person, would be especially deficient in *urbanity,* suave and polished manners. Similarly, a *bigot* would lack *tolerance.*

Critical Reading

23. (A) Since all rain is naturally acidic, the passage suggests that the name is inadequate. Although the paragraph says that the name may sound *sinister,* it does not suggest that acid rain is not a serious problem. Acid rain with a low pH is a serious problem.

24. (E) It is areas downwind of industrial polluters that are likely to be affected by acid rain.

25. (A) It can be inferred that an acidic reading of less than pH 2, which is *six to eight times more acidic than vinegar,* is less than one point lower than the pH of vinegar, since *each integer is 10 times more acidic* than the one before it. So the vinegar pH would be approximately 2.

26. (E) The record itself is not in doubt. What is questionable is if this record for intense pollution is a record anyone would want to set.

27. (E) The pH scale is neutral at 7, more acid below, and more alkaline above. So pH 11 would be the most alkaline.

28. (C) In the fifth paragraph, the passage points to *natural alkaline rock, like limestone,* that *helps to neutralize acid rain.*

29. (C) The word *eerily* means strangely or weirdly.

30. (B) Irony is a set of circumstances or result that is just the opposite of what might be expected. Here the expected result was the solution to a pollution problem (the smokestacks), and the result was increased pollution somewhere else.

31. (D) A *feat* is an exploit, a remarkable achievement.

32. (A) The *silver lining* here was the beneficial effect of the sulfur emissions in fertilizing the soil. The reference to *cloud* is especially apt in this case.

33. (B) The seventh paragraph suggests that the chief opponents in the acid rain debate are the environmentalists who want the pollution reduced and the industrialists who would probably have to pay the cost of reducing emissions.

34. (D) The passage implies that choices (A), (B), (C), and (E) would reduce acid rain but does not present reduction of the use of sulfur fertilizer as an opportunity to stem pollution.

35. (D) Because the rain falls on places far from the source of the pollutants, crossing international boundaries into Canada or throughout Europe, the solution will have to be political and international.

PRACTICE TEST 3

ANSWER SHEET FOR PRACTICE TEST 3
(Remove This Sheet and Use It to Mark Your Answers)

CUT HERE

SECTION 1

1 Ⓐ Ⓑ Ⓒ Ⓓ Ⓔ
2 Ⓐ Ⓑ Ⓒ Ⓓ Ⓔ
3 Ⓐ Ⓑ Ⓒ Ⓓ Ⓔ
4 Ⓐ Ⓑ Ⓒ Ⓓ Ⓔ
5 Ⓐ Ⓑ Ⓒ Ⓓ Ⓔ

6 Ⓐ Ⓑ Ⓒ Ⓓ Ⓔ
7 Ⓐ Ⓑ Ⓒ Ⓓ Ⓔ
8 Ⓐ Ⓑ Ⓒ Ⓓ Ⓔ
9 Ⓐ Ⓑ Ⓒ Ⓓ Ⓔ
10 Ⓐ Ⓑ Ⓒ Ⓓ Ⓔ

11 Ⓐ Ⓑ Ⓒ Ⓓ Ⓔ
12 Ⓐ Ⓑ Ⓒ Ⓓ Ⓔ
13 Ⓐ Ⓑ Ⓒ Ⓓ Ⓔ
14 Ⓐ Ⓑ Ⓒ Ⓓ Ⓔ
15 Ⓐ Ⓑ Ⓒ Ⓓ Ⓔ

16 Ⓐ Ⓑ Ⓒ Ⓓ Ⓔ
17 Ⓐ Ⓑ Ⓒ Ⓓ Ⓔ
18 Ⓐ Ⓑ Ⓒ Ⓓ Ⓔ
19 Ⓐ Ⓑ Ⓒ Ⓓ Ⓔ
20 Ⓐ Ⓑ Ⓒ Ⓓ Ⓔ

21 Ⓐ Ⓑ Ⓒ Ⓓ Ⓔ
22 Ⓐ Ⓑ Ⓒ Ⓓ Ⓔ
23 Ⓐ Ⓑ Ⓒ Ⓓ Ⓔ
24 Ⓐ Ⓑ Ⓒ Ⓓ Ⓔ
25 Ⓐ Ⓑ Ⓒ Ⓓ Ⓔ

SECTION 2

1 Ⓐ Ⓑ Ⓒ Ⓓ Ⓔ
2 Ⓐ Ⓑ Ⓒ Ⓓ Ⓔ
3 Ⓐ Ⓑ Ⓒ Ⓓ Ⓔ
4 Ⓐ Ⓑ Ⓒ Ⓓ Ⓔ
5 Ⓐ Ⓑ Ⓒ Ⓓ Ⓔ

6 Ⓐ Ⓑ Ⓒ Ⓓ Ⓔ
7 Ⓐ Ⓑ Ⓒ Ⓓ Ⓔ
8 Ⓐ Ⓑ Ⓒ Ⓓ Ⓔ
9 Ⓐ Ⓑ Ⓒ Ⓓ Ⓔ
10 Ⓐ Ⓑ Ⓒ Ⓓ Ⓔ

11 Ⓐ Ⓑ Ⓒ Ⓓ Ⓔ
12 Ⓐ Ⓑ Ⓒ Ⓓ Ⓔ
13 Ⓐ Ⓑ Ⓒ Ⓓ Ⓔ
14 Ⓐ Ⓑ Ⓒ Ⓓ Ⓔ
15 Ⓐ Ⓑ Ⓒ Ⓓ Ⓔ

16 Ⓐ Ⓑ Ⓒ Ⓓ Ⓔ
17 Ⓐ Ⓑ Ⓒ Ⓓ Ⓔ
18 Ⓐ Ⓑ Ⓒ Ⓓ Ⓔ
19 Ⓐ Ⓑ Ⓒ Ⓓ Ⓔ
20 Ⓐ Ⓑ Ⓒ Ⓓ Ⓔ

21 Ⓐ Ⓑ Ⓒ Ⓓ Ⓔ
22 Ⓐ Ⓑ Ⓒ Ⓓ Ⓔ
23 Ⓐ Ⓑ Ⓒ Ⓓ Ⓔ
24 Ⓐ Ⓑ Ⓒ Ⓓ Ⓔ
25 Ⓐ Ⓑ Ⓒ Ⓓ Ⓔ

26 Ⓐ Ⓑ Ⓒ Ⓓ Ⓔ
27 Ⓐ Ⓑ Ⓒ Ⓓ Ⓔ
28 Ⓐ Ⓑ Ⓒ Ⓓ Ⓔ
29 Ⓐ Ⓑ Ⓒ Ⓓ Ⓔ
30 Ⓐ Ⓑ Ⓒ Ⓓ Ⓔ

331

ANSWER SHEET FOR PRACTICE TEST 3
(Remove This Sheet and Use It to Mark Your Answers)

SECTION 3

1 Ⓐ Ⓑ Ⓒ Ⓓ Ⓔ	6 Ⓐ Ⓑ Ⓒ Ⓓ Ⓔ	11 Ⓐ Ⓑ Ⓒ Ⓓ Ⓔ
2 Ⓐ Ⓑ Ⓒ Ⓓ Ⓔ	7 Ⓐ Ⓑ Ⓒ Ⓓ Ⓔ	12 Ⓐ Ⓑ Ⓒ Ⓓ Ⓔ
3 Ⓐ Ⓑ Ⓒ Ⓓ Ⓔ	8 Ⓐ Ⓑ Ⓒ Ⓓ Ⓔ	13 Ⓐ Ⓑ Ⓒ Ⓓ Ⓔ
4 Ⓐ Ⓑ Ⓒ Ⓓ Ⓔ	9 Ⓐ Ⓑ Ⓒ Ⓓ Ⓔ	14 Ⓐ Ⓑ Ⓒ Ⓓ Ⓔ
5 Ⓐ Ⓑ Ⓒ Ⓓ Ⓔ	10 Ⓐ Ⓑ Ⓒ Ⓓ Ⓔ	15 Ⓐ Ⓑ Ⓒ Ⓓ Ⓔ

16

17

18

19

20

21

ANSWER SHEET FOR PRACTICE TEST 3
(Remove This Sheet and Use It to Mark Your Answers)

CUT HERE

22

	⊘	⊘	
⊙	⊙	⊙	⊙
	⓪	⓪	⓪
①	①	①	①
②	②	②	②
③	③	③	③
④	④	④	④
⑤	⑤	⑤	⑤
⑥	⑥	⑥	⑥
⑦	⑦	⑦	⑦
⑧	⑧	⑧	⑧
⑨	⑨	⑨	⑨

23

	⊘	⊘	
⊙	⊙	⊙	⊙
	⓪	⓪	⓪
①	①	①	①
②	②	②	②
③	③	③	③
④	④	④	④
⑤	⑤	⑤	⑤
⑥	⑥	⑥	⑥
⑦	⑦	⑦	⑦
⑧	⑧	⑧	⑧
⑨	⑨	⑨	⑨

24

	⊘	⊘	
⊙	⊙	⊙	⊙
	⓪	⓪	⓪
①	①	①	①
②	②	②	②
③	③	③	③
④	④	④	④
⑤	⑤	⑤	⑤
⑥	⑥	⑥	⑥
⑦	⑦	⑦	⑦
⑧	⑧	⑧	⑧
⑨	⑨	⑨	⑨

25

	⊘	⊘	
⊙	⊙	⊙	⊙
	⓪	⓪	⓪
①	①	①	①
②	②	②	②
③	③	③	③
④	④	④	④
⑤	⑤	⑤	⑤
⑥	⑥	⑥	⑥
⑦	⑦	⑦	⑦
⑧	⑧	⑧	⑧
⑨	⑨	⑨	⑨

ANSWER SHEET FOR PRACTICE TEST 3
(Remove This Sheet and Use It to Mark Your Answers)

SECTION 4

1 Ⓐ Ⓑ Ⓒ Ⓓ Ⓔ
2 Ⓐ Ⓑ Ⓒ Ⓓ Ⓔ
3 Ⓐ Ⓑ Ⓒ Ⓓ Ⓔ
4 Ⓐ Ⓑ Ⓒ Ⓓ Ⓔ
5 Ⓐ Ⓑ Ⓒ Ⓓ Ⓔ

6 Ⓐ Ⓑ Ⓒ Ⓓ Ⓔ
7 Ⓐ Ⓑ Ⓒ Ⓓ Ⓔ
8 Ⓐ Ⓑ Ⓒ Ⓓ Ⓔ
9 Ⓐ Ⓑ Ⓒ Ⓓ Ⓔ
10 Ⓐ Ⓑ Ⓒ Ⓓ Ⓔ

11 Ⓐ Ⓑ Ⓒ Ⓓ Ⓔ
12 Ⓐ Ⓑ Ⓒ Ⓓ Ⓔ
13 Ⓐ Ⓑ Ⓒ Ⓓ Ⓔ
14 Ⓐ Ⓑ Ⓒ Ⓓ Ⓔ
15 Ⓐ Ⓑ Ⓒ Ⓓ Ⓔ

16 Ⓐ Ⓑ Ⓒ Ⓓ Ⓔ
17 Ⓐ Ⓑ Ⓒ Ⓓ Ⓔ
18 Ⓐ Ⓑ Ⓒ Ⓓ Ⓔ
19 Ⓐ Ⓑ Ⓒ Ⓓ Ⓔ
20 Ⓐ Ⓑ Ⓒ Ⓓ Ⓔ

21 Ⓐ Ⓑ Ⓒ Ⓓ Ⓔ
22 Ⓐ Ⓑ Ⓒ Ⓓ Ⓔ
23 Ⓐ Ⓑ Ⓒ Ⓓ Ⓔ
24 Ⓐ Ⓑ Ⓒ Ⓓ Ⓔ
25 Ⓐ Ⓑ Ⓒ Ⓓ Ⓔ

26 Ⓐ Ⓑ Ⓒ Ⓓ Ⓔ
27 Ⓐ Ⓑ Ⓒ Ⓓ Ⓔ
28 Ⓐ Ⓑ Ⓒ Ⓓ Ⓔ
29 Ⓐ Ⓑ Ⓒ Ⓓ Ⓔ
30 Ⓐ Ⓑ Ⓒ Ⓓ Ⓔ

31 Ⓐ Ⓑ Ⓒ Ⓓ Ⓔ
32 Ⓐ Ⓑ Ⓒ Ⓓ Ⓔ
33 Ⓐ Ⓑ Ⓒ Ⓓ Ⓔ
34 Ⓐ Ⓑ Ⓒ Ⓓ Ⓔ
35 Ⓐ Ⓑ Ⓒ Ⓓ Ⓔ

SECTION 5

1 Ⓐ Ⓑ Ⓒ Ⓓ Ⓔ
2 Ⓐ Ⓑ Ⓒ Ⓓ Ⓔ
3 Ⓐ Ⓑ Ⓒ Ⓓ Ⓔ
4 Ⓐ Ⓑ Ⓒ Ⓓ Ⓔ
5 Ⓐ Ⓑ Ⓒ Ⓓ Ⓔ

6 Ⓐ Ⓑ Ⓒ Ⓓ Ⓔ
7 Ⓐ Ⓑ Ⓒ Ⓓ Ⓔ
8 Ⓐ Ⓑ Ⓒ Ⓓ Ⓔ
9 Ⓐ Ⓑ Ⓒ Ⓓ Ⓔ
10 Ⓐ Ⓑ Ⓒ Ⓓ Ⓔ

SECTION 6

1 Ⓐ Ⓑ Ⓒ Ⓓ Ⓔ
2 Ⓐ Ⓑ Ⓒ Ⓓ Ⓔ
3 Ⓐ Ⓑ Ⓒ Ⓓ Ⓔ
4 Ⓐ Ⓑ Ⓒ Ⓓ Ⓔ
5 Ⓐ Ⓑ Ⓒ Ⓓ Ⓔ

6 Ⓐ Ⓑ Ⓒ Ⓓ Ⓔ
7 Ⓐ Ⓑ Ⓒ Ⓓ Ⓔ
8 Ⓐ Ⓑ Ⓒ Ⓓ Ⓔ
9 Ⓐ Ⓑ Ⓒ Ⓓ Ⓔ
10 Ⓐ Ⓑ Ⓒ Ⓓ Ⓔ

11 Ⓐ Ⓑ Ⓒ Ⓓ Ⓔ
12 Ⓐ Ⓑ Ⓒ Ⓓ Ⓔ
13 Ⓐ Ⓑ Ⓒ Ⓓ Ⓔ

ANSWER SHEET FOR PRACTICE TEST 3
(Remove This Sheet and Use It to Mark Your Answers)

SECTION 7

1 Ⓐ Ⓑ Ⓒ Ⓓ Ⓔ	6 Ⓐ Ⓑ Ⓒ Ⓓ Ⓔ	11 Ⓐ Ⓑ Ⓒ Ⓓ Ⓔ
2 Ⓐ Ⓑ Ⓒ Ⓓ Ⓔ	7 Ⓐ Ⓑ Ⓒ Ⓓ Ⓔ	12 Ⓐ Ⓑ Ⓒ Ⓓ Ⓔ
3 Ⓐ Ⓑ Ⓒ Ⓓ Ⓔ	8 Ⓐ Ⓑ Ⓒ Ⓓ Ⓔ	13 Ⓐ Ⓑ Ⓒ Ⓓ Ⓔ
4 Ⓐ Ⓑ Ⓒ Ⓓ Ⓔ	9 Ⓐ Ⓑ Ⓒ Ⓓ Ⓔ	14 Ⓐ Ⓑ Ⓒ Ⓓ Ⓔ
5 Ⓐ Ⓑ Ⓒ Ⓓ Ⓔ	10 Ⓐ Ⓑ Ⓒ Ⓓ Ⓔ	15 Ⓐ Ⓑ Ⓒ Ⓓ Ⓔ

16   17   18

19   20   21

ANSWER SHEET FOR PRACTICE TEST 3
(Remove This Sheet and Use It to Mark Your Answers)

22

	⊘	⊘	
⊙	⊙	⊙	⊙
	⓪	⓪	⓪
①	①	①	①
②	②	②	②
③	③	③	③
④	④	④	④
⑤	⑤	⑤	⑤
⑥	⑥	⑥	⑥
⑦	⑦	⑦	⑦
⑧	⑧	⑧	⑧
⑨	⑨	⑨	⑨

23

	⊘	⊘	
⊙	⊙	⊙	⊙
	⓪	⓪	⓪
①	①	①	①
②	②	②	②
③	③	③	③
④	④	④	④
⑤	⑤	⑤	⑤
⑥	⑥	⑥	⑥
⑦	⑦	⑦	⑦
⑧	⑧	⑧	⑧
⑨	⑨	⑨	⑨

24

	⊘	⊘	
⊙	⊙	⊙	⊙
	⓪	⓪	⓪
①	①	①	①
②	②	②	②
③	③	③	③
④	④	④	④
⑤	⑤	⑤	⑤
⑥	⑥	⑥	⑥
⑦	⑦	⑦	⑦
⑧	⑧	⑧	⑧
⑨	⑨	⑨	⑨

25

	⊘	⊘	
⊙	⊙	⊙	⊙
	⓪	⓪	⓪
①	①	①	①
②	②	②	②
③	③	③	③
④	④	④	④
⑤	⑤	⑤	⑤
⑥	⑥	⑥	⑥
⑦	⑦	⑦	⑦
⑧	⑧	⑧	⑧
⑨	⑨	⑨	⑨

SECTION 1: MATHEMATICAL REASONING

Time: 30 Minutes
25 Questions

DIRECTIONS

Solve each problem in this section by using the information given and your own mathematical calculations, insights, and problem-solving skills. Then select the one correct answer of the five choices given and mark the corresponding circle on your answer sheet. Use the available space on the page for your scratchwork.

Notes

(1) All numbers used are real numbers.
(2) Calculators may be used.
(3) Some problems may be accompanied by figures or diagrams. These figures are drawn as accurately as possible EXCEPT when it is stated in a specific problem that a figure is not drawn to scale. The figures and diagrams are meant to provide information useful in solving the problem or problems. Unless otherwise stated, all figures and diagrams lie in a plane.

Data That May Be Used for Reference

Area

rectangle

$A = lw$

triangle

$A = \frac{1}{2}bh$

circle

$A = \pi r^2$

circumference

$C = 2\pi r$

Volume

rectangular solid

$V = lwh$

right circular cylinder

$V = \pi r^2 h$

Pythagorean Relationship

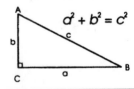

$a^2 + b^2 = c^2$

Special Triangles

30° – 60° – 90°

45° – 45° – 90°

A circle is composed of 360°
A straight angle measures 180°
The sum of the angles of a triangle is 180°

1. If $3m + n = 7$, then $9m + 3n =$
   (A) ⅐   (B) ⅓   (C) 10   (D) 21   (E) 63

2. If it takes 18 minutes to fill ⅔ of a container, how long will it take to fill the rest of the container at the same rate?
   (A) 6 minutes   (D) 27 minutes
   (B) 9 minutes   (E) 36 minutes
   (C) 12 minutes

3. What is the sales tax on $132.95 if the tax rate is 7%?
   (A) $0.93   (D) $63.06
   (B) $9.30   (E) $93.07
   (C) $9.31

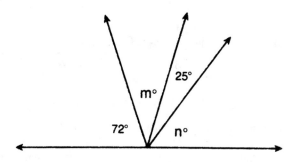

4. In the figure above, what is the number of degrees in the sum of $m + n$?
   (A) 103   (B) 97   (C) 93   (D) 83   (E) 72

5. The length of a rectangle is $6l$, and the width is $4w$. What is the perimeter?
   (A) $24lw$ (D) $12l + 8w$
   (B) $20lw$ (E) $6l + 4w$
   (C) $10lw$

6. If x is between 0 and 1, which of the following statements must be true?

   I. $x^2 > 1$
   II. $x^2 > 0$
   III. $x^2 > x$

   (A) I only   (D) I and II only
   (B) II only   (E) II and III only
   (C) III only

7. Tom is just 4 years older than Fran. The total of their ages is 24. What is the equation for finding Fran's age?

(A) $x + 4x = 24$

(B) $x + 4 = 24$

(C) $4x + x = 24$

(D) $x + (x + 4) = 24$

(E) $4x + 1 = 24$

8. If a plane travels 840 miles in 1½ hours, how many hours will it take for the plane to travel 3500 miles at the same speed?

(A) $2\frac{7}{9}$ (B) $4\frac{1}{16}$ (C) $5\frac{5}{6}$ (D) $6\frac{1}{4}$ (E) $6\frac{1}{2}$

9. What is 30% of $\frac{25}{18}$?

(A) $\frac{5}{108}$ (B) $\frac{5}{12}$ (C) $\frac{25}{54}$ (D) $\frac{25}{6}$ (E) $\frac{125}{3}$

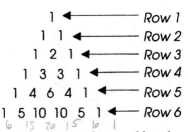

1 ← Row 1

1 1 ← Row 2

1 2 1 ← Row 3

1 3 3 1 ← Row 4

1 4 6 4 1 ← Row 5

1 5 10 10 5 1 ← Row 6

1 6 15 20 15 6 1

10. The seventh row in the diagram above could not have any

(A) even numbers

(B) odd numbers

(C) perfect numbers

(D) prime numbers

(E) perfect cube numbers

11. If $x = \frac{3}{4}$ and $y = \frac{4}{7}$, then $\dfrac{y - x}{y + x} =$

(A) -1 (B) $-\dfrac{5}{7}$ (C) $\dfrac{5}{37}$ (D) $\dfrac{1}{7}$ (E) $\dfrac{11}{21}$

12. In a class of 40 students, there are 24 girls. What percent of the class are boys?

(A) 16%   (B) 24%   (C) 40%   (D) 50%   (E) 60%

13. Bob is older than Jane, but he is younger than Jim. If Bob's age is b, Jane's age is c, and Jim's age is d, then which of the following is true?

(A) $c < b < d$

(B) $b < c < d$

(C) $b < d < c$

(D) $c < d < b$

(E) $d < c < b$

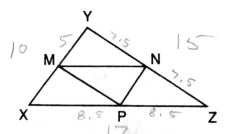

14. In △XYZ above, points M, N, and P are midpoints. If XY = 10, YZ = 15, and XZ = 17, what is the perimeter of △MNP?
    (A) 10⅔   (B) 14   (C) 16   (D) 21   (E) 42

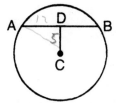

Note: Figure not drawn to scale.

15. On the circle above with center C, CD ⊥ AB, AB = 24, and CD = 5. What is the radius of the circle?
    (A) 19   (B) 17   (C) 13   (D) 12   (E) 7

16. George scored an average of 80% on three tests. What score must he get on the fourth test to bring his average to 85%?
    (A) 85%   (B) 88%   (C) 90%   (D) 95%   (E) 100%

17. The angles of a quadrilateral are in the ratio of 2:3:4:6. What is the degree measure of its largest angle?
    (A) 72°   (B)120°   (C) 144°   (D) 150°   (E) 180°

18. If $x(y - z) = t$, then $y =$
    (A) $(t/x) + z$ (D) $(t + z)/x$
    (B) tz/x (E) $t - x + z$
    (C) $t + x - z$

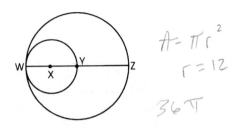

19. In the figure, X and Y are the centers of the two circles. If the area of the larger circle is 144π, what is the area of the smaller circle?
    (A) 72π (D) 12π
    (B) 36π (E) cannot be determined
    (C) 24π

20. If $m * n = \dfrac{m + n - 1}{n^2}$, then $2 * 3 =$

    (A) $\frac{4}{9}$ (B) $\frac{2}{3}$ (C) 1   (D) $1\frac{1}{3}$ (E) 2

21. If $\dfrac{a}{b} = \dfrac{c}{d}$ and $a, b, c,$ and d are positive integers, then which of the following is true?

    (A) $\dfrac{a}{b} = \dfrac{d}{c}$

    (B) $ac = bd$

    (C) $a + d = b + c$

    (D) $\dfrac{d}{b} = \dfrac{c}{a}$

    (E) $\dfrac{a}{d} = \dfrac{c}{b}$

$$6x - 12 = -6y$$
$$5y + 5x = 15$$

22. Which of the following is the number of solutions in the system of equations shown above?
    (A) More than three   (D) Exactly one
    (B) Exactly three   (E) None
    (C) Exactly two

23. If y varies directly as x and if $x = 18$ when $y = 12$, what is y when $x = 20$?
    (A) $11\frac{1}{5}$ (B) $13\frac{1}{3}$ (C) 14   (D) 16   (E) 30

24. If the diameter of circle R is 30% of the diameter of circle S, the area of circle R is what percent of the area of circle S?
    (A) 9%   (B) 15%   (C0 30%   (D) 60%   (E) 90%

25. The midpoint of xy is B. The coordinates of x are $(-4, 3)$, and the coordinates of B are $(5, -2)$. What are the coordinates of y?
    (A) $(\frac{1}{2}, \frac{1}{2})$ (D) $(14, -3)$
    (B) $(1, 1)$ (E) $(14, -7)$
    (C) $(6, -7)$

STOP. IF YOU FINISH BEFORE TIME IS CALLED, CHECK YOUR WORK ON THIS SECTION ONLY. DO NOT WORK ON ANY OTHER SECTION IN THE TEST.

SECTION 2: VERBAL REASONING

Time: 30 Minutes
30 Questions

In this section, choose the best answer for each question and blacken the corresponding space on the answer sheet.

Sentence Completion

DIRECTIONS

Each blank in the following sentences indicates that something has been omitted. Consider the lettered words beneath the sentence and choose the word or set of words that best fits the whole sentence.

1. As the boat drifted closer and closer to the rocks, the people on the beach became increasingly _____ about its safety.
   - (A) cowardly
   - (B) intrepid
   - (C) apprehensive
   - (D) eager
   - (E) receptive

2. If only a native can understand the dialect of this region, even the best foreign linguist will be _____ by the indigenous speakers.
   - (A) mistaken
   - (B) baffled
   - (C) misrepresented
   - (D) addressed
   - (E) translated

3. Carlson described the changes he had made in the story as merely _____, not censorship, because the alterations were made with the writer's prior knowledge and _____.
   - (A) editing . . . permission
   - (B) revising . . . prohibition
   - (C) expurgation . . . warrant
   - (D) corrections . . . disapproval
   - (E) decimation . . . connivance

4. The thousand-mile trek across the wilderness was a severe test of the children's _____ and their capacity to adapt.
   (A) proportion
   (B) immaturity
   (C) openness
   (D) weakness
   (E) resilience

5. A change in fashion to a very thin look is not just an innocent _____ or trend; it is a serious _____ for many women who may suffer from dangerous eating disorders.
   (A) victim . . . peril
   (B) prank . . . challenge
   (C) whim . . . undertaking
   (D) fad . . . hazard
   (E) idea . . . response

6. The public was _____ by the use of human bones and teeth in the jewelry and made their disapproval clear by refusing to buy any of the _____ items.
   (A) enthralled . . . unusual
   (B) fascinated . . . remarkable
   (C) horrified . . . ghoulish
   (D) repulsed . . . amiable
   (E) hypnotized . . . grisly

7. In the unsuccessful conference, none of the speakers _____ much response from the audience, but Dr. Schultz's address reached the _____ in tediousness.
   (A) aggrandized . . . pinnacle
   (B) elicted . . . nadir
   (C) attributed . . . record
   (D) raised . . . ebb
   (E) induced . . . medley

8. In a landscape so calm and beautiful, it was hard to believe that anything _____ could occur.
   (A) untoward
   (B) temperate
   (C) halcyon
   (D) seemly
   (E) refined

9. The land lying at even a slight distance from the river is not
_____, so the farming tribes _____ only the fields near its
banks.
(A) arable . . . cultivated
(B) barren . . . settled
(C) fallow . . . colonized
(D) fertile . . . shunned
(E) fertilizable . . . eschewed

Analogies

DIRECTIONS

In each question below, you are given a related pair of words or phrases.
Select the lettered pair that *best* expresses a relationship similar to that in
the original pair of words.

10. BOW : VIOLIN ::
(A) brass : tuba
(B) pedal : piano
(C) percussion : drum
(D) stop : clarinet
(E) drumstick : drum

11. SPEAR : SHIELD ::
(A) bomb : torpedo
(B) mace : trident
(C) fighter : aircraft carrier
(D) gun : bulletproof vest
(E) moat : portcullis

12. SKILLET : BACON ::
(A) palette : paints
(B) napkin : grease
(C) grass : lawnmower
(D) skeptic : doubt
(E) cocoon : twig

13. ARIA : OPERA::
(A) song : music
(B) waltz : dance
(C) chapter : novel
(D) artist : painting
(E) poem : epic

14. LOVER : ELOPE ::
    (A) thief : burglarize
    (B) army : retreat
    (C) convict : escape
    (D) coward : flee
    (E) embezzler : abscond

15. CALLOUS : TACT ::
    (A) certain : carelessness
    (B) dark : mourning
    (C) lethargic : speed
    (D) cheerful : joy
    (E) mature : growth

Critical Reading

DIRECTIONS

Questions follow each of the passages below. Using only the stated or implied information in each passage and in its introduction, if any, answer the questions.

Questions 16–22 are based on the following passage.

The rabies virus, which can cause disease in any mammal, is spread by the bite of an infected animal. It is lethal once symptoms develop but can be blocked by timely administration of a series of vaccine injections soon after an attack. The vaccine, which today
(5) may be given in an arm rather than the abdomen, is derived from a killed rabies virus. The inactivated virus prods the immune system to destroy active virus, especially when the injections are combined with application of rabies-specific antibodies to the wound area [see "Rabies" by Martin M. Kaplan and Hilary Koprowski;
(10) *Scientific American,* January 1980].

Unfortunately, in any year thousands of people who are probably uninfected undergo treatment because they do not know whether the animal that bit them had rabies. These high numbers are disturbing because therapy is costly and because vaccination of
(15) any kind carries a risk of side effects. (The expense is a major reason veterinarians and others who are very likely to encounter rabid animals are generally the only people immunized prophylactically.)

Even more distressing, most people who die of rabies are lost
(20) simply because they live in impoverished nations. Those who are
attacked by infected animals often lack access to therapy or cannot
pay for it.

Routine immunization of the animal species most likely to
transmit the virus to humans would be a more efficient, health-
(25) conscious way to save human lives and, not incidentally, to spare
animals from suffering. To an extent, such inoculation is already a
reality. In many wealthy nations, including the U.S., periodic
injection of pet dogs with vaccine has all but stopped canine
transmission to humans. Disease caused by cats can be limited in
(30) the same way.

In developing countries, however, obtaining veterinary care can
be extremely difficult, which is one reason why dogs continue to
account for at least 90 percent of all human deaths from rabies.
Another problem is that even where pet rabies is under good
(35) control, wild animals—not being very amenable to collection and
carting to the local veterinarian—pose a threat.

For these unattended groups, distribution of vaccine-laced baits
for animals to eat in the field is showing particular promise. This
approach is already halting the spread of rabies by foxes in many
(40) parts of western Europe and Canada. More preliminary work
suggests rabies in other species can be controlled as well.

Indeed, a vaccine-filled bait for raccoons is now being tested in
the U.S. If the results are good, the bait method might finally check
an epidemic of raccoon rabies that has been spreading up the East
(45) Coast from Florida since the 1950s. If baiting can be perfected for
distribution to dogs in developing countries, then the goal of
sharply curtailing human cases worldwide would finally seem
feasible.

This encouraging state of affairs stands in marked contrast to the
(50) situation in the 1960s, when research into vaccinating wild animals
started in earnest. By then immunization had already reduced the
incidence of dog rabies in the U.S. But infection by foxes, skunks,
raccoons and bats—the other significant rabies reservoirs in this
country—was a continuing concern. Compared with dogs, those
(55) groups have less direct contact with humans, but collectively they
are more abundant.

To control rabies in free-ranging animals, health officials in the
1950s had depended on thinning populations that harbored the
offending virus. They tried gassing of dens, poisoning, trapping and
(60) shooting, among other tactics. The workers reasoned that destruc-

tion of enough animals would so reduce a population that any
infected individuals would die without tangling with another
animal. When diseased creatures disappeared, only healthy ones
would remain. Yet the strategy halted the spread of the malady in
(65) target groups only some of the time.

16. All of the following could be infected with rabies EXCEPT
    (A) raccoons
    (B) cats
    (C) humans
    (D) skunks
    (E) carrion birds

17. The passage suggests that a human infected with rabies by a dog bite
    who did nothing for a long period of time would
    (A) be unable to spread the disease to another human
    (B) probably never be aware of having been infected
    (C) die
    (D) be cured by a vaccine injection
    (E) be cured by applying rabies-specific antibodies in the area of the
        bite

18. The passage suggests that throughout the world the largest cause of
    human exposure to the rabies virus is from
    (A) dogs that have not been immunized
    (B) dogs that have been immunized
    (C) cats that have not been immunized
    (D) cats that have been immunized
    (E) wild animals such as raccoons, foxes, or skunks

19. It can be inferred that the number of fatalities from rabies in the
    United States is small because

    I.   most dogs have been immunized by injections
    II. people exposed to the virus have access to immediate treatment
    III. the rabies virus is rare in the wild-animal populations of the United
         States

    (A) I only
    (B) I and II only
    (C) I and III only
    (D) II and III only
    (E) I, II, and III

20. As it is used in line 48, the word "feasible" means
    (A) unpredictable
    (B) inexpensive
    (C) hygienic
    (D) practicable
    (E) endurable

21. At present, humans infected with rabies virus can be treated by

    I. a vaccine injection in the abdomen
    II. a vaccine injection in the arm
    III. an oral recombinant vaccine

    (A) I only
    (B) II only
    (C) I and II only
    (D) II and III only
    (E) I, II, and III

22. Vaccine-laced baits would be most effective in preventing rabies among

    I. wild-animal populations susceptible to rabies
    II. domestic animals in areas where injections are impossible
    III. wild or domestic animals already infected with disease

    (A) III only
    (B) I and II only
    (C) I and III only
    (D) II and III only
    (E) I, II, and III

Questions 23–30 are based on the following passage.

The following passage is from the autobiography of a young black woman who was among the first women to attend the New England prep school St. Paul's.

     Outside my personal circle, the school that term seemed to buzz, buzz. Class officers, it seemed, were often called upon to talk. We talked day and evening, in club activities and rehearsals, in the houses, in the hallways, in our rooms, in the bathrooms, and in
(5) meetings after meetings. We gossiped. We criticized. We whined. We analyzed. We talked trash. We talked race relations, spiritual life, male-female relations, teacher-student trust. We talked confidentially. We broke confidences and talked about the results. We

talked discipline and community. We talked Watergate and social-
(10) fabric stuff.

I did not follow the Watergate hearings. I did not rush to the
third floor of the Schoolhouse for the ten-thirty *New York Times*
delivery to read about it; nor did I crowd around the common-room
TV to watch the proceedings. I could not bother to worry about
(15) which rich and powerful white people had hoodwinked which other
rich and powerful white people. It seemed of a piece with their
obsession with fairness.

I was unprepared, therefore, to dine at the Rectory with Mr.
Archibald Cox, the St. Paul's alumnus whom President Nixon had
(20) fired when, as U.S. Special Prosecutor, Mr. Cox began to reveal the
Watergate break-in and cover-up. Seated around him were the
Rector and a handful of faculty members and student leaders. I
said as little as possible in order to conceal my ignorance. Mr. Cox
was acute. He referred to the Watergate players and the major
(25) events in witty shorthand. I couldn't quite follow, so I ate and
smiled and made periodic conversation noises.

Then he wanted to hear about St. Paul's School. There had been
so many changes since his time. I found myself saying, in answer to
his question, or the Rector's signal, that I was more aware of being
(30) black at St. Paul's than I was of being a girl. I used a clever phrase
that I stole from somewhere and hoped he hadn't already heard:
"Actually, we're still more like . . . a boys' school with girls in it. But
black people's concerns—diversifying the curriculum and that sort
of thing—the truth is that that's more important to me than
(35) whether the boys have the better locker room."

Pompous it was, and I knew it, but better to be pompous in the
company of educated and well-off white folk, better even to be
stone wrong, than to have no opinion at all.

Mr. Cox thought a moment. God forbid he should go for the
(40) cross-examination. I added more. "Black concerns here at school
may look different, but are not really, from the concerns that my
parents have taught me all my life at home." I put that one in just
so he'd know that I had a family. "And believe me, sir, my mama
and daddy did not put President Nixon into the White House. *We*
(45) didn't do that!"

Mr. Cox wrinkled his lean, Yankee face into a mischievous smile.
His voice whispered mock conspiracy. He leaned toward me. "Do
you know who Nixon hates worst of all?"

I shook my head no. I had no idea.
(50)   "Our kind of people."

My ears felt hot. I wanted to jump on the table. I wanted go back home and forget that I'd ever come. I wanted to take him to West Philly, and drop him off at the corner of Fifty-second and Locust, outside Foo-Foo's steak emporium, right by the drug dealers, and
(55)   leave him there without a map or a bow tie. Then tell me about our kind of people.

The Rector gave me a look that urged caution. I fixed my face. "What kind of people are those?" I asked.

"Why, the educated Northeastern establishment," he said. The
(60)   Rector smiled as if relieved.

23. The speaker's lack of interest in the Watergate hearings is chiefly due to her
    (A) feeling alienated from the others at her school
    (B) concern with issues of gender rather than politics
    (C) belief that it was just another rich white person's problem
    (D) eagerness to be accepted by her peers at school
    (E) fear that it would separate her from her family's values

24. In line 16, the phrase "of a piece" means
    (A) consistent with
    (B) a small part of
    (C) indifferent to
    (D) partly to blame for
    (E) inconsistent with

25. The word "acute" in line 24 means
    (A) sharp-pointed
    (B) shrewd
    (C) critical
    (D) angular
    (E) severe

26. The speaker in line 40 uses the phrase "cross-examination" because
    (A) she wishes to amuse the others in the discussion
    (B) she feels she has committed a serious crime
    (C) she prefers to be wrong than to have no opinion at all
    (D) Archibald Cox is a lawyer
    (E) she has misunderstood Cox's questions

27. The speaker chooses which of the following words or phrases to deflate the seriousness or self-importance of what she has said?

      I. "social-fabric stuff" (lines 9–10)
     II. "conversation noises" (line 26)
   III. "that one" (line 42)

    (A) I only
    (B) II only
    (C) I and II only
    (D) I and III only
    (E) I, II, and III

28. When the speaker responds with the thoughts expressed in lines 51–55 ("my ears felt hot . . . people"), she is responding especially to what single word in the dialogue before?
    (A) "Nixon" (line 48)
    (B) "hates" (line 48)
    (C) "worst" (line 48)
    (D) "Our" (line 50)
    (E) "people" (line 50)

29. It can be inferred from the passage that the "Rector smiled as if relieved" (line 60) because he
    (A) has been afraid the speaker would say something shocking
    (B) disapproves of political arguments
    (C) has not understood what the speaker has been thinking
    (D) is too conventional to imagine a violent difference in opinion or in background
    (E) is amused by Archibald Cox's witty remark

30. The passage as a whole is characterized by the speaker's
    (A) lack of feeling and self-discipline
    (B) candor and self-awareness
    (C) bitterness and sense of unfairness
    (D) hypocrisy and self-deception
    (E) naivete and charm

STOP. IF YOU FINISH BEFORE TIME IS CALLED, CHECK YOUR WORK ON THIS SECTION ONLY. DO NOT WORK ON ANY OTHER SECTION IN THE TEST.

SECTION 3: MATHEMATICAL REASONING

Time: 30 Minutes
25 Questions

DIRECTIONS

This section is composed of two types of questions. Use the 30 minutes allotted to answer both question types. Your scratchwork should be done on any available space in the section.

Notes

(1) All numbers used are real numbers.
(2) Calculators may be used.
(3) Some problems may be accompanied by figures or diagrams. These figures are drawn as accurately as possible EXCEPT when it is stated in a specific problem that a figure is not drawn to scale. The figures and diagrams are meant to provide information useful in solving the problem or problems. Unless otherwise stated, all figures and diagrams lie in a plane.

Data That May Be Used for Reference

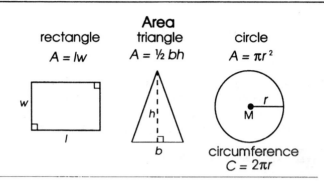

Area

rectangle	triangle	circle
$A = lw$	$A = \frac{1}{2}bh$	$A = \pi r^2$

circumference
$C = 2\pi r$

Volume

rectangular solid	right circular cylinder
$V = lwh$	$V = \pi r^2 h$

Pythagorean Relationship

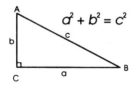

$$a^2 + b^2 = c^2$$

Special Triangles

30° – 60° – 90°   45° – 45° – 90°

A circle is composed of 360°
A straight angle measures 180°
The sum of the angles of a triangle is 180°

Quantitative Comparison

DIRECTIONS

In this section, you will be given two quantities, one in column A and one in column B. You are to determine a relationship between the two quantities and mark—

(A) if the quantity in column A is greater than the quantity in column B.
(B) if the quantity in column B is greater than the quantity in column A.
(C) if the quantities are equal.
(D) if the comparison cannot be determined from the information that is given.

AN (E) RESPONSE WILL NOT BE SCORED.

Notes

(1) Sometimes, information concerning one or both of the quantities to be compared is given. This information is not boxed and is centered above the two columns.

(2) All numbers used are real numbers. Letters such as a, b, m, and x represent real numbers.

(3) In a given question, if the same symbol is used in column A and column B, that symbol stands for the same value in each column.

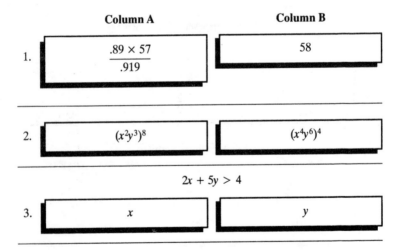

	Column A	**Column B**
1.	$\dfrac{.89 \times 57}{.919}$	58
2.	$(x^2 y^3)^8$	$(x^4 y^6)^4$

$$2x + 5y > 4$$

	Column A	**Column B**
3.	x	y

Column A	Column B

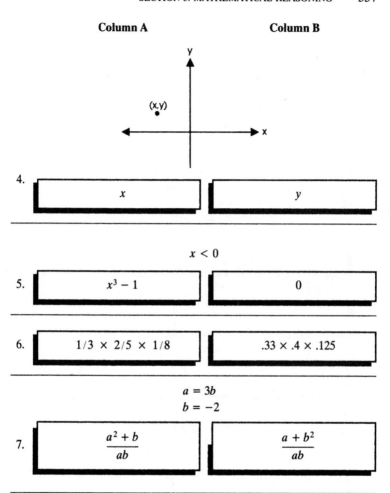

4.

x	y

$x < 0$

5.

$x^3 - 1$	0

6.

$1/3 \times 2/5 \times 1/8$	$.33 \times .4 \times .125$

$a = 3b$
$b = -2$

7.

$\dfrac{a^2 + b}{ab}$	$\dfrac{a + b^2}{ab}$

Questions 8–10 refer to the diagram.

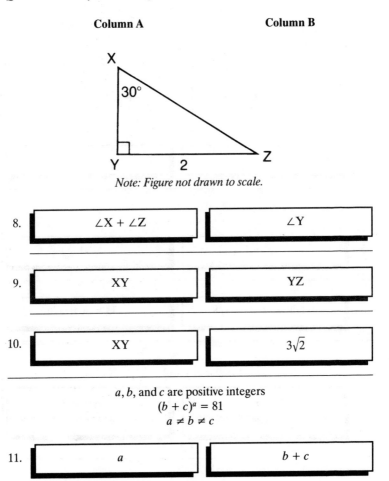

Column A   **Column B**

X

30°

Y   2   Z

Note: Figure not drawn to scale.

8. | ∠X + ∠Z | ∠Y |

9. | XY | YZ |

10. | XY | $3\sqrt{2}$ |

a, b, and c are positive integers
$(b + c)^a = 81$
$a \neq b \neq c$

11. | a | $b + c$ |

Questions 12–13 refer to the diagram.

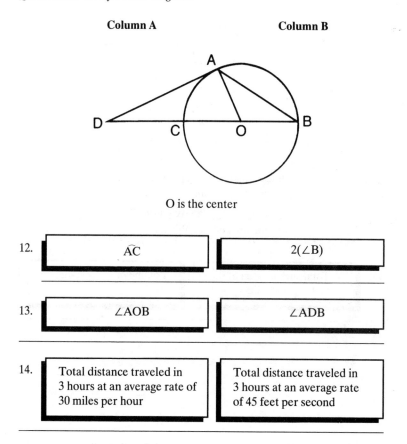

Column A   **Column B**

O is the center

12.

$\overarc{AC}$	$2(\angle B)$

13.

$\angle AOB$	$\angle ADB$

14.

Total distance traveled in 3 hours at an average rate of 30 miles per hour	Total distance traveled in 3 hours at an average rate of 45 feet per second

Column A   **Column B**

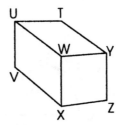

Note: Figure not drawn to scale.

Each dimension of the rectangular
solid above is an even number

The area of face **TUWY** is 20, and
the area of face **WXZY** is 8

15.   Total surface area of the   Volume of the rectangular
       rectangular solid   solid

Grid-in Questions

DIRECTIONS

Questions 16–25 require you to solve the problem and enter your answer by carefully marking the circles on the special grid. Examples of the appropriate way to mark the grid follow.

Answer: 3.7   **Answer: 1/2**

Answer: 1½

Do not grid in mixed numbers in the form of mixed numbers. **Always** change mixed numbers to improper fractions or decimals.

Change to 1.5   or   Change to 3/2

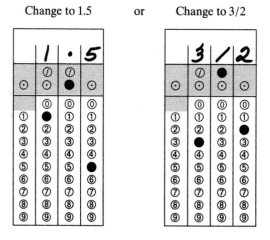

Answer: 123

Space permitting, answers may start in any column. Each grid-in answer below is correct.

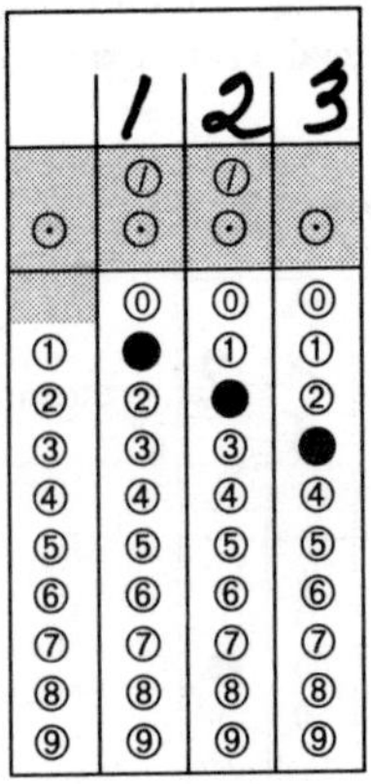

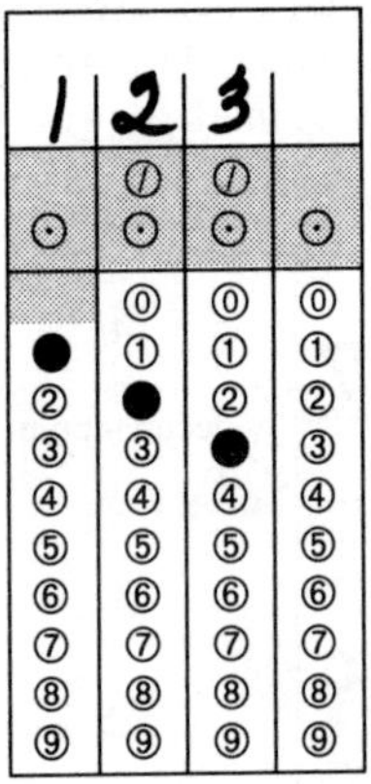

Note: Circles must be filled in correctly to receive credit. Mark only one circle in each column. No credit will be given if more than one circle in a column is marked. Example:

Answer: 258
No credit!!!!

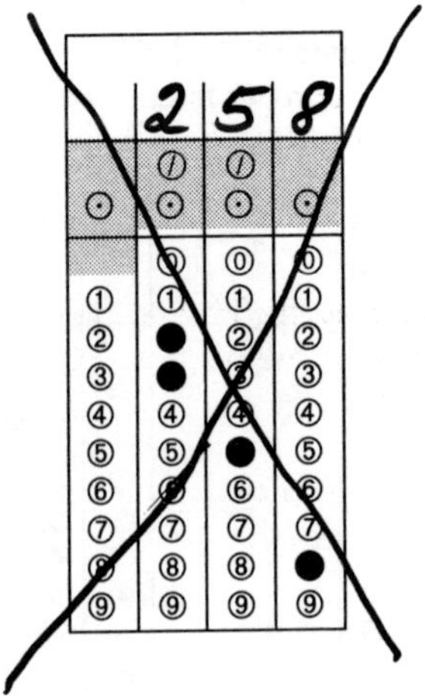

Answer: 8/9

Accuracy of decimals: Always enter the most accurate decimal value that the grid will accommodate. For example: An answer such as .8888 . . . can be gridded as .888 or .889. Gridding this value as .8, .88, or .89 is considered inaccurate and therefore **not acceptable**. The acceptable grid-ins of 8/9 are:

8/9   .888   .889

Be sure to write your answers in the boxes at the top of the circles before doing your gridding. Although writing out the answers above the columns is not required, it is very important to insure accuracy. Even though some problems may have more than one correct answer, grid only **one answer**. Grid-in questions contain no negative answers.

16. If $12a = 5b$, then $a/b =$

17. At a particular university, the ratio of males to females is 5 to 3. What percent of the students are female? (Disregard the % sign when gridding your answer.)

18. How many different outfits can be obtained from 5 shirts, 3 pairs of slacks, and 3 sports jackets?

19. If $\sqrt{m - 3} = 6$, then $m =$

Friendly Fruit Stand Price List

apples .... 60¢ each
bananas .... 20¢ each
cantaloupes .... 59¢ each or 2 for $1
oranges .... 39¢ each or 3 for $1

20. Mr. and Mrs. Adams are planning to attend a company picnic and need to make a fruit salad for the occasion. Their recipe calls for 5 apples, 10 bananas, 4 cantaloupes, and 5 oranges. Based on the prices given above, what is the least amount they could spend at the fruit stand to buy all the fruit they need for their salad? (Disregard the $ sign when gridding your answer.)

21. Ben's average for seven math exams is 89%. What percent must he score on the next exam to raise his average to 90%? (Disregard the % sign when gridding your answer.)

22. What is the area of a square whose diagonal has a length of 12?

Products	1980	1982	1984	1986	1988	1990
A	$4.20	$4.60	$5.00	$5.40	$5.80	$6.20
B	$6.30	$6.45	$6.60	$6.75	$6.90	$7.05

23. The chart above shows the prices of products A and B from 1980 to 1990. Using the chart, in what year will product A cost 40¢ more than product B?

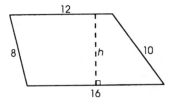

24. What is the height (*h*) of the trapezoid if its area is 98?

25. What is the length in centimeters of a chord that is 12 centimeters from the center of a circle whose radius is 20 centimeters?

STOP. IF YOU FINISH BEFORE TIME IS CALLED, CHECK YOUR WORK ON THIS SECTION ONLY. DO NOT WORK ON ANY OTHER SECTION IN THE TEST.

SECTION 4: VERBAL REASONING

Time: 30 Minutes
35 Questions

In this section, choose the best answer for each question and blacken the corresponding space on the answer sheet.

Sentence Correction

DIRECTIONS

Each blank in the following sentences indicates that something has been omitted. Consider the lettered words beneath the sentence and choose the word or set of words that best fits the whole sentence.

1. By banning cameras from the courtroom, the judge has _____ the public access to the most important civil-rights trial.
   (A) belied
   (B) denied
   (C) defied
   (D) afforded
   (E) disowned

2. The grocer reluctantly admitted that, despite his care, shoplifting was still _____.
   (A) exceptional
   (B) sporadic
   (C) commonplace
   (D) redundant
   (E) hackneyed

3. The work that once takes two men one week might well, one year later, take the same two men three weeks, since as Parkinson's law _____, "Work _____ so as to fill the time for its completion."
   (A) urges . . . grows easier
   (B) explains . . . becomes familiar
   (C) states . . . decreases
   (D) forbids . . . increases
   (E) asserts . . . expands

365

4. Although they loudly cheered the news of the renewed contract, the _____ of many workers was _____ by a fear that this would be the last year of government support.
    (A) sorrow . . . tempered
    (B) happiness . . . augmented
    (C) gladness . . . enervated
    (D) euphoria . . . moderated
    (E) buoyancy . . . debilitated

5. The local conversation was nothing if not _____, for no sentence was ever more than four words long.
    (A) ambiguous
    (B) timely
    (C) vague
    (D) terse
    (E) cordial

6. If both political parties can abandon _____ positions in the face of economic realities, a _____ may be achieved that will permit the government to function.
    (A) sensible . . . compromise
    (B) dogmatic . . . consensus
    (C) incisive . . . schism
    (D) irrational . . . dichotomy
    (E) reasoned . . . division

7. The universal Victorian preference of the more conventional morality of Charlotte Brontë to that of her sister is indicative of the nineteenth-century reader's _____ conformity.
    (A) impolitic
    (B) genteel
    (C) discordant
    (D) iconoclastic
    (E) individualistic

8. Though the first thirty pages are interesting and lively, chapter after chapter about obscure musicians grows _____, and the book never recovers the _____ of its opening chapter.
    (A) unmanageable . . . pace
    (B) tedious . . . verve
    (C) repetitive . . . torpor
    (D) dull . . . lethargy
    (E) boring . . . challenge

9. Some of the dangerous dishes on the menu are _____, but most are made without peppers or other spices and are as mild as most American restaurant food.
   (A) bland
   (B) palatable
   (C) torrid
   (D) insipid
   (E) piquant

10. As a young man, he regarded France as _____, but in his malcontent maturity, he considered visiting any place outside of Ireland to be _____.
    (A) hostile ... irritating
    (B) perfect ... jocund
    (C) irksome ... drab
    (D) Edenic ... perplexing
    (E) ideal ... painful

Analogies

DIRECTIONS

In each question below, you are given a related pair of words or phrases. Select the lettered pair that *best* expresses a relationship similar to that in the original pair of words.

11. SURFING : SKATEBOARDING ::
    (A) baseball : tennis
    (B) golf : football
    (C) bicycling : basketball
    (D) water-skiing : roller-skating
    (E) field hockey : ice hockey

12. VEGETARIAN : MEAT ::
    (A) dieter : food
    (B) teetotaler : alcohol
    (C) herbivore : grass
    (D) athlete : protein
    (E) dairy farmer : cheese

13. HONEYCOMB : WAX ::
    (A) worker : drone
    (B) beet : sugar
    (C) dress : designer
    (D) starch : shirt
    (E) kimono : fabric

14. TYPEWRITER : PENCIL ::
    (A) calculator : slide rule
    (B) paper clip : rubber band
    (C) mixer : refrigerator
    (D) rolling pin : ice tray
    (E) loaf pan : slotted spoon

15. QUIVER : ARCHER ::
    (A) pocket : wallet
    (B) holster : gun
    (C) forceps : surgeon
    (D) crossbow : arrow
    (E) dart : blowgun

16. DISINFECTANT : IODINE ::
    (A) gauze : adhesive tape
    (B) shampoo : styling gel
    (C) analgesic : aspirin
    (D) suture : surgeon
    (E) puncture : wound

17. DIGITAL : FINGER ::
    (A) aural : eye
    (B) orbital : planet
    (C) manual : hand
    (D) solar : star
    (E) radial : communication

18. SLOTH : RAIN FOREST ::
    (A) cow : barn
    (B) pride : ocean
    (C) Gila monster : desert
    (D) elephant : zoo
    (E) porpoise : water park

19. FOLLOW : ENSUE ::
    (A) request : litigate
    (B) inter : bury
    (C) ridicule : revere
    (D) propose : dispose
    (E) invoke : testify

20. DUCHY : DUKE ::
    (A) monarchy : queen
    (B) county : count
    (C) knighthood : knight
    (D) marchioness : marquis
    (E) estate : earl

21. QUILL : MANUSCRIPT ::
    (A) scalpel : operation
    (B) monk : prayer
    (C) brush : fresco
    (D) gearshift : automobile
    (E) editor : newspaper

22. DORSAL : VENTRAL ::
    (A) snowy : windy
    (B) dexterous : ambidextrous
    (C) red : crimson
    (D) retreating : advancing
    (E) oblique : indirect

23. VICTIM : MARTYR ::
    (A) trade : barter
    (B) action : crusade
    (C) zealot : fanatic
    (D) intention : purpose
    (E) liberty : freedom

Critical Reading

DIRECTIONS

Questions follow the passage below. Using only the stated or implied information in the passage and in its introduction, if any, answer the questions.

Questions 24–35 are based on the following passage.

Bilingual ballots have never enjoyed much public support because the public has never known much about their origin and rationale. For instance, it is often assumed that any non-English speaker is entitled to vote in his or her native tongue. The reality is
(5) that this right applies only to linguistic minorities who have historically faced discrimination at the polls—Hispanics, Asians, and Native Americans—and only in areas where they meet strict requirements. A language group must represent more than 5 percent of the local population and have below-average rates of
(10) voter turnout and English literacy. Moreover, the cost of assisting non-English-speaking voters is quite modest. San Francisco officials have estimated that the annual expense of trilingual English-Spanish-Chinese ballots comes to less than three cents per household. In 1984, a federal survey of eighty-three "covered" jurisdictions
(15) found that it cost them a grand total of $388,000, or 7.6 percent of election expenses, to provide bilingual ballots. Hardly an exorbitant price to safeguard what the Supreme Court has called a "fundamental right because it is preservative of all rights."

The trend toward bilingual ballots originated in the Voting
(20) Rights Act of 1965. This law suspended literacy requirements for voting in southern states where they had been systematically used to disfranchise African-Americans. A related provision, sponsored by Senator Robert F. Kennedy, prohibited such tests elsewhere for voters who had completed the sixth grade on U.S. soil in a school
(25) whose "predominant classroom language was other than English." In other words, native-born U.S. citizens could no longer be prevented from voting simply because they had grown up in a non-English-speaking environment. Puerto Ricans were the main beneficiaries of this section, particularly in New York, where a
(30) 1921 amendment to the state constitution (aimed principally at Yiddish-speaking Jews) had denied the franchise to anyone unable to read English.

Federal courts soon went further. Banning English literacy tests
was a hollow gesture, they reasoned, if formerly excluded voters
(35) still faced a language barrier at the polls. Accordingly, they
mandated bilingual election materials for Puerto Rican voters in
Philadelphia, Chicago, and New York. "It is simply fundamental,"
wrote one judge, "that voting instructions and ballots, in addition
to any other material which forms part of the official communica-
(40) tion to registered voters prior to an election, must be in Spanish as
well as in English, if the vote of Spanish-speaking citizens is not to
be seriously impaired."

Bilingual voting, like bilingual education, was designed to
compensate for decades of inequality, a goal that could not be
(45) achieved through strictly "equal" treatment. Simply prohibiting
the English literacy test, or ending the segregation of Mexican and
Chinese American students, was insufficient to restore rights that
linguistic minorities had lost through no fault of their own. For
such groups, affirmative measures were needed to guarantee equal
(50) opportunity. Clearly, this approach can lead to anomalies, as when
naturalized citizens of "Spanish origin" are entitled to bilingual
ballots but their Portuguese- or French-speaking neighbors are
not. Congressional critics of the expanded Voting Rights Act have
argued that its effect is "to mandate an 'unequal protection of the
(55) laws,' " privileging some minority voters over others from non-
English-speaking backgrounds—namely, that it favors nonwhite
immigrants and indigenous minorities over white Euro-ethnics.

Under current law an individual's need for a bilingual ballot
does not enter into the equation. Perhaps it should. Why encour-
(60) age immigrants to become U.S. citizens and then limit their ability
to participate in our political system? Why not make every effort to
eliminate language barriers to voting? It is true that most appli-
cants for naturalization must pass an English literacy test (except
for those aged fifty or older who have been legal U.S. residents for
(65) at least twenty years). But the level of proficiency required is quite
low. In 1982, an average year, the Immigration and Naturalization
Service turned down only twenty-nine out of 201,507 petitions for
citizenship because of inability to speak, read, or write the English
language. The literacy skills required to decipher voter registration
(70) notices or complex ballot propositions are normally the last to be
acquired in a second language.

24. It can be inferred from the passage that objections have been made to the use of bilingual ballots on the grounds that

   I. they cost too much taxpayer money
  II. any non-English speaker can demand a bilingual ballot
 III. any Spanish-speaking voter can demand a bilingual ballot

  (A) I only
  (B) I and II only
  (C) I and III only
  (D) II and III only
  (E) I, II, and III

25. Which of the following non-English-speaking groups could qualify for a bilingual ballot in an American election at the present time?
  (A) An Italian-speaking group making up 6 percent of the local population
  (B) A Samoan-speaking group making up 2 percent of the local population
  (C) A Portuguese-speaking group with above-average rates of English literacy
  (D) A Korean-speaking group making up 12 percent of the local population
  (E) A Spanish-speaking group with above-average rates of voter turnout

26. In the first paragraph, the concluding phrase, "fundamental right because it is preservative of all rights," refers to the fact that
  (A) laws are necessary to preserve order and justice in any society
  (B) the courts must be the final arbiter of what is and what is not permitted
  (C) by voting, citizens can guarantee that all their other rights are not lost
  (D) the rights of one class or group must be preserved for all classes or groups
  (E) the freedom of the citizenry is more important than the expenditure of a small sum of money

27. Under the Voting Rights Act of 1965, a native-born, Spanish-speaking American citizen who did not read English would
    (A) not be permitted to vote under any circumstances
    (B) not be permitted to vote if he or she had completed six grades in any school
    (C) be permitted to vote under any circumstances
    (D) be permitted to vote if he or she had completed six grades in a Spanish-speaking school in the United States
    (E) be permitted to vote if he or she passed a literacy test

28. The second paragraph suggests that, before 1965, there were laws designed to keep all of the following from voting EXCEPT
    (A) native-born Hispanics
    (B) Irish Catholics
    (C) African-Americans
    (D) Yiddish-speaking Jews
    (E) foreign-language speakers unable to speak English

29. The word "franchise" in line 31 means
    (A) ownership
    (B) marketing privilege
    (C) the right to vote
    (D) corporate rights
    (E) a team that represents a city

30. In line 34, the phrase "a hollow gesture" can be best interpreted to mean
    (A) a useless action
    (B) a resounding success
    (C) an empty boast
    (D) a sacred motion
    (E) a foolish joke

31. Which of the following statements could reasonably be used to argue against the belief that all the laws supporting bilingual voting should be repealed because they discriminate against white immigrants from Europe?

    I. Since many native English speakers have trouble understanding the complex language of ballots, non-English speakers are not at a serious disadvantage.
    II. Though the laws may be imperfect, it is better to spare a large number of other voters from discrimination.
    III. Elimination of bilingual voting would decrease the incidence of election fraud.

    (A) I only
    (B) II only
    (C) III only
    (D) I and II only
    (E) I, II, and III

32. Bilingual voting equality could not be achieved by strictly equal treatment of all foreign-language speakers because
    (A) some minorities had been subject to unequal treatment for many years
    (B) the complexity of Asian languages is greater than that of European languages
    (C) the costs of printing languages such as Korean or Chinese are higher than those for printing Spanish
    (D) some minorities control more of the wealth than others
    (E) under any circumstances, equal treatment is impossible because all minorities are different

33. Which of the following citizens would probably have the most difficulty in obtaining a bilingual ballot in his or her native language?
    (A) A Hispanic immigrant from Argentina
    (B) A white immigrant from Spain
    (C) A white immigrant from Greece
    (D) A non-white immigrant from Taiwan
    (E) A Hispanic immigrant from El Salvador

34. The effect of the final paragraph of the passage is to suggest that

   I. the literacy test required of naturalized citizens is an inadequate
      test of the literacy required of a voter
   II. the Voting Rights Act of 1965 is inadequate and additional laws
       should be enacted to enable all voters to vote
   III. the availability of a bilingual ballot should be determined chiefly by
        the voters' need for language assistance

   (A) III only
   (B) I and II only
   (C) I and III only
   (D) II and III only
   (E) I, II, and III

35. From this passage, the reader can infer that the author's attitude
    toward the "English Only" movement, a group urging the elimination
    of bilingual schools and ballots, is one of
    (A) enthusiastic approval
    (B) guarded approval
    (C) approval in theory, but not in practice
    (D) guarded disapproval
    (E) strong disapproval

STOP. IF YOU FINISH BEFORE TIME IS CALLED, CHECK YOUR
WORK ON THIS SECTION ONLY. DO NOT WORK ON ANY
OTHER SECTION IN THE TEST.

SECTION 5: MATHEMATICAL REASONING

Time: 15 Minutes
10 Questions

DIRECTIONS

Solve each problem in this section by using the information given and your own mathematical calculations, insights, and problem-solving skills. Then select the one correct answer of the five choices given and mark the corresponding circle on your answer sheet. Use the available space on the page for your scratchwork.

Notes

(1) All numbers used are real numbers.
(2) Calculators may be used.
(3) Some problems may be accompanied by figures or diagrams. These figures are drawn as accurately as possible EXCEPT when it is stated in a specific problem that a figure is not drawn to scale. The figures and diagrams are meant to provide information useful in solving the problem or problems. Unless otherwise stated, all figures and diagrams lie in a plane.

Data That May Be Used for Reference

Area

rectangle	triangle	circle
$A = lw$	$A = \frac{1}{2}bh$	$A = \pi r^2$

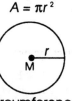

circumference
$C = 2\pi r$

Volume

rectangular solid
$V = lwh$

right circular cylinder
$V = \pi r^2 h$

Pythagorean Relationship

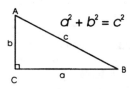

$a^2 + b^2 = c^2$

Special Triangles

30° – 60° – 90°

45° – 45° – 90°

A circle is composed of 360°
A straight angle measures 180°
The sum of the angles of a triangle is 180°

1. If $3/x = 6$, then $x - 1 =$
   (A) 1   (B) ½   (C) −½   (D) −⅔   (E) −1½

2. What is the reciprocal of $\dfrac{.25 \times \dfrac{2}{3}}{.06 \times 15}$?

   (A) ³⁄₂₀   (B) ⁵⁄₂₇   (C) ⅔   (D) ²⁷⁄₅   (E) ²⁰⁄₃

3. Harmon's new sports car averages 35 miles per each gallon of gasoline. Assuming that Harmon is able to maintain his average miles per gallon, how far can he drive on 12 gallons of gas?
   (A) Almost 3 miles   (D) 420 miles
   (B)   42 miles   (E) 700 miles
   (C) 350 miles

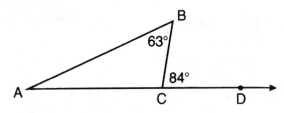

4. Given △ABC with ∠BCD = 84° and ∠B = 63°, what is the measure of ∠A?
   (A) 21°   (B) 27°   (C) 84°   (D) 96°   (E) 116°

5. Teachers will be assigned special camp duty one day of the week during a seven-day camping trip. If all the days of the week (Monday through Sunday) are tossed into a cap and each teacher chooses one day of the week, what is the probability that the first teacher will randomly select a weekday (Monday through Friday)?
   (A) ⅐   (B) 2⁄7   (C) ⅕   (D) 5⁄7   (E) ½

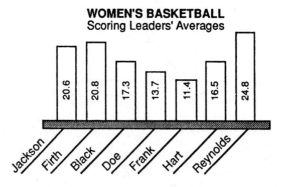

WOMEN'S BASKETBALL
Scoring Leaders' Averages

Jackson 20.6 Firth 20.8 Black 17.3 Doe 13.7 Frank 11.4 Hart 16.5 Reynolds 24.8

6. According to the bar graph above, Reynolds's average score exceeds Doe's average score by how many points?
   (A) 13.4   (B) 11.1   (C) 8.3   (D) 7.4   (E) 2.3

7. Given positive integer y, which of the following CANNOT be evenly divisible by y?
   (A) $y + 1$ (D) $y - 1$
   (B) $y + 2$ (E) $y + ½$
   (C) $2y + 1$

8. What is the total surface area in square meters of a rectangular solid whose length is 7 meters, width is 6 meters, and depth is 3 meters?
   (A) $32m^2$ (D) $162m^2$
   (B) $81m^2$ (E) $252m^2$
   (C) $126m^2$

9. A girl runs k miles in n hours. How many miles will she run in x hours at the same rate?
   (A) knx (B) k/n (C) kx/n (D) kx (E) kn/x

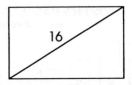

Note: Figure not drawn to scale.

10. If the diagonal of a rectangle is 16, then what is its area in square units?
    (A) 32   (D) 256
    (B) 64   (E) cannot be determined
    (C) 160

STOP. IF YOU FINISH BEFORE TIME IS CALLED, CHECK YOUR WORK ON THIS SECTION ONLY. DO NOT WORK ON ANY OTHER SECTION IN THE TEST.

SECTION 6: VERBAL REASONING

Time: 15 Minutes
13 Questions

In this section, choose the best answer for each question and blacken the corresponding space on the answer sheet.

Critical Reading

DIRECTIONS

Questions follow the two passages below. Using only the stated or implied information in each passage and in its introduction, if any, answer the questions.

Questions 1–13 are based on the following passages.

The following are critical commentaries by two well-known American film reviewers on the 1960s film The Graduate.

Passage 1

The Graduate is a director's picture because even its mistakes are the proofs of a personal style. Style is more an attitude toward things than the things themselves. It can be a raised eyebrow or a nervous smile or a pair of shrugged shoulders. It can even be an
(5)   averted glance. By playing down some of the more offensive qualities of the book, Nichols expresses his own attitude toward the material. The main trouble with the book is its reduction of the world to the ridiculous scale of an overgrown and outdated Holden Caulfield. Charles Webb's Benjamin Braddock expresses himself
(10)   with a monosyllabic smugness that becomes maddeningly self-indulgent as the book unravels into slapstick passion. He is superior to his pathetic parents and adults generally. He is kind to the wife of his father's law partner even though she seduces him with cold-bloodedly calculating carnality. Ben then falls in love with
(15)   Elaine, his mistress's daughter, and makes her marry him through the sheer persistence of his pursuit.

The screenplay has been improved by a series of little changes and omissions constituting a pattern of discretion and abstraction. The hero is made less bumptious, the predatory wife less calculat-
(20)   ing, the sensitive daughter less passive, and the recurring parental admonitions are reduced in number and intensity. The very end of

381

the movie is apparently the result of an anti-cliché improvisation. In the book, Ben interrupts Elaine's wedding (to another) before the troths have been plighted. In the movie, the bride kisses the
(25) groom before Ben can disrupt the proceeding, but the bride runs off just the same. And this little change makes all the difference in dramatizing the triumph of people over proceedings. An entire genre of Hollywood movies had been constructed upon the suspenseful chase-to-the-altar proposition that what God hath
(30) joined together no studio scriptwriter can put asunder. *The Graduate* not only shatters this monogamous mythology; it does so in the name of a truer love. . . . I was with *The Graduate* all the way because I responded fully to its romantic feelings. Some people have complained that the Bancroft-Hoffman relationship is more
(35) compelling than the subsequent Ross-Hoffman relationship. I don't agree. It is easier to be interesting with an unconventional sexual relationship than with a conventional love pairing. *The Graduate* is moving precisely because its hero passes from a premature maturity to an innocence regained, an idealism recon-
(40) firmed. That he is so much out of his time and place makes him more of an individual and less of a type. Even the overdone caricatures that surround the three principals cannot diminish the cruel beauty of this love story.

Passage 2

Part of the fun of movies is in seeing "what everybody's talking
(45) about," and if people are flocking to a movie, or if the press can con us into thinking that they are, then ironically, there is a sense in which we want to see it, even if we suspect we won't enjoy it, because we want to know what's going on. Even if it's the worst inflated pompous trash that is the most talked about (and it usually
(50) is) and even if that talk is manufactured, we want to see the movies because so many people fall for whatever is talked about that they make the advertisers' lies true.

An analyst tells me that when his patients are not talking about their personal hang-ups and their immediate problems they talk
(55) about the situations and characters in movies like *The Graduate,* and they talk about them with as much personal involvement as about their immediate problems. The high-school and college students identifying with Dustin Hoffman's Benjamin are not that different from the stenographer who used to live and breathe with
(60) the Joan Crawford-working girl and worry about whether that rich boy would really make her happy—and considered her pictures

"great." They don't see the movie as a movie but as part of the soap opera of their lives. The person who responds this way does not respond more freely but less freely and less fully than the person
(65) who is aware of what is well done and what badly done in a movie, who can accept some things in it and reject others, who uses all his senses in reacting, not just his emotional vulnerabilities. The small triumph of *The Graduate* was to have domesticated alienation and the difficulty of communication, by making what Benjamin is
(70) alienated from a middle-class comic strip and making it absurdly evident that he has nothing to communicate—which is just what makes him an acceptable hero for the large movie audience. *The Graduate* isn't a *bad* movie, it's entertaining, though in a fairly slick way. What's surprising is that so many people take it so seriously.
(75) What's funny about the movie are the laughs on that dumb sincere boy who wants to talk about art in bed. But then the movie begins to pander to youthful narcissism, glorifying his innocence, and making the predatory (and now crazy) woman the villainess. Commercially this works: the inarticulate dull boy becomes a
(80) romantic hero for the audience to project into with all those squishy and now conventional feelings of look, his parents don't communicate with him; look, he wants truth not sham, and so on. But the movie betrays itself and its own expertise, sells out its comic moments that click along with the rhythm of a hit Broadway show,
(85) to make the oldest movie pitch of them all—asking the audience to identify with the simpleton who is the latest version of the misunderstood teen-ager and the pure-in-heart boy next door. It's almost painful to tell kids who have gone to see *The Graduate* eight times that once was enough for you because you've already seen it
(90) [in other versions]. How could you convince them that a movie that sells innocence is a very commercial piece of work when they're so clearly in the market to buy innocence? *The Graduate* only wants to succeed and that's fundamentally what's the matter with it. This kind of moviemaking shifts values, shifts focus, shifts emphasis,
(95) shifts everything for a sure-fire response. Mike Nichols's "gift" is that he lets the audience direct him; this is demagoguery in the arts.

What's interesting about the success of *The Graduate* is sociological: the revelation of how emotionally accessible modern youth is
(100) to the same old manipulation. The recurrence of certain themes in movies suggests that each generation wants romance restated in slightly new terms, mooning away in fixation on themselves and thinking this fixation meant movies had suddenly become an art, and *their* art.

1. It can be inferred from the first paragraph of Passage 1 that Charles Webb is
   (A) the director of the film *The Graduate*
   (B) the author of the novel on which the film *The Graduate* is based
   (C) the author of the screenplay of *The Graduate*
   (D) the actor playing Benjamin Braddock in the film *The Graduate*
   (E) a character in *The Catcher in the Rye*

2. In Passage 1, line 5, the phrase "playing down" means
   (A) concluding
   (B) minimizing
   (C) making unscrupulous use of
   (D) excluding
   (E) participating in

3. By referring to the novel *The Graduate*'s "reduction of the world to the ridiculous scale of an overgrown and outdated Holden Caulfield" (the hero of Salinger's *The Catcher in the Rye*), the author of the Passage 1 suggests that

   I. the characterization of Benjamin Braddock in the novel is inferior to that in the film
   II. the Salinger novel is overgrown and outdated
   III. the film is superior to the novel *The Graduate*

   (A) III only
   (B) I and II only
   (C) I and III only
   (D) II and III only
   (E) I, II, and III

4. As it is used in Passage 1, the word "bumptious" (line 19) means
   (A) passive
   (B) slovenly
   (C) yokel-like
   (D) arrogant
   (E) jolting

5. According to the critic of Passage 1, the most original event in the plot of the film is having
   (A) Benjamin fall in love with Elaine, the daughter of his mistress
   (B) the older woman the seducer of the younger man
   (C) Benjamin pursue Elaine despite her engagement to another man
   (D) Benjamin interrupt Elaine's wedding after vows are exchanged
   (E) the young lovers united at the end

6. According to Passage 1, the theme of the film *The Graduate* is the
   (A) recovery of idealism through love
   (B) self-indulgent narcissism of youth
   (C) older generation's failure to nurture the younger
   (D) myth of the monogamous marriage
   (E) superiority of institutions to people

7. The argument of the first paragraph of Passage 2 (lines 44–52) is that
   (A) the advertising for films is often false
   (B) too many people believe advertisers and go to bad movies as a result
   (C) people go to movies partly to discover what has made a film popular or talked about
   (D) people waste time and money at trashy movies because they cannot see the falsity of advertising
   (E) more people would go to better films if advertising were more honest

8. According to the critic of Passage 2, the popular success of *The Graduate* is due to the fact that Benjamin
   (A) is empty-headed
   (B) is alienated
   (C) is unable to communicate with his parents
   (D) matures in the course of the film
   (E) is sincere

9. In Passage 2, the meaning of the word "gift" in line 95 is
   (A) present
   (B) talent
   (C) secret
   (D) idea
   (E) blessing

10. When Passage 2 says that Mike Nichols "lets the audience direct him" (line 96), it is saying that
    (A) a good director has a firm hold on all the details of a film
    (B) Nichols's films are badly directed because they are too difficult for many audiences to follow
    (C) Nichols does not pay enough attention to the needs of his actors
    (D) Nichols gives the audience what he knows it likes
    (E) Nichols is indifferent to commercial success

11. According to Passage 2, *The Graduate* is sociologically valuable because it
    (A) exposes the sentimentality of a generation
    (B) expresses the universality of alienation in the modern world
    (C) teaches mutual respect between the sexes
    (D) expresses the nature of the difficulties generations that cannot communicate must face
    (E) reveals how different the generation of the late 1960s is from older generations

12. Of the following phrases from Passage 2, all might be applied by their author to the author of the first passage EXCEPT
    (A) a critic who is "not that different from the stenographer who used to live and breathe with the Joan Crawford-working girl" (lines 58–60)
    (B) a critic who sees a movie as "part of the soap opera of" his life (lines 62–63)
    (C) a critic who "uses all his senses in reacting, not just his emotional vulnerabilities" (lines 64–65)
    (D) a critic "clearly in the market to buy innocence" (line 92)
    (E) a critic "emotionally accessible . . . to the same old manipulation" (lines 99–100)

13. With which of the following comments on the film would the authors of both Passage 1 and Passage 2 agree?

    I. The presentation of Ben's parents is a caricature.

    II. The older woman who seduces Ben is presented as predatory.

    III. The latter part of the movie attempts to present Ben as an exemplar of innocence.

  (A) II only

  (B) I and II only

  (C) I and III only

  (D) II and III only

  (E) I, II, and III

STOP. IF YOU FINISH BEFORE TIME IS CALLED, CHECK YOUR WORK ON THIS SECTION ONLY. DO NOT WORK ON ANY OTHER SECTION IN THE TEST.

SECTION 7: MATHEMATICAL REASONING

Time: 30 Minutes
25 Questions

DIRECTIONS

This section is composed of two types of questions. Use the 30 minutes allotted to answer both question types. Your scratchwork should be done on any available space in the section.

Notes

(1) All numbers used are real numbers.
(2) Calculators may be used.
(3) Some problems may be accompanied by figures or diagrams. These figures are drawn as accurately as possible EXCEPT when it is stated in a specific problem that a figure is not drawn to scale. The figures and diagrams are meant to provide information useful in solving the problem or problems. Unless otherwise stated, all figures and diagrams lie in a plane.

Data That May Be Used for Reference

Area

rectangle	triangle	circle
$A = lw$	$A = \frac{1}{2} bh$	$A = \pi r^2$

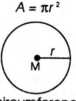

circumference
$C = 2\pi r$

Volume

rectangular solid	right circular cylinder
$V = lwh$	$V = \pi r^2 h$

Pythagorean Relationship

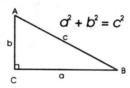

$$a^2 + b^2 = c^2$$

Special Triangles

30° – 60° – 90°

45° – 45° – 90°

A circle is composed of 360°
A straight angle measures 180°
The sum of the angles of a triangle is 180°

Quantitative Comparison

DIRECTIONS

In this section, you will be given two quantities, one in column A and one in column B. You are to determine a relationship between the two quantities and mark—

(A) if the quantity in column A is greater than the quantity in column B.
(B) if the quantity in column B is greater than the quantity in column A.
(C) if the quantities are equal.
(D) if the comparison cannot be determined from the information that is given.
AN (E) RESPONSE WILL NOT BE SCORED.

Notes

(1) Sometimes, information concerning one or both of the quantities to be compared is given. This information is not boxed and is centered above the two columns.
(2) All numbers used are real numbers. Letters such as a, b, m, and x represent real numbers.
(3) In a given question, if the same symbol is used in column A and column B, that symbol stands for the same value in each column.

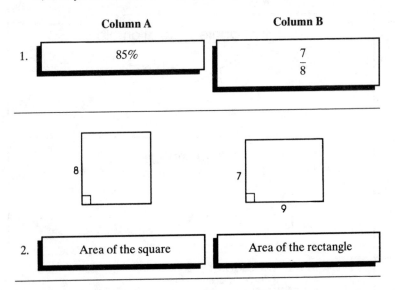

	Column A	**Column B**
1.	85%	$\dfrac{7}{8}$

| 2. | Area of the square | Area of the rectangle |

Column A	Column B

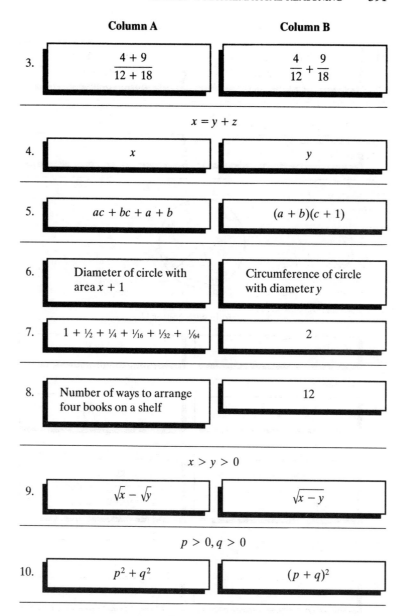

3.
$$\frac{4 + 9}{12 + 18}$$
$$\frac{4}{12} + \frac{9}{18}$$

$$x = y + z$$

4.
x
y

5.
$ac + bc + a + b$
$(a + b)(c + 1)$

6.
Diameter of circle with area $x + 1$
Circumference of circle with diameter y

7.
$1 + \frac{1}{2} + \frac{1}{4} + \frac{1}{16} + \frac{1}{32} + \frac{1}{64}$
2

8.
Number of ways to arrange four books on a shelf
12

$$x > y > 0$$

9.
$\sqrt{x} - \sqrt{y}$
$\sqrt{x - y}$

$$p > 0, q > 0$$

10.
$p^2 + q^2$
$(p + q)^2$

	Column A	**Column B**

11.

Number of inches in one mile	Number of minutes in one year

$$a > b > c$$

12.

$a - b - c$	$a + b - c$

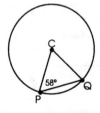

Circle with center C

13.

CP	PQ

14.

$\sqrt{3^{18}}$	$(\sqrt{27^3})^2$

15.

The length of a diagonal of a square with side of length 10	The length of a diagonal of a rectangle with sides of lengths 9 and 12

Grid-in Questions

DIRECTIONS

Questions 16–25 require you to solve the problem and enter your answer by carefully marking the circles on the special grid. Examples of the appropriate way to mark the grid follow.

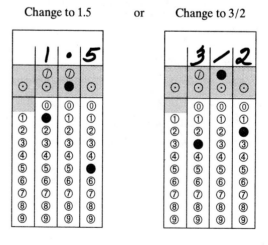

Answer: 3.7   **Answer: 1/2**

decimal point

fraction bar

Answer: 1½

Do not grid in mixed numbers in the form of mixed numbers. **Always** change mixed numbers to improper fractions or decimals.

Change to 1.5   or   Change to 3/2

Answer: 123

Space permitting, answers may start in any column. Each grid-in answer below is correct.

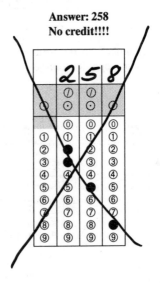

Note: Circles must be filled in correctly to receive credit. Mark only one circle in each column. No credit will be given if more than one circle in a column is marked. Example:

Answer: 258
No credit!!!!

Answer: 8/9

Accuracy of decimals: Always enter the most accurate decimal value that the grid will accommodate. For example: An answer such as .8888 . . . can be gridded as .888 or .889. Gridding this value as .8, .88, or .89 is considered inaccurate and therefore **not acceptable.** The acceptable grid-ins of 8/9 are:

8/9   .888   .889

Be sure to write your answers in the boxes at the top of the circles before doing your gridding. Although writing out the answers above the columns is not required, it is very important to insure accuracy. Even though some problems may have more than one correct answer, grid only **one answer.** Grid-in questions contain no negative answers.

16. If $F = \frac{9}{5}C + 32$, what is F when $C = 19$?

17. Red, green, and white jellybeans are combined in a ratio of 5:4:3, respectively. What is the ratio of green jelly beans to the total number of jelly beans?

18. A picture 8 inches by 10 inches is bordered by a frame that is $1\frac{1}{2}$ inches wide. What is the total area of the picture and the frame in square inches?

Review Test Areas

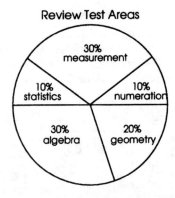

19. According to the graph above, if the test contains 5 numeration problems, then how many algebra problems would be expected?

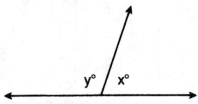

Note: Figure not drawn to scale.

20. If, in the figure above, $y = 3x$, then $x =$

21. If 150% of y is equal to 60% of z, and y and z are not zero, then $y/z =$

22. Three-fourths of a circle is divided into six equal parts. What fractional part of the whole circle does each piece represent?

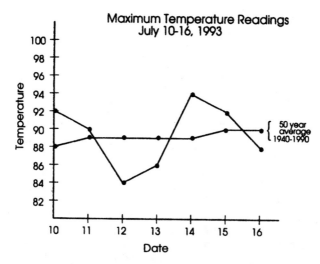

23. Of the seven days shown, what percent of the days did the maximum temperature exceed the average temperature? (Disregard the % sign when gridding your answer.)

24. How many days would it take for two people working together to complete a job if it takes one person 6 days working alone and it takes the other person 10 days working alone to complete the same job?

25. A fraction is equivalent to ⅔. If its numerator is decreased by 2 and its denominator is increased by 3, the new fraction is equivalent to ⅓. What is the original fraction?

STOP. IF YOU FINISH BEFORE TIME IS CALLED, CHECK YOUR WORK ON THIS SECTION ONLY. DO NOT WORK ON ANY OTHER SECTION IN THE TEST.

SCORING PRACTICE TEST 3

ANSWER KEY

Section 1 Mathematical Reasoning	Section 2 Verbal Reasoning	Section 3 Mathematical Reasoning	Section 4 Verbal Reasoning
1. D	1. C	1. B	1. B
2. B	2. B	2. C	2. C
3. C	3. A	3. D	3. E
4. D	4. E	4. B	4. D
5. D	5. D	5. B	5. D
6. B	6. C	6. A	6. B
7. D	7. B	7. A	7. B
8. D	8. A	8. C	8. B
9. B	9. A	9. A	9. C
10. D	10. E	10. B	10. E
11. B	11. D	11. D	11. D
12. C	12. A	12. C	12. B
13. A	13. C	13. A	13. E
14. D	14. E	14. B	14. A
15. C	15. C	15. A	15. C
16. E	16. E	16. 5/12	16. C
17. C	17. C	17. 37.5	17. C
18. A	18. A	18. 45	18. C
19. B	19. B	19. 39	19. B
20. A	20. D	20. 878	20. A
21. D	21. C	21. 97	21. C
22. E	22. B	22. 72	22. D
23. B	23. C	23. 2000	23. B
24. A	24. A	24. 7	24. E
25. E	25. B	25. 32	25. D
	26. D		26. C
	27. E		27. D
	28. D		28. B
	29. A		29. C
	30. B		30. A
			31. B
			32. A
			33. C
			34. E
			35. E

398

ANSWER KEY

Section 5 Mathematical Reasoning	Section 6 Verbal Reasoning	Section 7 Mathematical Reasoning
1. C	1. B	1. B
2. D	2. B	2. A
3. D	3. C	3. B
4. A	4. D	4. D
5. D	5. D	5. C
6. B	6. A	6. D
7. E	7. C	7. B
8. D	8. A	8. A
9. C	9. B	9. B
10. E	10. D	10. B
	11. A	11. B
	12. C	12. D
	13. E	13. B
		14. C
		15. B
		16. 66.2
		17. 1/3
		18. 143
		19. 15
		20. 45
		21. 2/5
		22. 1/8
		23. 57.1
		24. 3.75
		25. 6/9

ANALYZING YOUR TEST RESULTS

The charts on the following pages should be used to carefully analyze your results and spot your strengths and weaknesses. The complete process of analyzing each subject area and each individual problem should be completed for each practice test. These results should then be reexamined for trends in types of errors (repeated errors) or poor results in specific subject areas. **This reexamination and analysis is of tremendous importance to you in assuring maximum test preparation benefit.**

Verbal Reasoning Analysis Sheet

Section 2	possible	completed	right	wrong
sentence completion	9			
analogies	6			
critical reading	15			
Subtotal	30			

Section 4	possible	completed	right	wrong
sentence completion	10			
analogies	13			
critical reading	12			
Subtotal	35			

Section 6	possible	completed	right	wrong
critical reading	13			
Subtotal	13			

Overall Verbal Totals	78			

Mathematical Reasoning Analysis Sheet

Section 1	possible	completed	right	wrong
multiple choice	25	25	21	4
Subtotal	25	25	21	4

24

Section 3	possible	completed	right	wrong
quantitative comparison	15			
grid-ins	10			
Subtotal	25			

Section 5	possible	completed	right	wrong
multiple choice	10			
Subtotal	10			

Section 7	possible	completed	right	wrong
quantitative comparison	15			
grid-ins	10			
Subtotal	25			

Overall Math Totals	85			

You can now use the Score Range Approximator on page 439 to convert your raw scores to an **approximate** scaled score.

WHY??????????????????????????????????

Analysis/Tally Sheet for Problems Missed

One of the most important parts of test preparation is analyzing **why** you missed a problem so that you can reduce the number of mistakes. Now that you have taken the practice test and checked your answers, carefully tally your mistakes by marking them in the proper column.

Reason for Mistakes

	Total Missed	Simple Mistake	Misread Problem	Lack of Knowledge	Lack of Time
Section 2: Verbal					
Section 4: Verbal					
Section 6: Verbal					
Subtotal					
Section 1: Math					
Section 3: Math					
Section 5: Math					
Section 7: Math					
Subtotal					
Total Math and Verbal					

Reviewing the above data should help you determine **why** you are missing certain problems. Now that you've pinpointed the type of error, compare it to other practice tests to spot other common mistakes.

COMPLETE ANSWERS AND EXPLANATIONS
FOR PRACTICE TEST 3

SECTION 1: MATHEMATICAL REASONING

1. (D) Multiplying each side by 3

$$3m + n = 7$$
$$3(3m + n) = 3(7)$$

Therefore, $9m + 3n = 21$

2. (B) If ⅔ of the container is full, there remains ⅓ of the container to fill. The time to fill ⅓ of the container will be half as long as the time needed to fill ⅔ of the container. Hence, ½(18 minutes) = 9 minutes.

3. (C) To find the tax at 7% on $132.95, simply round off and multiply (the rule for rounding off is "5 or above rounds up"): 7% times $133.

$$.07 \times \$133 = \$9.31$$

Using a calculator without rounding off,

$$.07 \times \$132.95 = \$9.306, \text{ or } \$9.31$$

4. (D) Since the sum of the angles is 180°,

$$m + n + 72 + 25 = 180$$
$$m + n + 97 = 180$$
$$m + n = 180 - 97$$
$$m + n = 83$$

Hence, the sum of $m + n$ is 83°.

5. (D) The perimeter of a rectangle is equal to the sum of the dimensions of its sides. For this rectangle,

$$\text{perimeter} = 6l + 4w + 6l + 4w$$
$$= 6l + 6l + 4w + 4w$$
$$= 12l + 8w$$

6. (B) Since the square of a positive number is a positive number, choice (B) is the correct answer.

7. **(D)** If Tom is 4 years older than Fran, if we call Fran's age x, Tom's age must be 4 years more, or $x + 4$. Therefore, since the total of their ages is 24, Fran's age + Tom's age = 24.

$$x + (x + 4) = 24$$

8. **(D)** $\dfrac{840 \text{ miles}}{1\frac{1}{2} \text{ hours}} = \dfrac{3500 \text{ miles}}{x \text{ hours}}$

Cross multiplying yields
$$840x = 3500 \cdot 1\frac{1}{2}$$
$$840x = 5250$$
$$x = 5250 \div 840$$
$$x = 6\frac{1}{4} \text{ hours}$$

9. **(B)** $\dfrac{\text{percent}}{100} = \dfrac{\text{is number}}{\text{of number}}$

$$\frac{30}{100} = \frac{x}{{}^{25}\!/_{18}}$$

Cross multiplying
$$100x = \frac{\overset{5}{\cancel{30}}}{1} \times \frac{25}{\underset{3}{\cancel{18}}}$$

$$100x = \frac{125}{3}$$

$$x = \frac{\overset{5}{\cancel{125}}}{3} \times \frac{1}{\underset{4}{\cancel{100}}}$$

$$x = \frac{5}{12}$$

10. **(D)** The seventh row will be 1-6-15-20-15-6-1, which contains no prime numbers.

11. (B) $\dfrac{y - x}{y + x} = \dfrac{\dfrac{4}{7} - \dfrac{3}{4}}{\dfrac{4}{7} + \dfrac{3}{4}}$

Multiplying by the lowest common denominator, which is 28,

$$= \dfrac{28\left(\dfrac{4}{7} - \dfrac{3}{4}\right)}{28\left(\dfrac{4}{7} + \dfrac{3}{4}\right)}$$

$$= \dfrac{16 - 21}{16 + 21}$$

$$= \dfrac{-5}{37}$$

12. (C) There are $40 - 24 = 16$ boys in the class.

$$\dfrac{\text{is number}}{\text{of number}} = \dfrac{\text{percent}}{100}$$

$$\dfrac{16}{40} = \dfrac{x}{100}$$

$$40x = 1600$$
$$x = 40$$

Hence, 40% of the class are boys.

13. (A) b = Bob's age, c = Jane's age, d = Jim's age.

Since Bob is older than Jane, $c < b$.
Since Bob is younger than Jim, $b < d$.
Hence, $c < b$, and $b < d$, or $c < b < d$.

14. (D) Perimeter of $\triangle MNP$ = ½(perimeter of $\triangle XYZ$)

$$= \text{½}(XY - YZ + XZ)$$

$$= \text{½}(10 + 15 + 17)$$

$$= \text{½}(42)$$

perimeter of $\triangle MNP$ = 21

15. (C) Using the Pythagorean theorem, $a^2 + b^2 = c^2$.

$$(BC)^2 = (CD)^2 + (DB)^2$$
$$= 5^2 + 12^2$$
$$= 25 + 144$$
$$= 169$$
$$(BC) = \sqrt{169} = 13$$

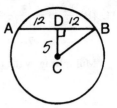

Hence, the radius of the circle is 13.

16. (E) So far, George has averaged 80% on each of three tests. Therefore, his *total* points scored equals three times 80, or 240 points. In order to average 85% for four tests, George needs a total point score of four times 85, or 340 points. Since George presently is 100 points short of 340, he needs to get 100 points, or 100%, on the fourth test.

17. (C) Let $2x$ = first angle, $3x$ = second angle, $4x$ = third angle, and $6x$ = fourth angle. Since the sum of the measures of the angles in a quadrilateral must be 360°,

$$2x + 3x + 4x + 6x = 360°$$
$$15x = 360$$

$$\frac{15x}{15} = \frac{360}{15}$$

$$x = 24°$$
$$2x = 48° = \text{first angle}$$
$$3x = 72° = \text{second angle}$$
$$4x = 96° = \text{third angle}$$
$$6x = 144° = \text{fourth angle}$$

Hence, the largest angle of the quadrilateral has a measure of 144°.

18. (A) If $x(y - z) = t$,

$$\frac{\cancel{1}{x}(y - z)}{\cancel{x}_1} = \frac{t}{x}$$

$$y - z = t/x$$
$$y - z + z = (t/x) + z$$
$$y = (t/x) + z$$

19. (B) Area of larger circle = 144π. Since area = πr^2, then

$$\pi r^2 = 144\pi$$
$$r^2 = 144$$
$$r = 12$$

radius of larger circle = 12
diameter of smaller circle = 12
radius of smaller circle = 6

area of smaller circle = πr^2
$$= \pi(6)^2$$
$$= 36\pi$$

20. (A) Substituting 2 for m and 3 for n gives

$$2 * 3 = \frac{2 + 3 - 1}{3^2}$$

$$= \frac{5 - 1}{9}$$

$$= 4/9$$

21. (D) If $\dfrac{a}{b} = \dfrac{c}{d}$, then, by cross multiplying, $ad = bc$.

If $\dfrac{d}{b} = \dfrac{c}{a}$, then cross multiplying gives the same result, $ad = bc$.

Hence, if $\dfrac{a}{b} = \dfrac{c}{d}$, then $\dfrac{d}{b} = \dfrac{c}{a}$.

22. (E) First, rearrange and simplify the first equation as follows. Add $+12$ and $+6y$ to both sides of the equation $6x - 12 = -6y$, and you get

$$
\begin{array}{rcl}
6x - 12 & = & -6y \\
+\,12 + 6y & = & +6y + 12 \\
\hline
6x \quad + 6y & = & 12
\end{array}
$$

Now, dividing through by 6 leaves

$$x + y = 2$$

Next, rearrange and simplify the second equation as follows.

$5y + 5x = 15$ is the same as $5x + 5y = 15$

Now, dividing through by 5 leaves

$$x + y = 3$$

The equations $x + y = 2$ and $x + y = 3$ have no solutions in common because you can't add the same two numbers and get two different answers.

23. **(B)** Since y varies directly as x, $y = kx$ for some constant k. Since $x = 18$ when $y = 12$,

$$12 = k \cdot 18$$
$$k = 12/18 = 2/3$$

and
$$y = (2/3)x$$

Hence, when $x = 20$,

$$y = (2/3)(20)$$
$$= 40/3$$
$$= 13\frac{1}{3}$$

24. **(A)** Ratio of diameters = ratio of radii.

$$\frac{d_1}{d_2} = \frac{r_1}{r_2} = \frac{30}{100} = 3/10$$

Ratio of area = (ratio of radii)^2.

$$\frac{A_1}{A_2} = \left(\frac{r_1}{r_2}\right)^2$$

$$\frac{A_1}{A_2} = 9/100$$

Hence, the area of circle R is $9/100$, or 9%, of the area of circle S.

25. (E) If the coordinates of two points x and y are (x_1, y_1) and (x_2, y_2), respectively, then the coordinates of the midpoint B (m_1, m_2) of xy are

$$\left(\frac{x_1 + x_2}{2}, \frac{y_1 + y_2}{2}\right) = (m_1, m_2)$$

Hence, $\qquad m_1 = \dfrac{x_1 + x_2}{2} \qquad$ and $\qquad m_2 = \dfrac{y_1 + y_2}{2}$

$$5 = \frac{-4 + x_2}{2} \qquad \text{and} \qquad -2 = \frac{3 + y_2}{2}$$

$$(2)(5) = (2)\frac{(-4 + x_2)}{2} \qquad \text{and} \qquad (2)(-2) = (2)\frac{(3 + y_2)}{2}$$

$$10 = -4 + x_2 \qquad\qquad\qquad -4 = 3 + y_2$$
$$10 + 4 = -4 + x_2 + 4 \qquad\qquad -4 - 3 = 3 + y_2 - 3$$
$$14 = x_2 \qquad\qquad\qquad\qquad -7 = y_2$$

Hence, the coordinates of y are $(x_2, y_2) = (14, -7)$.

SECTION 2: VERBAL REASONING

Sentence Completion

1. (C) The adjective needed here will describe the growing fear of the watchers of the endangered boat. Choice (B) *intrepid* means fearless, and *cowardly* (A), although it describes a fearful person, is for those who fear for themselves, not others. The best choice is *apprehensive*, meaning uneasy, anxious, or troubled by fears.

2. (B) *Native* and *indigenous* here mean the same thing. Since even the best language students who are foreign will not understand the native speaker, the missing word must mean something like puzzled or bewildered. The best choice, then, is *baffled.*

3. (A) With the use of *merely* and *not censorship,* the sentence implies that the missing first word describes some minor changes in a text, something like *editing,* or *revising,* or *corrections* but not so serious as *expurgation* or *decimation.* The phrase *with the writer's prior knowledge and* suggests that the last word must mean something like approval. In (B) the use of *prohibition* and in (C) the use of *disapproval* won't work, so the correct choice must be (A) *permission.*

4. (E) The missing noun probably describes a strength, since it is being tested and is parallel to the phrase *capacity to adapt.* The best choice is *resilience,* that is, the capacity to bounce back, to recover strength or good spirits.

5. (D) The first noun is probably a synonym for *trend,* but although (D) *fad* looks like the best choice, *prank* or *whim* might work. The second noun describes a serious threat (*not* an *innocent* or harmless *trend*). Either *peril* (A) (danger) or *hazard* (D) (risk) will do, but since (D) has the better first answer, it is the better choice.

6. (C) Since the second half of the sentence tells us of the public's *disapproval,* the missing participle must reflect this attitude. Either *horrified* (C) or *repulsed* (D) will fit. Only *ghoulish* continues the expression of condemnation. A *repulsed* public would not find the jewelry *amiable.*

412

7. (B) The first term, a verb, has *response* as its object; choices (A) and C do not fit this context. The second term, a noun, describes a point that can be reached. Only choices (A), (B), and (C) might fit here. Thus, the correct choice is (B). *Elicited* means evoked or drew, while *nadir* means the lowest point.

8. (A) Since the missing word must be surprising in an atmosphere of *calm* and beauty, choices (B), (C), (D), and (E) are all unsuitable. But *untoward,* that is, perverse, unseemly, unexpected, fits well.

9. (A) The two blanks must be filled together, and you can solve this question only by looking at both answers. Choice (A) makes sense, since the first blank describes lands that are *not* something, in this case, not *arable,* or capable of cultivation, and the second missing term, the verb, is logically one that means planted. (B) looks bad because, if the fields far from the river are *not* barren, why settle elsewhere? The adjectives in (D) and (E) would work, but the verbs are wholly inappropriate. A field is not *shunned, eschewed,* or *colonized* (C).

Analogies

10. (E) In this question, *bow* is a noun referring to the part that is drawn across the strings of the *violin* to produce sound. The analogy here is the *drumstick* which is used to produce sound from a *drum.* The *pedal* of a *piano* controls the volume but does not produce the sound.

11. (D) A *spear* is an offensive weapon; a *shield* is protective armor, a defensive device. The parallel pair is (D); the *gun* is an offensive weapon, while the *bulletproof vest* is a defensive item. None of the other pairs uses the offensive-defensive difference.

12. (A) A *skillet* is a round, flat pan, a frying pan, the utensil in which *bacon* is usually prepared. A *palette* is the oval board on which an artist prepares *paints.*

13. (C) An *aria* is a melody or song in an *opera,* a part of the whole. Similarly, a *chapter* is a section of a *novel,* a part of the whole.

14. (E) To *elope* is to run away secretly, a verb used of *lover*s who run away to get married. To *abscond* is to run away secretly, especially in order to escape the law. The verb is used of *embezzler*s (thieves who take money by fraud). When a *convict escape*s, it may or may not be secret, and the verb itself has no suggestion of the surreptitious.

15. (C) The first term here is an adjective; the second is a noun describing a quality which a person described by this adjective would *not* have. A *callous,* unfeeling, insensitive person would lack *tact.* Similarly, a *lethargic,* sluggish person would lack *speed.*

Critical Reading

16. (E) The passage mentions raccoons, cats, humans, and skunks as rabies victims. Since the first paragraph explicitly limits the disease to any *mammal,* carrion birds are not susceptible to the virus.

17. (C) Unless rabies is treated by *timely* injections of vaccine, it is a fatal disease (lines 2–4).

18. (A) Although dogs are no longer the major carriers in countries with good veterinary services and laws requiring inoculation, they still account for *90 percent of all human deaths from rabies,* chiefly in developing nations.

19. (B) The number of fatalities from the disease is small in the United states because most dogs have been immunized, people are aware of the danger of the disease, and those at risk of having been infected are treated before the symptoms of the disease can develop. The virus is not rare in wild-animal populations. In line 44, the passage refers to an epidemic among raccoons in America.

20. (D) The word *feasible* means practicable or possible.

21. (C) The treatment of humans can now include vaccine injections (in the abdomen or arm) and application of rabies-specific antibodies in the wound area. The passage makes no mention of an oral recombinant vaccine.

22. (B) The vaccine-laced bait should be useful in dealing with wild populations and with dogs in countries where large-scale inoculation is impossible. The vaccine would not be useful in animals already infected, since once the symptoms of the disease develop, it is too late to save the victim.

23. (C) In lines 11–17, the speaker says she did not follow the Watergate proceedings because it was just a case of one set of rich white people hoodwinking another set.

24. (A) *Of a piece* means part of, consistent with, or in keeping with.

25. (B) In this context, the word *acute* means shrewd or clever. Although some of the other meanings can apply in other contexts, the word here is opposed to *ignorance* and associated with wit.

26. (D) The words here are the thoughts of the speaker, not what she says. Throughout the passage, the reader knows both what she says and also what she thinks but does not say. Aware here of the *pompous* remarks she has just made, she is not eager to elaborate on these second-hand ideas, and remembering that Cox is a lawyer, she hopes to herself that he will not cross-examine her further.

27. (E) All three are deliberately used to undercut any pretentiousness of the passage. The phrases are conversational, even slangy in tone, and are characteristic of the writing in the passage, which is at pains to appear natural.

28. (D) The comic scene she imagines—Cox left in West Philly *without a map or a bow tie*—is her response to his inclusive *Our.* The speaker does not feel of a piece with the white New England establishment, and it is the pronoun which inspires her thoughts.

29. (A) The Rector, a shrewd observer throughout the passage, has some idea of what is going on in the speaker's mind. For a moment, he is afraid she will blurt out something that will embarrass the school. He is relieved that the moment has passed without incident.

30. (B) Because the passage was written some time after the events and allows the reader to know the thoughts of the speaker, the selection as a whole is very frank, even self-critical. The author understands herself and reveals this understanding very candidly. None of the other choices is appropriate.

SECTION 3: MATHEMATICAL REASONING

Quantitative Comparison

1. **(B)** By inspection, if you multiply $(.89/.919) \times 57$, this must be less than 57 (as you are multiplying 57 by a fraction less than 1). Therefore, it must be less than 58. The correct answer is **(B)**.

2. **(C)** Simplifying columns A and B leaves $x^{16}y^{24} = x^{16}y^{24}$. Note that when you have a number with an exponent to a power, you simply multiply the exponents together.

3. **(D)** This problem is best solved by inspection or insight. Since there are two variables in this single inequality, there are many possible values for x and y. Therefore, a comparison cannot be made.

4. **(B)** Since the given point lies in quadrant II, $x < 0$ and $y > 0$. Hence, $y > x$.

5. **(B)** Substituting -1 for x gives

$$(-1)^3 - 1 = -1 - 1 = -2$$

Now, trying -2 for x gives

$$(-2)^3 - 1 = -8 - 1 = -9$$

It is evident that this phrase will always generate negative values if $x < 0$. Therefore, the correct answer is **(B)**. The cube of a negative is negative. One less than a negative is negative. Any negative is less than 0.

6. **(A)** Change column A to decimals.

$$\frac{1}{3} \times \frac{2}{5} \times \frac{1}{8}$$

gives $.33\frac{1}{3} \times .4 \times .125$, which, by inspection, is greater than column B. Another method would be to change column B to all fractions and then compare.

7. (A) Since $a = 3b$ and $b = -2$, then $a = 3(-2) = -6$, substituting into the numerator of each expression (since the denominators are positive and alike, they can be eliminated),

$$\frac{a^2 + b}{\cancel{ab}}$$ $$\frac{a + b^2}{\cancel{ab}}$$

$$(-6)^2 + -2$$ $$-6 + (-2)^2$$
$$36 + -2$$ $$-6 + 4$$

Therefore,

$$34 \quad > \quad -2$$

8. (C) Since a triangle has 180° in the interior angles, if one angle is 90°, then the other two must total 90°.

9. (A) In the triangle, $\angle Z$ must be 60° and $\angle X$ is given as 30°. Since the side across from the larger angle in a triangle is the longer side, then $XY > YZ$.

10. (B) The ratio of the sides of a 30°-60°-90° triangle is 1, 2, $\sqrt{3}$, and since the side across from 30° is 2, the side across from 90° is $2\sqrt{3}$. Compare each column by squaring the number outside and multiply by the numbers under the radical.

$$2\sqrt{3}$$ $$3\sqrt{2}$$
$$\sqrt{3 \cdot 4}$$ $$\sqrt{2 \cdot 9}$$
$$\sqrt{12} \quad < \quad \sqrt{18}$$

11. (D) There are only two ways for a positive integer to a positive power to equal 81: 9^2 or 3^4. Thus, $(b + c)^a$ could be, say, $(3 + 6)^2$. Or it could be $(1 + 2)^4$. In the first case, $b + c$ is greater than a. But in the second instance, $b + c$ is less than a. Therefore, the answer is (D).

12. (C) $\overset{\frown}{AC} = 2(\angle B)$ because an inscribed angle is half of the arc it subtends (connects to).

13. **(A)** Since ∠AOB is a central angle, it equals the measure of $\overset{\frown}{AB}$, and since ∠ADC is outside the circle but connects to $\overset{\frown}{AB}$, it is less than half of $\overset{\frown}{AB}$. Therefore,

$$\angle AOB \qquad > \qquad \angle ADC$$

Alternate method: The external angle AOB must be larger than either of the remote interior angles.

14. **(B)** Converting the rate of 30 miles per hour to its equivalent rate in feet per second,

$$30 \text{ miles per hour} = \frac{30 \times 5280 \text{ feet}}{3600 \text{ seconds}}$$

$$= \frac{158{,}400 \text{ feet}}{3600 \text{ seconds}}$$

$$= 44 \text{ feet per second}$$

Since the time is the same in both problems, the distance traveled would be greater at a rate of 45 feet per second.

15. **(A)** Since the area of face TUWY is 20, the dimensions must be 2 × 10. Remember, each dimension must be an even number. The dimensions of face WXZY must therefore be 2 × 4. Since edge WY is common to both faces, the dimensions of face UVXW are 10 × 4.

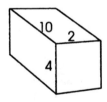

The surface area of the rectangular solid is

$$
\begin{aligned}
2 \times 20 &= 20 \text{ (doubled)} = &40 \\
2 \times 4 &= 8 \text{ (doubled)} = &16 \\
10 \times 4 &= 40 \text{ (doubled)} = &\underline{80} \\
& &136
\end{aligned}
$$

Volume equals 2 × 10 × 4 = 80

Therefore, the surface area is greater.

Grid-in Questions

16. Answer: 5/12—Dividing both sides of the equation $12a = 5b$ by $12b$,

$$\frac{12a}{12b} = \frac{5b}{12b}$$

$$a/b = 5/12$$

17. Answer: 37.5—Since the female students make up 3 parts out of the total 8 parts, the percent of students that are female is

$$\frac{3}{8} = \frac{x}{100}$$

$$8x = 300$$

$$x = \frac{300}{8}$$

$$x = 37\tfrac{4}{8}$$

$$x = 37\tfrac{1}{2} = 37.5$$

18. Answer: 45—Since each of the 5 shirts may be matched with each of the 3 pair of slacks, and these combinations may in turn be matched with each of the 3 sports jackets, the total number of combinations possible is

$$5 \cdot 3 \cdot 3 = 45$$

19. Answer: 39—Squaring both sides of the original equation yields

$$(\sqrt{m - 3})^2 = 6^2$$
$$m - 3 = 36$$
$$m = 39$$

Checking the answer in the original equation for extraneous solutions,

$$\sqrt{m - 3} = \sqrt{39 - 3}$$
$$= \sqrt{36}$$
$$= 6$$

Hence, $m = 6$ is the solution for the given equation.

20. Answer: 8.78—

5 apples:	$5 \times .60 = \$3.00$
10 bananas:	$10 \times .20 = \$2.00$
4 canteloupes:	$2 \times 1.00 = \$2.00$ (4 = 2 × 2 for $1)
5 oranges:	$\$1.00 + 2 \times .39 = \$1.78$ (3 for $1 and 39¢ each for the other two)

To find the total, add

$$\$3.00 + \$2.00 + \$2.00 + \$1.78 = \$8.78$$

21. Answer: 97—To average 89% for seven exams, Ben must have a total of (89)(7), or 623 points. To average 90% for eight exams, Ben must have a total of (90)(8), or 720 points. Hence, his score on the eighth exam must be

$$720 - 623 = 97\%$$

22. Answer: 72—The length of the side of a square with diagonal 12 is

$$12 \div \sqrt{2} = \frac{12}{\sqrt{2}}$$

The area of a square with side length x is

$$A = x^2$$
$$= \left(\frac{12}{\sqrt{2}}\right)^2$$
$$= \frac{144}{2}$$
$$= 72$$

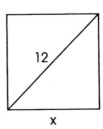

23. Answer: 2000—Simply continue the chart as follows, adding 40¢ for each two years to Product A and 15¢ for each two years to Product B.

Products	1992	1994	1996	1998	2000
A	$6.60	$7.00	$7.40	$7.80	$8.20
B	$7.20	$7.35	$7.50	$7.65	$7.80

It is evident that the correct answer is 2000.

24. Answer: 7—The area of a trapezoid is

$$A = \frac{1}{2}h(b_1 + b_2)$$
$$98 = \frac{1}{2}h(12 + 16)$$
$$98 = \frac{1}{2}h(28)$$
$$98 = 14h$$
$$7 = h$$

25. Answer: 32—By the Pythagorean theorem,

$$x^2 + 12^2 = 20^2$$
$$x^2 + 144 = 400$$
$$x^2 = 256$$
$$x = 16$$

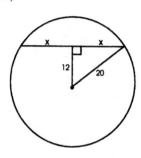

Hence, the length of the chord is

$$2x = 32 \text{ centimeters}$$

SECTION 4: VERBAL REASONING

Sentence Completion

1. (B) The clue in the sentence is *banning.* If cameras have been banned, the public will not see the whole story, so their *access,* right to approach, has been curtailed. The best word here is *denied* (B). *Belied* means lied about.

2. (C) The adverb *reluctantly* and the phrase *despite his care* suggest that the adjective that modifies *shoplifting* here is one that distresses the grocer and, so you can infer, one that means frequent. The only word that is close is *commonplace,* that is, common or ordinary.

3. (E) The sentence presents the example of the same number of workers taking more time for the same job as an example of Parkinson's law. The missing word in the law must explain this phenomenon. If work does something to fill the time for its completion, and the time for its completion has increased, then work must grow larger to fill the longer time. The missing word cannot be *decreases* or *grows easier.* The right answer must be (D) or (E), and *expands* (E) goes better with *fill.* The missing verb must be a synonym for *states* or says. Choices (B), (C), and (E) would work, but (E) also has the best second answer.

4. (D) The noun must reflect the mood of loud cheering, something happy such as *happiness* (B), *gladness* (C), *euphoria* (D), or *buoyancy* (E). But the second word must qualify this mood because the first clause begins with *although.* A proper word here could be *tempered* (A) or *moderated* (D). The words *enervated* and *debilitated,* although they can mean weaken, cannot be used in this context. They refer to physical weakness. Only (D) has two good choices; *euphoria* is a feeling of well-being.

5. (D) The clues in the sentence tell you that the missing word must describe a conversation with no sentence longer than four words. The correct answer is *terse,* that is brief, to the point. None of the other choices is plausible.

6. (B) The second term, a noun, must be a word that accords with a functioning government, so you can eliminate *schism, dichotomy,* and *division.* Either *compromise* or *consensus* (agreement) will fit. The first term, an adjective, describes a position that should be abandoned. Thus *dogmatic* is a much better choice than *sensible.*

422

7. (B) The words *conventional, morality,* and *conformity* suggest that the missing adjective to modify *conformity* will express the correctness of the Victorian reader. Choice (B) *genteel* means polite, refined, well bred—just what would be expected. The incorrect answers are all adjectives describing the opposite of what is suggested by *conventional morality.*

8. (B) The opening clause with its *though* at the beginning suggests that the missing adjective will be the opposite of *lively* and *interesting.* The second missing word refers to the *lively* first chapter, so it must be a noun synonym for liveliness. The choice of *tedious* (B), *repetitive* (C), *dull* (D), or *boring* (E) would do for the first blank, but only *pace* (A) or *verve* (B) are possible for the second. The right response must be (B). Words like *torpor* and *lethargy* are the opposite of what is needed for the second noun, while *verve* means vigor or energy.

9. (C) The useful clues here are *dangerous, without peppers or other spices,* and *mild,* with the latter two set in opposition to the missing adjective by the word *but.* Choices (A), (B), and (D) are just what you don't want. Both (C) *torrid,* that is fiery, very hot, or (E) *piquant* are possible, but as *piquant* suggests an agreeable tartness and these dishes are *dangerous, torrid* is better.

10. (E) The second adjective, expressing the response of a malcontent (a dissatisfied or rebellious person), must be disparaging, while the first adjective, coming before the *but,* must be opposite in effect. The favorable first adjectives are (B) *perfect,* (D) *Edenic,* and (E) *ideal,* while the pejorative second words are (A) *irritating,* (C) *drab,* and (E) *painful.* The correct choice must be (E).

Analogies

11. (D) *Surfing* and *skateboarding* are individual (as opposed to team) sports, the one on water, the other on land. Similarly, *water-skiing* and *roller-skating* are sports for individuals, the one on water, the second on land. The other choices include at least one team sport and sometimes two.

12. (B) A *vegetarian* is a person who does not consume *meat.* A *teetotaler* is a person who does not consume *alcohol.* A *dieter* may restrict the *food* he or she eats, but a *dieter* does eat some *food.*

13. (E) A *honeycomb* is the part of the beehive where the honey is stored. It is made of *wax*. The parallel here is *kimono,* which is made of *fabric.*

14. (A) A *typewriter* is a mechanism used for writing; a *pencil* is an instrument used for writing by hand. A *calculator* is a mechanism for making mathematical computations; a *slide rule* is an instrument used for making mathematical computations by hand.

15. (C) A *quiver* is used by an *archer* to hold arrows. The first noun refers to an object and the second to a person who uses or is associated with that object. Only (C) has as its second term a word referring to a person. A *forceps* is an object used by a *surgeon.*

16. (C) An example of a *disinfectant* is *iodine.* An example of an *analgesic* (something that allays pain) is *aspirin.*

17. (C) A digit is a numeral from zero to nine, but it also means *finger* or toe; the adjective form is *digital,* of, or constituting, or like a *finger.* The adjective *manual* means of a *hand.* The adjective *aural* means of the ear, not the *eye.* The root of *solar* is sun, not *star.*

18. (C) A *sloth* is a South-American animal whose natural habitat is the *rain forest.* Although a *cow* can be found in a *barn,* it is not the natural habitat. The same applies to *porpoise* and *water park.* The *Gila monster* is a poisonous lizard whose natural habitat is the *desert.*

19. (B) To *follow* and to *ensue* are synonyms. A second pair of synonyms is *inter* and *bury.*

20. (A) A *duchy* is the area that is ruled by a *duke* or by a duchess. A *count* does not rule a *county,* but a *queen* is a monarch, and she rules a *monarchy.*

21. (C) A *quill,* a feather from a bird, was at an earlier time used as a pen with which to write. A *manuscript* was at that time a document written by hand. A writer used a *quill* to produce a *manuscript.* The parallel pair here is *brush* and *fresco.* A *fresco* is a painting on a plaster surface which the artist makes by using a *brush.*

22. (D) The adjectives *dorsal* and *ventral* refer to the back and front of a human. They are, then, adjectives denoting opposite sides. The best parallel is *retreating* (going away from) and *advancing* (coming toward), actions that are also opposed and which, coincidentally, would reveal the *dorsal* and the *ventral* sides of a person.

23. (B) A *victim* is someone or something killed or injured. A *martyr* is a *victim* who suffers for principles or beliefs. An *action* is the doing of something. A *crusade* is an *action* undertaken on behalf of some cause or idea, so in both cases, the second term adds a moral or religious motive to the idea of the first.

Critical Reading

24. (E) Most of the first paragraph deals with what has been *often assumed* about bilingual ballots but which is untrue. The author attempts to respond to objections about the high costs and bilingual ballots on demand by pointing out what the costs are and what rules govern the qualifications for bilingual ballots.

25. (D) Since the rules specify that a language group must make up *more than 5 percent of the local population,* choice (B) would not qualify. Since the minorities who might qualify are Hispanic, Asian, and Native Americans, choices (A) and (C) will not qualify. Choice (E) is disqualified because the group does not have a *below average* rate *of voter turnout.* An Asian minority of 12 percent would qualify if it had a below-average voter turnout and English literacy.

26. (C) The phrase refers to voting, a *fundamental right* of all citizens which is the means the people have to preserve all their other rights. A watchful public seeing that a candidate or a law might limit its rights can vote against that candidate or law. Some of the other answers may be true, but they are not the point of the phrase in the passage.

27. (D) In lines 22–25, the passage explains that a condition of the Voting Rights Act was the suspension of literacy tests for foreign-language speakers whose *predominant classroom language was other than English* who had completed six grades in an American school.

28. (B) The second paragraph refers to laws intended to exclude voters who were Hispanic (line 28), African-American (line 22), Yiddish speakers (line 31), and nonspeakers of English (lines 26–28) but makes no reference to Irish Catholics, who would presumably be English-speaking whites.

29. (C) As it used in line 31, the word *franchise* means the right to vote, the central issue in the passage.

30. (A) The phrase *a hollow gesture* means an action with no consequence, a useless motion, an empty gesture. Choice (A) is the best of the five definitions.

31. (B) The second statement is a responsible reply to the argument that all bilingual voting materials should be abolished. Granting that some discrimination may now exist, it argues that by repeal of the laws those who are injured now would not be helped and those who are now enfranchised would lose their votes. The first statement, even if true, is not an argument against bilingual voting. The third statement, if true, would support the argument against bilingual voting.

32. (A) If everyone starts from the same position, equal treatment should be the fairest way. But if some groups start with a serious disadvantage, equal treatment will simply preserve the disadvantage. Thus, to achieve equality, those groups who have not had a head start need to be helped more to catch up.

33. (C) The fourth paragraph deals with the disadvantage of non-English-speaking white Europeans (save Hispanics). The only example of the white non-Hispanic European in this list is (C), the Greek.

34. (E) The final paragraph suggests all three. If only one in nearly seven thousand fails the literacy in English test, the test must be seriously flawed. Questions like *Why not make every effort to eliminate language barriers to voting?* call for the reader's assent, and *Perhaps it should* suggests that *need* should be taken into account when determining who should have a bilingual ballot.

35. (E) As the last paragraph makes clear, the author of this passage favors liberalizing the laws to make bilingual ballots more available. The author would, you can be sure, strongly disapprove of a movement which attempted to restrict or abolish the use of bilingual ballots in American elections.

SECTION 5: MATHEMATICAL REASONING

1. (C) Since $3/x = 6/1$, cross multiplying gives

$$6 \cdot x = 3$$
$$x = \tfrac{1}{2}$$

Therefore, $\quad x - 1 = (\tfrac{1}{2}) - 1 = -\tfrac{1}{2}$

2. (D)

$$\frac{.25 \times \dfrac{2}{3}}{0.6 \times 15} = \frac{\dfrac{25}{100} \times \dfrac{2}{3}}{\dfrac{6}{100} \times \dfrac{15}{1}}$$

$$= \frac{\dfrac{1}{4} \times \dfrac{2}{3}}{\dfrac{3}{50} \times \dfrac{15}{1}} = \frac{\dfrac{1}{6}}{\dfrac{9}{10}} = \frac{1}{6} \times \frac{10}{9} = \frac{5}{27}$$

Hence the reciprocal of $\dfrac{.25 \times \dfrac{2}{3}}{0.6 \times 15}$ is the reciprocal of $\frac{5}{27}$, or $\frac{27}{5}$.

3. (D) Since Harmon's sports car averages 35 miles for each gallon of gas, on 12 gallons, he'll be able to drive 12×35, or 420 miles.

4. (A) $\angle BCD = \angle A + \angle B$ (exterior angle of a triangle equals the sum of the opposite two).

Then $\qquad\qquad 84° = \angle A + 63°$
and $\qquad\qquad \angle A = 21°$

5. (D) Using the probability formula,

$$\text{probability} = \frac{\text{number of ``lucky'' chances}}{\text{total number of chances}}$$

The chance of choosing a weekday = 5 weekdays/7 total days = 5/7.

6. (B) Reynold's average score was 24.8, and Doe's average score was 13.7. Therefore, $24.8 - 13.7 = 11.1$.

7. (E) If y is a positive integer, y could be 1. Choices (A), (B), (C), and (D) are all evenly divisible by 1. Only choice (E), $1\tfrac{1}{2}$, is not evenly divisible by 1.

8. (D) A rectangular solid consists of six rectangular faces. This one in particular has two 7 × 6, two 6 × 3, and two 7 × 3 rectangles with areas of 42, 18, and 21, respectively. Hence, the total surface area will be

$$2(42) + 2(18) + 2(21) = 84 + 36 + 42 = 162 \text{ square meters}$$

9. (C) Distance = rate × time.

$$d = rt$$
$$k = m$$
$$r = (k/n) \text{ miles per hour}$$

Hence,
$$d = rt$$
$$d = (k/n)(x) = kx/n$$

10. (E) Since there are many different rectangles with a diagonal of 16, the lengths of the sides cannot be determined, and therefore the area of the rectangle cannot be determined.

 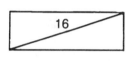 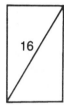

SECTION 6: VERBAL REASONING

Critical Reading

1. (B) Mike Nichols is the director of the film based upon the novel *The Graduate* by Charles Webb. The critic prefers Nichols's film to Webb's novel.

2. (B) To *play down* is to minimize, to reduce the importance of. To exclude goes one step further.

3. (C) The critic suggests that there are several limitations in the characterization of Ben Braddock in the novel; it is, in fact, its *main trouble.* Since Nichols's film avoids or mitigates these faults, the film is better than the book. Though the phrase criticizes Webb's hero, it does not accuse Salinger's novel of being overgrown and outdated.

4. (D) The word *bumptious* means arrogant, offensively conceited. It is not related to the word bumpkin, which means yokel.

5. (D) The critic says Ben's arriving at the wedding too late to prevent the final vows and then running away with the bride *shatters . . .* a *monogamous mythology* of an *entire genre of Hollywood movies.*

6. (A) *The Graduate,* according to the Passage 1, is the story of a passage *from a premature maturity to an innocence regained, an idealism reconfirmed,* a passage made possible by love.

7. (C) Although the author of the passage would probably agree with (A), (B), and (D), the first paragraph is about why people go to movies that are talked about, even though they may expect them to be bad. They go not to see a good movie but to find out what everyone is talking about.

8. (A) The critic in an unflattering remark about the taste of the mass audience says (lines 71–72) that Benjamin *has nothing to communicate— which is just what makes him an acceptable hero for the large movie audience.* Brains, the passage implies, are not box-office.

9. (B) Nichols's *"gift"* (which the critic puts in ironic quotation marks) is his talent, his singular ability.

10. (D) The line is a denigration of the director. Nichols has no point of view of his own, the passage suggests; he anticipates just what an audience wants and gives that to them. His object is the *sure-fire response* and nothing more.

11. (A) The last paragraph of Passage 2 finds sociological interest in the success of the film because it reveals that an educated generation is just as sentimental and self-satisfied as older generations who doted on romance in film.

12. (C) Choices (A), (B), (D), and (E) are essentially the same; they are complaining of moviegoers who identify too intensely with the heroes or heroines of film and see films only as emotional reflections of their own lives, not as works of art, or craft, or fiction. Choice (C) describes a critic who sees a film objectively, who does not became so emotionally involved that he cannot separate reality from cinema.

13. (E) Both critics imply that Ben's parents are caricatures. The first refers to the *overdone caricatures that surround the three principals* (lines 41–42) and the second to the *middle-class comic strip* (line 70). Both critics use the word *predatory* to describe the older woman (lines 19 and 78). Both see Ben as an exemplar of innocence (lines 39, 77, 91), although the first praises this aspect of the film, while the second regards it as trite.

SECTION 7: MATHEMATICAL REASONING

Quantitative Comparison

1. (B) $85\% = {}^{85}\!/_{100} = 0.85$ ${}^{7}\!/_{8} = 7 \div 8 = 0.875$

    Since 0.85 $<$ 0.875

             85% $<$ ${}^{7}\!/_{8}$

2. (A) The area of a square is equal to the length of its side squared. The area of the given square is

$$s^2 = 8^2 = 64$$

The area of a rectangle is the product of its base times its height. The area of the given rectangle is

$$bh = (9)(7) = 63$$

Hence, the area of the square is greater than the area of the rectangle.

3. (B) $\dfrac{4 + 9}{12 + 18} = \dfrac{13}{30}$ $\dfrac{4}{12} + \dfrac{9}{18} = \dfrac{1}{3} + \dfrac{1}{2}$

$$= \dfrac{2}{6} + \dfrac{3}{6}$$

$$= \dfrac{5}{6} = \dfrac{25}{30}$$

    Hence, $\dfrac{13}{30}$ $<$ $\dfrac{25}{30}$

    and $\dfrac{4 + 9}{12 + 18}$ $<$ $\dfrac{4}{12} + \dfrac{9}{18}$

4. (D) The relationship between the values of x and y cannot be determined without knowing what kind of number z is.

$$\text{If } z = 0, \text{ then } x = y.$$
$$\text{If } z > 0, \text{ then } x > y.$$
$$\text{If } z < 0, \text{ then } x < y.$$

5. (C) Solve by factoring column A into $c(a + b) + (a + b)$. Using the distributive property gives $(c + 1)(a + b)$, which is the same as column B. Or substitute in numbers and you will notice that both columns consistently come out equal. Let's try $a = 0, b = 1, c = 2$.

$0(2) + 1(2) + 0 + 1$		$(0 + 1)(2 + 1)$
$2 + 1$		$1(3)$
3	$=$	3

6. (D) Since the values of x and y are not known, and there is no relationship between x and y, no comparison can be made.

7. (B) The easiest method is by inspection (and/or addition). Column A is approaching 2 but will not get there. Mathematically, getting a common denominator and adding gives

$1 + \frac{1}{2} + \frac{1}{4} + \frac{1}{16} + \frac{1}{32} + \frac{1}{64}$		2
$1 + \frac{32}{64} + \frac{16}{64} + \frac{4}{64} + \frac{2}{64} + \frac{1}{64}$		
$1 + \frac{55}{64}$		
$1\frac{55}{64}$	$<$	2

8. (A) To find the number of ways four books can be arranged on a shelf, multiply $4 \times 3 \times 2 \times 1$, getting 24, which is greater than column B.

9. (B) Substitute $x = 9$ and $y = 4$. (Note that these are square numbers and that they can make solving easier when dealing with square roots.)

$\sqrt{x} - \sqrt{y}$		$\sqrt{x - y}$
$\sqrt{9} - \sqrt{4}$		$\sqrt{9 - 4}$
$3 - 2$		$\sqrt{5}$
1	$<$	2.23

Now, try $x = 16$ and $y = 1$.

$\sqrt{16} - \sqrt{1}$		$\sqrt{16 - 1}$
$4 - 1$		$\sqrt{15}$
3	$<$	3.87

Column B will always be greater.

10. **(B)** $\qquad\qquad\qquad\qquad\qquad (p + q)^2 = p^2 + 2pq + q^2$

Since $p > 0$ and $q > 0$, $2pq > 0$, and

	$p^2 + q^2$	$<$	$p^2 + 2pg + q^2$
Hence,	$p^2 + q^2$	$<$	$(p + q)^2$

11. **(B)** First set up the numbers for each side.

Number of inches in one mile	Number of minutes in one year
(12″ in 1 ft) × (5280 ft in 1 mi)	(60 min in 1 hr) × (24 hr in 1 day) × (365 days in 1 yr)
12 × 5280	60 × 24 × 365

Now, dividing out a 10 and 12 leaves

1 × 528	6 × 2 × 365
528	12 × 365

Column B is obviously greater.

12. **(D)** You should substitute small numbers following the condition $a > b > c$. Let $a = 2, b = 1$, and $c = 0$. Then

(2) − (1) − 0		(2) + (1) − 0
1	$<$	3

Now, try different values. Let $a = 1, b = 0$, and $c = -1$.

(1) − (0) − (1)		(1) + (0) − (1)
0	$=$	0

Since different answers occur depending on the values chosen, the correct answer is (D). You could have worked this problem by first elminating a and $-c$ from each side and comparing b and $-b$ with different values.

13. (B) In the given circle, CP = CQ because they are radii of the same circle. △CPQ is an isosceles triangle, and $\angle P = \angle Q = 58°$. Since the sum of the measures of the angles of a triangle is 180°.

$$\angle C + \angle P + \angle Q = 180°$$
$$\angle C + 58° + 58° = 180°$$
$$\angle C + 116° = 180°$$
$$\angle C = 64°$$

Since $\angle Q < \angle C$,

      CP   <   PQ

14. (C) Simplifying columns A and B gives

$$\sqrt{3^{18}} \qquad\qquad (\sqrt{27^3})^2$$
$$\qquad\qquad\qquad\qquad 27^3$$
$$\qquad\qquad\qquad\qquad (3 \cdot 3 \cdot 3)^3$$
$$3^9 \qquad = \qquad (3^3)^3$$

The correct answer is (C).

15. (B) By the Pythagorean theorem, the diagonal of a square with side of length 10 is

$x^2 = 10^2 + 10^2$
$x^2 = 100 + 100$
$x^2 = 200$
$x = \sqrt{200} = 10\sqrt{2}$
   $\cong 10(1.41)$
   $\cong 14.1$

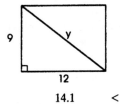

$y^2 = 9^2 + 12^2$
$y^2 = 81 + 144$
$y^2 = 225$
$y = \sqrt{225}$
   $= 15$

      14.1   <   15

Hence, the length of the diagonal of the square is less than the length of the diagonal of the rectangle.

Grid-in Questions

16. Answer: 66.2—Since $F = \frac{9}{5}C + 32$ and $C = 19$,

$$
\begin{aligned}
F &= \left(\tfrac{9}{5}\right) \cdot \left(\tfrac{19}{1}\right) + 32 \\
&= \left(\tfrac{171}{5}\right) + 32 \\
&= 34.2 + 32 \\
&= 66.2
\end{aligned}
$$

17. Answer: 1/3—The total combination of red, green, and white jellybeans is made up of $5 + 4 + 3 = 12$ parts. Since the green jellybeans make up 4 parts of the total 12 parts, the portion of green jellybeans in the combination is $4/12 = 1/3$.

18. Answer: 143—Since the width of the frame is 1½ inches, the dimensions of the rectangle containing both the frame and the picture are

    width = $8 + 1\frac{1}{2} + 1\frac{1}{2} = 11$ inches
    length = $10 + 1\frac{1}{2} + 1\frac{1}{2} = 13$ inches

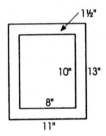

    The area of this rectangle is the product of its base times its height. So

$$\text{area} = bh = (11)(13) = 143 \text{ square inches}$$

19. Answer: 15—Numeration is 10%. Algebra is 30%. This means that there should be three times as many algebra problems. So if there are 5 numeration problems, there should be

$$5 \times 3 = 15 \text{ algebra problems}$$

20. Answer: 45—$x + y = 180°$ (x plus y form a straight line, or straight angle). Since $y = 3x$, substituting gives

$$
\begin{aligned}
3x + x &= 180° \\
4x &= 180° \\
x &= 45°
\end{aligned}
$$

21. Answer: 2/5—Since 150% of y is equal to 60% of z,

$$\frac{150}{100}y = \frac{60}{100}z$$

Multiplying both sides of the equation by the LCD of 100 yields

$$100\left(\frac{150}{100}y\right) = 100\left(\frac{60}{100}z\right)$$

$$150y = 60z$$

$$\frac{150y}{150z} = \frac{60z}{150z}$$

$$\frac{y}{z} = \frac{60}{150}$$

$$\frac{y}{z} = \frac{2}{5}$$

22. Answer: 1/8—Let n = whole circle. Three-fourths of the circle divided by 6 is

$$\tfrac{3}{4}n \div 6 = \tfrac{3}{4}n \cdot \tfrac{1}{6}$$

$$= \tfrac{3}{24}n$$

$$= \tfrac{1}{8}n$$

Hence, each piece will be 1/8 of the whole circle.

23. Answer: 57.1—There were 4 days (July 10, 11, 14, and 15) on which the maximum temperature exceeded the average. Thus, $\tfrac{4}{7}$ is 57.1%.

24. Answer 3.75—Let x = number of days to complete the job working together. The first person will complete $x/6$ part of the job in x days, while the other person will complete $x/10$ part of the job in x days. Since they complete the job in x days working together,

$$\frac{x}{6} + \frac{x}{10} = 1$$

Multiplying both sides of the equation by 30 yields

$$30\left(\frac{x}{6} + \frac{x}{10}\right) = (30)(1)$$

$$5x + 3x = 30$$
$$8x = 30$$
$$x = {}^{30}\!/_{8}$$
$$x = 3\tfrac{3}{4} = 3.75$$

Hence, it will take the two people 3.75 days to complete the job working together.

25. Answer: 6/9—Let x = numerator of original fraction and y = denominator of original fraction.

Hence, $x/y = {}^{2}\!/_{3}$ and $x = {}^{2}\!/_{3}y$.

The new fraction is

$$\frac{x - 2}{y + 3} = \frac{1}{3}$$

$$3(x - 2) = 1(y + 3)$$

Since $x = {}^{2}\!/_{3}y$, $3x - 6 = y + 3$

$$3({}^{2}\!/_{3}y) - 6 = y + 3$$
$$2y - 6 = y + 3$$
$$y - 6 = 3$$
$$y = 9$$

Hence, $x = {}^{2}\!/_{3}y = ({}^{2}\!/_{3})(9) = 6$

and the original fraction is $x/y = 6/9$

SCORE RANGE APPROXIMATOR

The following charts are designed to give you only an approximate score range, not an exact score. When you take the actual SAT I, you will have questions that are similar to those in this book; however, some questions may be slightly easier or more difficult. Needless to say, this may affect your scoring range.

Because one section of the SAT I is experimental (it doesn't count toward your score), **for the purposes of this approximation, do not count Section 7.** Remember, on the actual test, the experimental section could appear anywhere on your test.

How to approximate your score in

Verbal Reasoning

1. Add the total number of correct responses for the three verbal sections. Remember, *for the purposes of this approximation, do not count Section 7.*

2. Add the total number of incorrect responses (only those attempted or marked in) for those sections.

3. The total number of incorrect responses for the verbal sections should be divided by 4, giving you an adjustment factor (round off to the nearest whole number if necessary).

4. Subtract this adjustment factor from the total number of correct responses to obtain a raw score.

5. This raw score is then scaled to a range of 200 to 800.

   Example:

   - If the total number of correct answers was 40 out of a possible 78,
   - and 20 problems were attempted by missed,
   - dividing the 20 by 4 gives an adjustment factor of 5.
   - Subtracting this adjustment factor of 5 from the original 40 correct gives a raw score of 35.
   - This raw score is then scaled to a range of 200 to 800.

6. Now use the following table to match your raw score for Verbal Reasoning and the corresponding approximate score range.

Raw Score	Approximate Score Range
75–78	720–800
61–74	580–720
46–60	480–580
31–45	390–480
16–30	290–390
0–15	200–290

Keep in mind that this is only an **approximate score range.**

How to approximate your score in

Mathematical Reasoning

1. Add the total number of correct responses for the three math sections. Remember, *for the purposes of this approximation, do not count Section 7.*

2. Add the total number of incorrect responses for the multiple-choice questions.

3. The total number of incorrect responses for these multiple-choice questions should be divided by 4, giving you an adjustment factor for multiple choice (round off to the nearest whole number).

4. Now total the incorrect responses for the quantitative comparison questions and divide this total by 3, giving you an adjustment factor for quantitative comparison (round off to the nearest whole number).

5. Add the adjustment factors for multiple choice and quantitative comparison together, giving you a single adjustment factor.

6. Subtract this adjustment factor from the total number of correct responses to obtain a raw score.

7. This raw score is then scaled to a range of 200 to 800.

   Example:
   - If the total number of correct answers was 30 out of a possible 60
   - and 16 multiple-choice problems were attempted but missed,
   - dividing the 16 by 4 gives an adjustment factor for multiple choice of 4.
   - Now suppose that 6 quantitative comparison problems were attempted but missed.
   - Dividing these 6 problems by 3 gives an adjustment factor for quantitative comparison of 2.
   - Add the adjustment factors for multiple choice and quantitative comparison (4 + 2), giving you a single adjustment factor of 6.

- Subtracting this adjustment factor of 6 from the original 30 correct gives a raw score of 24.
- This raw score is then scaled to a range of 200 to 800.

Note: The reason for this unusual calculation is that there is ¼ point deducted for each incorrect multiple-choice question and ⅓ point deducted for each incorrect quantitative comparison question. There is no deduction for incorrect grid-in responses.

8. Now use the following table to match your raw score for Mathematical Reasoning and the corresponding approximate score range.

Raw Score	Approximate Score Range
56–60	730–800
41–55	570–720
26–40	440–560
11–25	310–430
−5–10	200–300

Keep in mind that this is only an **approximate score range.**

FINAL PREPARATION: "The Final Touches"

1. Make sure that you are familiar with the testing center location and nearby parking facilities.
2. The last week of preparation should be spent primarily on reviewing strategies, techniques, and directions for each area.
3. Don't *cram* the night before the exam. It's a waste of time!
4. Remember to bring the proper materials to the test—identification, admission ticket, three or four sharpened Number 2 pencils, a watch, a good eraser, and a calculator.
5. Start off crisply, working the ones you know first and then coming back and trying the others.
6. If you can eliminate one or more of the choices, make an educated guess.
7. Mark in reading passages, underline key words, write out information, make notations on diagrams. Take advantage of being permitted to write in the test booklet.
8. Make sure that you are answering "what is being asked" and that your answer is reasonable.
9. Using the **Successful Overall Approaches** (page 9) is the key to getting the ones right that you should get right—resulting in a good score on the SAT I.

LIST OF SOURCES

(actual size)

(actual size)

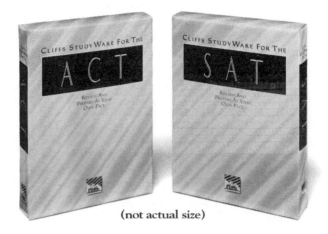

(not actual size)

Everything You Need for Your College Entrance Exam

Do your best on your SAT or ACT with the most comprehensive study program. Cliffs StudyWare is an interactive computerized program that will help you learn more through a Cliffs Test Preparation Guide, hundreds of on-screen questions, complete answer analyses, color graphics, test-taking strategies and more.

Sharpen your skills with Cliffs StudyWare. It has all the answers.

CLIFFS
StudyWare